EXILES
ON
MISSION

EXILES

ON

MISSION

How Christians Can Thrive in a Post-Christian World

PAUL S. WILLIAMS

Brazos Press
a division of Baker Publishing Group
Grand Rapids, Michigan

© 2020 by Paul S. Williams

Published by Brazos Press
a division of Baker Publishing Group
PO Box 6287, Grand Rapids, MI 49516-6287
www.brazospress.com

Printed in the United States of America

Library of Congress Cataloging-in-Publication Data
Names: Williams, Paul S., 1966– author.
Title: Exiles on mission : how Christians can thrive in a post-Christian world / Paul S. Williams.
Description: Grand Rapids : Brazos Press, a division of Baker Publishing Group, 2020. | Includes bibliographical references and index.
Identifiers: LCCN 2019031839 | ISBN 9781587434358 (paperback)
Subjects: LCSH: Christianity and culture. | Mission of the church.
Classification: LCC BR115.C8 W55 2020 | DDC 261—dc23
LC record available at https://lccn.loc.gov/2019031839

ISBN 978-1-58743-463-1 (casebound)

20 21 22 23 24 25 26   7 6 5 4 3 2 1

To Nigel Swinford,
who set me on this course by helping me identify heroes
and meet Lesslie Newbigin,
and to Rodger and Carol Woods,
whose encouragement and support helped me finish this book.

Contents

Acknowledgments ix
Prologue: Longing and Shame xi

Part 1: Enduring Faith: Christians and the Contemporary World

  1. The Legacy of Modernity 3
  2. Are We in Exile? 24
  3. Two Temptations 41
  4. Judgment and Mission 53

Part 2: Fostering Hope: From Alien to Ambassador

  5. Learning to Lament 67
  6. Calling, Citizenship, and Commission 80
  7. Establish an Embassy 99
  8. Know the Mission 115

Part 3: Ambassadors of Love: Exiles on Mission

  9. Learn the Language 137
  10. Stories of the West 156
  11. Cultural Translation 184
  12. Pilgrimage: A Way of Being 213

Bibliography 231

Acknowledgments

The material in this book was embodied and shaped through the work of the Regent College Marketplace Institute, through live events and conferences, web resources, the creation of the *ReFrame* film series, and most of all through my colleagues and friends Russell Pinson, Soohwan Park, Grace Zhang, Mark Sampson, Mark Mayhew, Constance Chan, Nathan and Bronwyn McLellan, Jen Gill, Steve and Ginnie Shaw, Kathy Kwon, Graham Pritz-Bennet, Ceri Rees, and Rebecca Pousette.

I am also grateful to Michael Hodson, Gary Hewitt, Preston Manning, and John Stackhouse for their wisdom and expertise, and for the support and advice of Institute friends Jon Scott, Peter Mogan, Rodger and Carol Woods, Bob and Evie Rolston, and Rosie Perera.

Thanks especially to those students I taught and learned from during my years of full-time teaching at Regent College (2005–15), especially in Christian Thought and Culture; Mission and Vocation; Vocation, Work and Ministry; Marketplace Theology; and Gospel and Culture courses.

Thank you to Bill Reimer and Kim Boldt of the Regent College Bookstore for your advice and wisdom, and to Michael Thomson, Paul Spilsbury, and Craig Bartholomew for your support of the project at crucial moments.

Special thanks also to my TA Rachel Tweet and friends Jon Reimer, Bronwyn McLellan, Pete Lynas, and Natalie Collins, who provided much needed feedback and editing of early drafts, as well as to friends Paul Woolley and James Featherby of the British and Foreign Bible Society, who did so for later drafts.

I have been enormously privileged to have Katelyn Beaty and James Korsmo as my editors for this project. The whole team at Brazos has been remarkably professional and fun to work with: thanks also to Mason Slater, Kara Day, Brandy Scritchfield, Paula Gibson, Jean Entingh, Maureen Ruge, Alex Nieuwsma, Michael Walkup, and Shelley MacNaughton.

I remain deeply grateful to my best friend and beautiful wife, Sarah, for her constant encouragement, prayer, and insightful editing given consistently over many years.

Prologue

Longing and Shame

What would it be like for the church to serve the purposes of God in this generation?

I, for one, want to see this. I want to see Christians in the Western world confident of God's presence in our midst and confident in the power of his gospel. I want to see believers experiencing the power of the Holy Spirit working through them in their workplaces and neighborhoods and in the public square. I want to see Christian communities known in our societies as communities of healing, justice, and wisdom. I want us to be known by our love for one another.

This is a book for people who share these desires. It is for those perplexed by the missional challenges of contemporary life and frustrated by the consumerism and disunity of much contemporary Western Christianity. It is for those who feel uncovered and unprotected by their leaders, and are disaffected by the apparent irrelevance of traditional Christian practice and belief. It is for those who long for humble, intelligent, anointed leadership.

These desires are not limited to Christians. There is also an inarticulate heart cry "for the children of God to be revealed" (Rom. 8:19). Despite the incredible sophistication of modern science and technology and the unprecedented wealth enjoyed in the developed world, Westerners are increasingly prone to loneliness, meaninglessness, and despair. Our culture is riven by conflict and disunity both within and between nations. We are experiencing a profound breakdown in trust and confidence. Might the church offer any kind of hope, purpose, and life?

The perspective I offer in response to these desires and questions has been shaped by my own somewhat eclectic journey. My first career after graduating from Oxford University was as a professional economist (in strategy consulting, public-policy development, and real-estate investment banking). After fifteen years working in this way, I made a significant change to move from Oxford to Vancouver and took up a position as part of the theology faculty of Regent College, an international graduate school of Christian studies affiliated with the University of British Columbia. The emphasis of my questions changed from "How do I relate my faith to my work?" to "How does the church engage missionally in contemporary culture?"

Part of my role at Regent involved launching and leading the Marketplace Institute—a think tank aiming to promote a theological vision for life in the marketplace and to equip the church to do the same. This meant that I had both the privilege of teaching young adults who came from all over the world to study theology for a few years and the experience of speaking to Christian leaders throughout North America, Europe, and Asia Pacific.

I've heard from many church leaders who want advice on how to help their congregation better connect faith and life. At the same time, I've met countless Christians working in secular contexts who have a great hunger for faith-work integration and whole-life discipleship but who also hold a deep disappointment and frustration with church life. For many of these believers, there is a shocking gap of irrelevance between Sunday and Monday that for some will end in nonattendance and possibly nonbelief.

These experiences have taken place for me alongside a parallel exposure to the broadly evangelical theological academy, particularly in North America. When I put those conversations "out there" in the church and the marketplace alongside those "in here" among the faculty and "ministerial" graduates of the theological academy, I've been led back frequently to some troubling questions:

- Why aren't the church and the Christian academy solving this critical problem of the faith-life divide, despite its growing urgency for believers and unbelievers alike?
- Is the sacred-secular divide connected to the missional challenges facing the church in the Western world?

Since the 1960s, most of Western Europe and the former European colonies of Australia, New Zealand, and the Americas have progressively rejected Christianity not only in terms of the formal influence of the church in public life but also in terms of any perceived positive cultural contribution of Christian faith. With vanishingly few exceptions (and these largely involving the shrinking conservative heartland of the United States), it is now not a cultural advantage to be known as a Christian or to engage in "God talk" in these societies but rather a positive hindrance to communication, likely to be misunderstood and possibly detrimental to one's reputation.

This Western turn *against* Christian faith constitutes a significant change of context and is interwoven with what appears to be a seismic shift in world history that is at least as significant as the sixteenth-century Reformation. Cultural historians use words like "momentous" and "unprecedented" to describe the changes convulsing Western societies since the 1960s. The term "postmodern" signifies not just the *end* of a modern period—characterized by confidence in reason, science, and technological progress to usher in ever-increasing wealth and happiness—but also a rejection of the vestiges of the Christian culture which that modern world inherited from the Middle Ages. Where this decisive turn toward nonreligion, amorphous spirituality, moral relativism, and authoritarian secularism will lead is unclear, which is why we can only describe our current time as "post-."

Just as these huge changes are fundamentally altering the internal character of Western culture, Western political and economic power is losing its dominant role on the world stage. In different ways, the emerging BRIC[1] nations of Brazil, Russia, India, and China are changing the global balance of power and altering Western cultural dominance. Meanwhile, Islamic fundamentalism has emerged as a destabilizing and often violent challenge to the Western cultural narrative.

The church thus faces a double barrier to effective mission.

The first is that almost the entire institutional infrastructure of the church and the assumptions that underlie it are now outmoded. Seminary education, the process of selecting and appointing trainees and church leaders, the form of many church services, and the theological assumptions in much preaching and pastoral care all *inhibit* effective missional engagement with Western culture because they are based on a set of cultural assumptions that no longer hold.

Second, that culture is now not simply increasingly pagan but is pagan with an anti-Christian flavor. Christianity is typically derided as the enemy of free thought and rational science by secular critics like Richard Dawkins but is at the same time blamed for its part in the rise of modern science and the market economy by advocates of the environmental movement.[2] Christians who work for justice in the social arena can easily be critiqued by those who fear a renewed attempt at a Christian theocracy or those who recall the previous entanglement of missions with colonialism. Tainting everything is the ongoing scandal of institutional child sexual abuse.

Essentially, all the church's past sins are coming back to haunt us, even if the criticisms are incoherent and self-contradictory (for example, it's hard to be implicated in the rise of modern science and technology and at the same time be anti-rational). Part of the reason for this is that Western culture is not a unified whole that has now rejected Christianity. Rather, having

1. An acronym coined in 2001 by former Goldman Sachs Chief Economist Jim O'Neill ("Building Better Global Economic BRICs"). I agree with O'Neill that including South Africa makes little conceptual sense, though it may be a politically astute way for these four nations to engage the African continent.

2. Most influential of the latter argument was the 1967 lecture "The Historical Roots of Our Ecologic Crisis" given by Lynn White to the American Association for the Advancement of Science, in which he blamed Christian theology for the exploitative nature of the Industrial Revolution.

rejected the faith that once held it together, Western culture is fragmenting into incoherent and incommensurable discourses, but each fragment has a different grudge against the church. We find ourselves in an incredibly difficult and ambiguous position.

This situation constitutes a strategic crisis for the church in the West. I say this not as a pessimist foreseeing the inevitable decline of Christian faith in the West. The narrative of inevitable decline is a historically inaccurate piece of wishful thinking on the part of secular humanists that we must not internalize. Rather, I want the church to face realities and seek God together for faith to respond in our generation with the same striking countercultural combination of humility, boldness, and expectation of the manifestation of God's presence that characterized early Christianity and other periods of renewal and vitality. If this crisis is to become an opportunity, this is the space we must occupy.

Believers must face two core underlying questions:

- Has the church lost confidence in the gospel?
- Do we believe the gospel is good news for our societies?

We might feel our society doesn't really need the gospel. *Does* the gospel have anything to offer? Have we outgrown Jesus now that we have nanotechnology, artificial intelligence, and DNA sequencing? Alternatively, we might see Western culture as a lost cause, so impervious to change and so morally degenerate that the only hope for it is a swift end (but one that comes, we hope, after we've enjoyed a few more years of the twilight of Western civilization in some quiet backwater).

The heart of this book, then, is a response to a paradox: though we *long* for the kingdom, we are often *ashamed* of the gospel.

In many situations, we find Jesus and the Bible embarrassing. Frequently, we feel intimidated by the increasingly commonplace criticisms of and hostility toward Christianity. Unprotected and uncovered by our leaders, we feel ashamed and daunted. We become anxious and doubtful, with the result that many abandon the institutional church as a "sinking ship," retreat within it to form a "holy huddle" and wait for the end, or "man the barricades" and defend what is left of cultural Christianity. None of these responses can provide the kind of hope or direction that God intends.

It is in this context that the church needs to be able to sing "Salvation belongs to our God, who sits on the throne" (Rev. 7:10). For such a song to be sung as an authentic expression of the gospel requires that God meet us in the midst of our longing and shame and empower us to sing. This is the challenge of "sing[ing] the songs of the LORD while in a foreign land" (cf. Ps. 137:4). It is the challenge of being exiles on mission.

I am by no means the first to make theological use of the biblical concept of exile in recent times.[3] In my experience though, much more can and needs to be made of it. I will make the case in chapter 2 that "exile" not only captures well our existential moment but is also a dominant model throughout Scripture for a theology of mission that has practical and conceptual power.

As I've heard my colleague at Regent College J. I. Packer say, "True theology leads to doxology." I've written this book to help us worship, in all of life, in the contemporary world—to "sing" in a foreign land, with faith, hope, and love. To sing with *faith* means that our song can't be sung as mere wishful thinking—an attempt to make ourselves feel better. It means that we must sing it with the conviction arising from confidence in the character of God and the truth of his word. To sing with biblical *hope* is, again, not simply a wish about what might be but a sure expectation that God will indeed act in the world, in our culture and time, based on his promises. To sing with biblical hope is a prophetic act—we are declaring reality before it is visible. Finally, to sing of God's salvation with *love* means that our shame and anger must be purged and sanctified so that

3. My thinking has been shaped by a sermon series by Charles Simpson I heard in 1990, a student paper I wrote on Daniel for Eugene Peterson in 1994, and reading Walter Brueggemann's *Cadences of Home: Preaching among Exiles* and William Stringfellow's *An Ethic for Christians and Other Aliens in a Strange Land*. Later I also gained much from reading Stanley Hauerwas and William Willimon's *Resident Aliens*, N. T. Wright's *Jesus and the Victory of God*, and various tomes by Alan Hirsch and Mike Frost. I engage with these and other writers in subsequent chapters.

we are able to love those who mock us and misunderstand us and those who persecute us and seem to be our enemies. To be able to sing like this requires a journey of humility, brokenness, and courage. It is to invite an outpouring of God's Spirit and saving power in our societies. To be able to sing like this is truly to be the church.

This book is divided into three parts. The parts roughly correspond to the biblical virtues of faith, hope, and love. Part 1 explores what it means for God's people to be in exile in the contemporary world. "Exile" challenges and shapes our sense of identity and mission. It forces us to decide what we will believe and who we will listen to. It requires faith. Part 2 is all about the biblical shift of identity that we can experience—a shift from "alien" to "ambassador"—and what this means for a prophetic approach to discipleship, the local church, and our understanding of mission. This shift fosters hope. Finally, part 3 focuses back on contemporary culture, showing how the ambassadorial paradigm of exile provokes and invites innovation in the way we reach out to others and empowers every believer in their own context. We become ambassadors of love.

During the final stages of writing this book, I took on a new role as chief executive of the British and Foreign Bible Society. The research I've done and the concerns I've summarized above have driven me toward a greater engagement with Scripture and desire to see Bible confidence built in the church. So I make no apology for the extensive use of Scripture throughout this book. By conviction and experience I believe that there is great power in Scripture, not simply at the level of the overall message of the Bible, but also in the detail of how that message is conveyed. I pay detailed attention to the biblical motif of exile because I am convinced that in doing so it is possible to find not simply better thinking or fresh vision but also the empowerment and encouragement that come when we know we've been encountered by God's presence and voice.

My hope is that while you read this book and wrestle for yourself with the Scripture, Jesus will come alongside you just as he did for those despondent disciples on the road to Emmaus. Their context and mind-set was one of being aliens in exile in their own land, and their outward circumstances didn't change during their time with Jesus. The Romans (and the corrupt religious authorities) were still in charge at the end of the story, just as they were at the beginning. What transformed their entire outlook was a rereading of Scripture during which their hearts burned within them (cf. Luke 24:32) and after which they suddenly could recognize Jesus where before they could not see him. We too need a transformation not just in our thinking and perspective but also through a fresh encounter with the living God. This is my prayer for you.

PART ONE

ENDURING FAITH

Christians and the Contemporary World

1

The Legacy of Modernity

With all the resources available to the church in the West, and the incredible history of foreign missions throughout the nineteenth and twentieth centuries, how did we end up in a situation where the church in the West is so out of touch with its own missional and cultural context that even committed believers find most Sunday services difficult or irrelevant? To answer this, we must understand the kind of responses we have made to the "legacy of modernity." To begin, we need to step back briefly into the era of Christendom that preceded it.

The End of Christendom

Christendom can perhaps best be thought of as a *symbiotic* relationship between church and state.[1] This mutually beneficial relationship grew out of the accession of Constantine as Roman emperor in AD 312. Constantine brought an end to centuries of persecution of Christian believers by Rome and ultimately established Christianity as the official religion of the empire.

---

1. I have taken this basic idea of Christendom as symbiosis from David Bosch (*Transforming Mission*, 274). It comports well with historian Sir Richard Southern's definition of the medieval period as "the identification of the church with the whole of organized society" (*Western Society and the Church in the Middle Ages*, 16).

When the western part of the empire fell to the "barbarian" invaders about a century later, Europe fragmented into a diversity of smaller and more isolated kingdoms.

However, seeded across these territories were a network of monasteries and religious communities that preserved the classical culture of the ancient world and spearheaded mission to the tribal peoples living throughout the European continent. The majority of these peoples converted from pagan worldviews in which society, religion, and power were inseparable. As such, conversion tended to occur in groups, not by isolated individuals. When tribal peoples did convert, Christianity became the religion of their entire territory.

Both the Constantinian and tribal legacies of Christian expansion in Europe thus lent themselves to a union of political and religious authority. Over time, this manifested itself in established churches powerfully shaping national politics and law. Society became culturally "Christian" without individuals necessarily having encountered God or believed the gospel. The task of the local church became focused on helping people develop their personal faith and practice in line with the gospel, rather than thinking missionally about the surrounding culture.

These fundamental assumptions of symbiosis persisted beyond the sixteenth-century Protestant Reformation. It was as natural for established Protestant churches—whether the Anglican in Britain, Reformed in Holland, or Lutheran in Germany and Scandinavia—to think of their nations as "Christian" and *assume* a high level of influence in political, cultural, and social affairs as it was for Catholic churches in Italy, Portugal, and Spain.

Christendom made manifest a new kind of longing. A longing for peace (from persecution and, later, tribal warring) developed into a longing for a unified order expressed most evidently in Charlemagne's temporary successes and the eventual flowering of the medieval synthesis of faith and reason in the thirteenth and fourteenth centuries in the work of Thomas Aquinas and Dante Alighieri. The attempt to achieve this order through political power and force also gave rise to the shame of coercive conversions, the violence of the Crusades, the corruption of Christian ideals by political power and material wealth, and the eventual disunity and division of the church itself.

The Rise of Modernity

In response to a church at war with itself across Europe, seventeenth- and eighteenth-century thinkers sought a framework for order and peace that was less contentious than the theologically charged positions used to justify war. Gradually an early form of "secular reason" came to replace theology in national and international politics.

Over time, the European Enlightenment decisively weakened the ties between church and state. But much of the mind-set of Christendom, including the cultural Christianity of the West, persisted into the modern period. It was natural for churches to identify mission as the *geographic* expansion of faith enabled by European colonization. This assumption was not confined to the churches but was also interwoven with political power. A commonplace assumption of nineteenth- and early–twentieth-century mission and political economy alike was the concomitant geographic extension of Christianity, civilization, and commerce.

Modernity was dominated by a longing for peace and order but also by a vision of progress in science, technology, wealth creation, and social equality. Christians were centrally involved in these developments. This is why we can now be accused by environmentalists of supporting unsustainable and exploitative models of economic growth but also rightly be proud of Christian social reformers such as William Wilberforce, Lord Shaftesbury, Elizabeth Fry, and Josephine Butler. Alongside these and other social achievements of Christianity in the modern period must be put the shame of the entanglement of foreign missions with colonialism and imperialism and the church's involvement in the twentieth-century experience of total war. Parts of the church were unable to resist the Nazi regime in Germany, and even the "Christian" allied powers engaged in systematic bombing of civilians and made use of the terrifying destructive power of nuclear energy to defeat Japan. The church in Britain and the United States, as elsewhere, was visibly implicated in these actions.

As well as revealing the compromise of the church, European imperialism and twentieth-century total war also dealt a death blow to the intellectual credibility of modernity, with its confidence in human reason to assure societal progress, peace, and human happiness.

The point of this summary is not to diminish those Christians who stood against these compromises, to say that no good was done, or even to suggest that better choices could easily have been made at crucial turning points. Rather, the point is to understand that churches in the contemporary Western context face *particular* missional challenges. The legacy of Christendom has left a fear of the political use of theological authority. The church's entanglement with the imperialism and total war of modernity has significantly damaged its reputation as a community that can resist harmful ideologies and act on behalf of the weak and marginalized. This shame is magnified by churches' involvement in institutional child sexual abuse.

The legacy of modernity meant, in part, that the fortunes of both Enlightenment modernity *and* Christianity were locked together. A loss of confidence in one meant a loss of faith in the other. The rise of a postmodern consciousness that began in the 1960s was a response to the ideology and power abuses of modernity. Postmodernity celebrates not a unified order but a diverse individualism. It rejects unifying stories and insists on a "value-neutral" liberal secularism. It is deeply suspicious of power and seeks always to give voice to those considered marginalized and alienated.

Mission after Hiroshima

Since the 1960s, Christian thinkers and leaders have responded to these changes, spawning a growing literature and a divergent range of missional practices. Twentieth-century total war was particularly galvanizing to a wide range of Christians. The decisive shift in societal practices took place in the 1960s, but it was evident in the postwar period that Western culture was experiencing a huge loss of faith (in Christianity *and* in the modern project).

Three intertwining strands of theological discourse emerged as missional responses in the wake of World War II and flowered particularly in the 1970s and 1980s—the prophetic, the evangelistic, and the pastoral. I want to trace the development of these strands to help us better understand the practical, institutional, and discursive outworkings that we've seen over the last twenty to thirty years. Reviewing the literature and organizational history briefly at this point will help us in several ways. We will see the themes of longing and shame manifest in various ways. While we will notice the fragmentation of the debate and the piecemeal focus of particular traditions, we'll also be able to see the good in each part of those debates. With the benefit of hindsight, we will be able to pull these strands together and thereby paint a clearer picture not only of how God has been at work in the Western churches in the postwar period but also of lessons still to be learned.

Prophetic

More than any other, the prophetic strand was energized by the experience of Christian accommodation to the Nazi regime in the Second World War. Around 85 percent of those who voted Hitler into power were churchgoers, and a similar proportion of the German church capitulated to Nazi pressure to endorse the regime. Awareness of this shame galvanized many leaders in the German confessing church to mount a faithful resistance, and the legacy of the writings that emerged form the substance of this discourse. Karl Barth is the key figure in this strand, particularly through his influence on writers such as Dietrich Bonhoeffer, Jacques Ellul, William Stringfellow, and Stanley Hauerwas. The major concern of this strand is the avoidance of compromise and the purity of Christian witness, expressed through concerns for radical discipleship in community, radical critique of the ideology of Western culture, and resistance to any syncretism arising from theological assimilation to Western cultural norms. Classic texts include Bonhoeffer's *The Cost of Discipleship* (1948) and *Life Together* (1954), Ellul's *The Presence of the Kingdom* (1951), Stringfellow's *An Ethic for Christians and Other Aliens in a Strange Land* (1973), and Hauerwas's *Resident Aliens* (1989), coauthored with William Willimon.

Evangelistic

With origins in the 1910 Edinburgh Missionary Conference, the evangelistic strand responded to the widespread loss of faith in the wake of World War II by focusing on the "evangelization of the world in this generation."[2] Billy Graham is the key figure in this strand, especially through the Lausanne movement following the 1966 World Congress on Evangelism held in Berlin.[3] From the outset, the Lausanne movement has struggled with a degree of confusion over the nature and meaning of evangelism and the relationship of evangelism to social concern. Around 2,700 evangelical leaders from more than 150 nations met at the 1974 congress in Lausanne.

This internationalism, a great strength of the movement, increasingly brought Western evangelicals into close contact with their counterparts in the developing world. The latter were far less infected by the legacy of the late-nineteenth-century reaction to the liberal social gospel that had led many Western evangelicals to withdraw into a private and personal version of faith and adopt a sacred-secular dichotomy. Accordingly, they were prominent in challenging Western theological dualism on these matters.

The classic texts of this strand are the series of covenants and declarations issuing from successive Lausanne gatherings. There is a clear progression of ideas away from sacred-secular dualism and toward a more holistic understanding of the gospel as we move from the *Wheaton Declaration* (1966) to the *Lausanne Covenant* (1974, authored by John Stott) and then to the *Thailand Statement* (1980), to the 1982 Grand Rapids *Consultation on the Relationship between Evangelism and Social Responsibility*

2. The rallying cry of the Student Volunteer Movement, itself begun in the late nineteenth century by Dwight Moody.

3. The church-growth movement, inspired by Donald McGavran, is also part of this strand. It too was formed out of a wrestling with the priority of evangelism over social concern. Over time, and partly under the influence of C. Peter Wagner, it became distorted into a technique-obsessed focus on pragmatic strategies to build large churches, often with little remaining focus on mission or conversion.

(CRESR, jointly sponsored by the Lausanne movement and the World Evangelical Fellowship), and finally to the *Wheaton Statement* (1983).[4] The consensus emerging from this protracted dialogue is that the gospel requires both public *proclamation*, in words, and public *demonstration*, in social concern and transformation.

Pastoral

The third and final strand of postwar theological discourse I identify as "pastoral."[5] Its primary concern is for the application of biblical teaching in the lives of ordinary believers. As such, it is not surprising that this strand is less obviously responding to World War II but is much more concerned to safeguard and pass on biblical truths to a new generation.[6] This group's predominant influence has been from Dutch Reformed leaders like Abraham Kuyper and Herman Dooyeweerd. More generally, this strand has followed the emphasis in Reformed thought on relating theology to all of life. Its main themes are, first, the vast scope of the gospel and the claims of Christ's lordship over the entire creation and, second, the necessity for human beings to operate within some kind of worldview that seeks to bring meaning and coherence to life. The classic texts in this strand are James Sire's study of competing worldviews, *The Universe Next Door* (1976), and Al Wolters's explication of the Christian worldview, *Creation Regained* (1985). This strand has provided Christians with a significant resource for

4. A detailed and insightful summary of this progression can be found in Bosch, *Transforming Mission*, 403–8.

5. It might be noticeable by now that I am taking my descriptors for these broad categories of Christian response to the end of Christendom from the list of appointed gifts given by Christ to the church as recorded in Eph. 4:11–12. Technically, the fourth charism in the list is the "pastor-teacher." While I absolutely hold that this phrase is intended to signify one gift, and not two, such that teaching is the primary means by which the pastoral ministry of a shepherd of God's sheep is to be discharged, "pastor" makes for a more elegant descriptor.

6. The juxtaposition in this sentence bears brief reflection. On the one hand, there is clearly something right about the idea of faithfully handing on the apostolic teaching as relevant in any era. On the other hand, an experience like the capitulation of many German Christians to the Nazi regime demonstrates that how we read Scripture is very much influenced by our cultural context and that we need the help of other believers to break out of our own cultural horizons in ways that allow the text to confront us.

understanding competing belief systems, combatting the sacred-secular divide, and gaining a biblical narrative framework for public theology.

I present these three strands as such in order to highlight the positive contribution that each has made to the global church. As they emerged in the wake of the Second World War and flowered in the 1970s and 1980s, each began at once, though in small measure, to influence and cross-fertilize one another. This process was accelerated by the introduction of a powerful catalyst in the form of British missionary and theologian Lesslie Newbigin (1909–98).

Newbigin's influence in this entire postwar missional movement has been *apostolic*. His ministry and writing powerfully articulate central elements from each of the three strands I've identified and combine them into a coherent strategy for the pursuit of God's mission in the contemporary Western world. Converted while studying economics at Cambridge University, Newbigin became bishop of the Church of South India and was active in the ecumenical dialogue associated with the World Council of Churches. On returning to Britain in 1974, he saw Western culture through missionary eyes—not so much as a secular society without gods but as a pagan society with false gods. He bemoaned the failure of the church in the West to achieve an effective missionary encounter at home, even while it was focusing on missions everywhere else. Newbigin's combination of theological orthodoxy and generous ecumenism has enabled his thinking to engage believers across an incredibly wide range of Christian traditions, including mainline Protestants; independent evangelical, charismatic, and Reformed groups; Anglicans; and Catholics. His most influential works include *The Open Secret* (1978), *The Other Side of 1984* (1983), *Foolishness to the Greeks* (1986), *The Gospel in a Pluralist Society* (1989), and *Proper Confidence* (1995).

Those in the prophetic strand find support in Newbigin for their emphasis on ecclesiology and the missional witness of the church as an alternative community and in their critique of the ideological "powers" dominating Western culture. Newbigin, however, also challenges their tendency toward excessive idealism and confrontation and their failure to engage in mission as dialogue and reconciliation. Those in the evangelistic strand discover robust support in Newbigin's work for the proclamation of the gospel as public truth (not simply the private opinion of Christian religionists), but they also find a powerful challenge to stop neglecting the mission field at home and stop narrowing the scope of the gospel's claims. Finally, those in the pastoral strand find encouragement for their worldview focus in Newbigin's insistence that the cross and resurrection of Jesus Christ only make sense as the starting point of an entirely new way of understanding the cosmos and in his assertion that the gospel's claims are cosmic and universal, but they also find in his work a challenge to move beyond personal discipleship and cultural transformation and orient these truths toward a missionary encounter with our culture that is personal, communal, and public. Newbigin's most visible legacy is the Gospel and Our Culture Networks (GOCN) that developed first in the United Kingdom and New Zealand in the 1980s and 1990s and subsequently in the United States, though his influence extends well beyond these areas.

Recent Responses

These three theological responses to the loss of faith following the Second World War—the prophetic, the evangelistic, and the pastoral—have interacted together since the 1970s and 1980s. Synthesized and catalyzed by thinkers and practitioners like Newbigin, the following missional responses have emerged over the last few decades: retrenchment, ecclesial mission, and "lay" ministry.[7]

7. Our common usage of the term "lay" to refer to Christians who are not clergy or church leaders is biblically and theologically problematic insofar as it designates a group of believers who are not "full-time" or "ministers." Such a notion is completely alien to Scripture and to the actual meaning and use of the Greek words underlying these English terms in the New Testament. *Laos* refers to the whole household of God. *Kleros* refers to those who are called. All ministry (*diakonos*) is service to God. Thus, all believers are *laos*, *kleros*, and *diakonos*. Our continued use of "lay" and "laity" in the way we often use the terms and the split between the ecclesial and lay ministry discourses that I am identifying are both therefore symptomatic of the continued influence of the sacred-secular divide and of Christendom models of church leadership.

11

Retrenchment

As a response to these developments, retrenchment exists in relatively toxic and benign forms, but what is common to them is a desire to hold on to the historic mind-set of Christendom, to turn the tide back on ebbing Christian influence in society, or simply to continue doing what we've been doing without any reference to the significantly changed cultural context of Western societies.

The more benign form of this response is activist in nature. It seeks essentially to "try harder" to save a degenerate culture by evangelizing more or by praying more fervently for revival. It is hard to criticize either of these emphases in themselves. Clearly the empowering of the Holy Spirit is fundamental to the church, and effective evangelism is a foundational fruit of an empowered church. However, on its own, this kind of activism tends to see missional problems as "outside" the church, while holding to a very narrow view of the gospel (in which a "decision for Christ" is all that matters) and adopting a naive view of culture (thus being unaware of the challenges to effective mission presented by the cultural captivity of the church itself to unbiblical modes of thought and practice). This benign activism has been able to reach some on the edge of church who had backslidden or who still had some latent memory of the Christian story. This is something to be thankful for, but it is inadequate on its own.

The more toxic form of retrenchment is essentially Christian-energized culture wars. It is not so much "try harder" as "shout louder." In essence, this is the impulse to use political power to defend what remains of the legacy of Christian moral and cultural norms as embedded in Western institutional life and legal requirements. It is toxic because, while the norms that it seeks to defend or advance are generally good in themselves (thus enabling activists to appeal to a broad mass of moderate orthodox believers), the *way* in which they are defended or advanced is often inimical to the gospel. Further, the fact that they are being so defended only reinforces the stereotypes of Christianity and the church in the eyes of its detractors, thus undermining Christians' reputation even further. Too often it ends up communicating the opposite of Jesus' command to love your enemies.

Ecclesial Mission

A second response to the postwar theological conversation is ecclesial mission, which is concerned to rethink and reform how we "do church" in the light of the huge changes in Western culture that I've sketched above. There are two main parts to this that can helpfully be distinguished in theory, though not always be divided in practice: the emerging-church "conversation," a strand that fundamentally concerns itself with the dialogue between Christianity and postmodern culture, and the missional-church movement, which is animated by a renewed recognition that every aspect of church life needs to be a contextualized expression of the gospel in its surrounding culture. Both of these types of ecclesial response developed in the 1990s, and both have drawn on Newbigin's groundbreaking work.

The emerging-church conversation can be traced back to a gathering in the late 1990s of North American leaders who sought to discuss the church's response to postmodernity.[8] Early leaders included Doug Pagitt, Brian McLaren, Chris Seay, Tony Jones, Dan Kimball, and Andy Jones. In particular, the writings of Brian McLaren, such as *A New Kind of Christian* (2001) and *The Story We Find Ourselves In* (2003), acted as a lightning rod by drawing in many other like-minded Christians in the wider Anglosphere who were having similar conversations. This broad global conversation about new forms of church in the postmodern West coalesced into distinct groupings, most helpfully categorized by missiologist Ed Stetzer as Relevants, Reconstructionists, and Revisionists.[9] "Relevants" seek to make church more relevant to a younger, postmodern generation by changing the style of practices such as worship, preaching, and leadership without changing basic evangelical theology. "Reconstructionists" are also theologically orthodox but more radical in wanting to

---

8. For a short firsthand account see Driscoll, "A Pastoral Perspective on the Emergent Church," 87–93.

9. See Stetzer and Putnam, *Breaking the Missional Code*, 188–90.

see a wholesale reimagining of the form of church to one that can genuinely change lives and reach society by advocating organic, incarnational communities in place of megachurches and other structures that fail to centralize genuine relationality and community engagement. Finally, "Revisionists" embrace postmodernity to the extent of adopting theologically liberal positions on a range of issues including salvation, gender orientation, the authority of Scripture, and evangelism. This third group has attracted a great deal of critique and led many theologically orthodox believers to disassociate themselves from the "emerging" label. It is this "Revisionist" group, led by Pagitt, McLaren, Seay, and Tony Jones, who have developed the Emergent Village organization in the United States and the United Kingdom.[10]

The missional-church movement shares concerns with the emerging-church conversation, but its different provenance lends it a somewhat different trajectory. At its core, the missional-church movement is not so much driven to respond to a particular culture (postmodernity) as it is determined to work out a missional ecclesiology for whatever culture a church may be situated in. Newbigin (alongside other missiologists such as David Bosch and Lamin Sanneh) stands firmly at the origin of this movement, which can be said to have begun in the United Kingdom in the 1980s when Newbigin began writing on this theme and initiated the creation of the Gospel and Our Culture Networks (GOCN) in the United Kingdom and then New Zealand. The resultant wave of church-planting activity began to be documented and directed through reports such as the Church of England's *Breaking New Ground* (1994) and *Mission-Shaped Church* (2004) and the Fresh Expressions organization that followed. A well-funded GOCN was founded in the United States in the early 1990s, a move that generated the landmark publication *Missional Church: A Vision for the Sending of the Church in North America* (1998), edited by Darrell Guder. Key North American leaders and organizations in this broad movement include Alan Roxburgh, Timothy Keller, the Verge Network, the Gospel

---

10. Thus, "emergent" is to be distinguished as only one part of the "emerging" conversation.

Coalition, and most recently the Missio Alliance.[11] The following decade saw a major contribution to the movement from Australians Alan Hirsch and Michael Frost, who have authored and coauthored numerous books on the missional church and cofounded the Forge Mission Training Network, now active in the United States, Canada, Scotland, Germany, Ecuador, Russia, and Australia.[12]

As will be obvious, the missional-church and emerging-church conversations are overlapping categories, and depending on who is using the terminology, they may be distinguished or equated. Individual authors may likewise self-identify with, or be claimed by, one or both labels.

Two further observations are in order. First, we might draw another distinction between these two categories. On balance, the core emerging-church conversation is a product of the *evangelistic* response to the postmodern context. Moreover, it is best seen as largely in *reaction* to it. Much of this reaction is understandable, both because the evangelistic strand has remained infected with the dualist mind-set of the sacred-secular divide far more extensively than other strands and because much of that strand, especially in the United States, held on to a foundationalist epistemology long after it had any plausible use as an apologetic strategy.[13] The emerging-church conversation

11. Some readers will be surprised to see me including the Gospel Coalition as part of the missional-church movement in North America because of its early debates and concerns with the missional church's meaning of the gospel. Although I am aware of these differences and explore them more fully in chap. 8, they don't alter my conclusion that the Gospel Coalition is an expression of the missional-church type of response to the end of Christendom.

12. For a fuller bibliography of missional church literature, see the online reading room at Tyndale Seminary: https://www.tyndale.ca/seminary/mtsmodular/reading-rooms/missional.

13. It is questionable whether the biblical foundationalism of fundamentalism was ever a good apologetic strategy, given that it accepted the Enlightenment quest for certainty acquired through the application of reason to evidence, differing only in that it allowed Scripture as providing admissible evidence. The strategy had some short-lived success in helping some people retain a biblical faith but has now detached many believers from the more biblical stance of the tradition—namely, that all knowledge begins with trust, not Enlightenment doubt, and ends in a humble confidence, not an arrogant certainty. The biblical stance of "faith seeking understanding" is also a more effective way to resist postmodern relativism and engage apologetically in postmodern culture. The argument between foundationalist evangelicals and relativistic emergent Christians is thus particularly distressing given that the entire conversation is taking place in a theological dead-end in which both sides appear ignorant of the intellectual history of their epistemological claims.

thus has something of great importance to teach us, and it is vital that in disassociating themselves from the extremes of the "liberal" wing of the emerging conversation, others do not abandon or neglect these important theological and philosophical critiques of an overly modernist evangelicalism. In contrast, the missional-church movement has tended to draw more heavily on the *prophetic* strand and is more *radical* in orientation, in the literal sense that it is calling for a return to the fundamental root nature of church.

A second observation concerns the different nature of the discourse in the United States as compared with the rest of the Anglosphere and Europe. In the former case, much discussion and practice has focused on reforming existing churches, whereas in the latter the emphasis has been more on church planting. This is to be expected given that cultural Christianity remains a significant vestigial force in the United States, more so than in any other Western country.

Lay Ministry

Taken together, the emerging-church conversation and the missional-church movement constitute a highly visible ecclesial outworking of the various strands of postwar theological reflection. Less prominent, but equally significant, has been the development of a diverse and somewhat eclectic renewal of lay ministry. Whereas the ecclesial response has been driven primarily by the prophetic strand in dialogue with the evangelical one, the lay-ministry response has found its inspiration primarily in the pastoral and evangelical strands. Before focusing on its recent expression, I will briefly rehearse its postwar antecedents.

Amid the general loss of faith that gathered momentum in the postwar period, church leaders and theologians were focused on Christianity's purity of witness and public proclamation. However, laypeople and some missionaries and theologians drew attention to the dramatic changes taking place in the workplace and society, as well as the growing gap between ordinary Christians' daily lives and the topics addressed in Sunday sermons. In response to these realities, the 1950s witnessed the birth of

16

formal theologies of work and the laity. Anglican Alan Richardson published *The Biblical Doctrine of Work* in 1952, building on lay leader J. H. Oldham's *Work in Modern Society* (1950), and Dutch Reformed missionary Hendrik Kraemer authored the classic work *A Theology of the Laity* (1958).[14] These essentially pastoral writings were designed to help clergy and laypeople understand the daily life and work of ordinary believers in the context of Christian ministry to the world. This conversation was further reinforced by a series of theological and ministerial affirmations of lay ministry emerging from the Second Vatican Council in the 1960s.

Overall, this postwar renewal of lay ministry had three substantive drivers: a pastoral concern to help laypeople connect their faith with their daily life, a practical concern to show the relevance of Christian faith to all areas of life, and an ecclesiological concern that the church be missional *by* supporting lay ministry in the world. In other words, lay ministry was an attempt to retain faith in the social relevance and impact of the gospel. Many Christian professional groups were formed as a result, alongside organizations such as the Full Gospel Businessmen's Fellowship, International Christian Leadership,[15] and Laity Lodge. Nevertheless, in his groundbreaking and careful study of lay ministry in the United States, David Miller concludes that this postwar renewal movement petered out by the 1980s for four primary reasons: its focus and culture became increasingly clericalized; the energy of the movement was channeled toward more lay involvement in the life of the church (rather than equipping them for their outward life); the theological academy regarded it as peripheral to its core focus; and in many denominations the prophetic impulse of preachers tended to involve critique of the business world without offering any theological resources for constructive engagement, leaving the clear impression that work in the modern economy was intrinsically compromised.[16]

---

14. Yves Congar's *Jalons pour un théologie du laïcat* is acknowledged as an influence by Hendrik Kraemer.

15. ICL is the organization behind the national prayer-breakfast initiatives.

16. Miller, *God at Work*. Miller identifies three modern waves of the movement, which he characterizes as "the Social Gospel era" (1890s–1945), "the Ministry of the Laity era" (1945–85), and "the Faith at Work era" (1985–present).

Despite this, ordinary Christians still longed for resources to help them live an integrated life. And if anything, the gap between the Christian culture of church on Sunday and the increasingly secularized culture they lived in during the rest of the week was now even wider. This Sunday–Monday gap, and the deep desire to bridge it, drove laypersons to seek for themselves the integration that church leaders were not providing. This led to a further modern phase of this lay response best described under the umbrella term of the faith-at-work (FAW) movement.[17]

Much of the initial emphasis of the FAW movement was on overcoming the idea that secular work was a second-best or inferior option for a Christian, undertaken only by those less committed to the faith. Richard Mouw's *Called to Holy Worldliness* (1980) and R. Paul Stevens's *Liberating the Laity* (1984) captured well the sense that thousands of ordinary believers felt but lacked the theological resources to support: they believed God valued and desired their service to him in and through their daily work. The classic texts that emerged in the 1980s and 1990s to resource this movement include Leland Ryken's *Work and Leisure in Christian Perspective* (1987), Lee Hardy's *The Fabric of This World* (1990), Miroslav Volf's *Work in the Spirit* (1991), William Diehl's *Ministry in Daily Life* (1996), Os Guinness's *The Call* (1998), and Paul Stevens's provocatively titled *Abolition of the Laity* (2000). These authors sought to undermine the false but incredibly widespread unspoken hierarchy of Christians that has pastor, missionary, and other "full-time workers" at the top, living out the highest Christian calling; doctors, nurses, and health care professionals followed by manual workers in the middle; and finally, businesspeople and professionals like accountants and lawyers at the bottom, where work was sanctified only by its ability to help pay the bills. They also sought to develop a firm foundation for ministry in daily life and work, either by recovering and updating the Reformation doctrine of vocation or, in the case of Volf and Stevens,

---

17. I agree with David Miller that "faith at work" is the best generic descriptor of this movement. The definitional issues, and the varieties of labels used, are discussed in Miller, *God at Work*, 14–21. In this book, I am only concerned with the Christian part of the broader FAW movement considered by Miller, and within that my focus is on orthodox Protestantism, recognizing when I can the debts due to Catholic and Orthodox thinkers and movements.

by emphasizing instead the charismatic anointing to work transformatively in the power of the Spirit.[18]

The FAW movement thus has as its foundational principle the notion of affirmation and commission: working in the world with integrity and calling is as valid an expression of Christian discipleship and mission as any other. God can be expected to be present there, to lead and guide there, to answer prayer there, and to bless and make fruitful the work done there in the same way we would expect him to in the more traditional spheres of mission. This core conviction only became more relevant and attractive to Christians during the 1990s and 2000s as ethical failures in business, politics, health care, and other areas of society became more obvious and the entire society became increasingly open to spirituality as part of its growing search for meaning. Accordingly, the FAW movement has grown rapidly over the last few decades: the number of dedicated workplace ministry organizations has increased from an estimated "handful" in the 1980s to over one thousand, many of them offering specialized websites, magazines, and resources. With this growth, it has become large enough to attract the attention of both the secular media and specialists in business and management within the academy.[19]

Although there is a great deal of diversity within the movement, the majority of FAW ministries have increasingly come to see work, undertaken in faith in God, as an expression of service *to* God and of mission *by* God through the worker. In other words, work, when undertaken in obedient response to God, is an aspect of God's mission to reconcile all things in Christ. What follows from this understanding of work as mission is the extension of ministry *into* the workplace (Christian "*intra*preneurs" undertaking workplace ministry inside secular and Christian organizations) and *by* the work organization (Christian entrepreneurs developing kingdom business as mission). One variant to this pattern arises from the ongoing

18. Volf is especially critical of the Reformation doctrine of vocation, considering it unscriptural and inadequate. I assess these issues in chap. 6.

19. For a more detailed assessment of the movement, consult Miller, *God at Work*, 105–23.

legacy of the evangelistic strand's ambivalence toward the sacred-secular divide and the primacy of evangelism. Some workplace ministries interpret workplace ministry solely in terms of evangelizing coworkers. Most workplace ministries repudiate this approach as utilitarian and misguided, without being against evangelism per se.[20]

Echoing David Miller in *God at Work*, I believe the faith-at-work movement is gaining momentum in our generation. But it is also clear that once again, church leaders and the theological academy tend to marginalize the movement and co-opt its energy to increase lay participation in the programs and ministries of the gathered church.

This is disappointing, because it suggests that the energy of the missional-church movement could shift toward retrenchment. The missional-church and faith-at-work movements are the most positive responses yet to our contemporary crisis. I believe that both of these are works of the Holy Spirit in our generation. Unfortunately, though, they remain largely separate discourses and activities. Only limited cross-fertilization of ideas occurs between their proponents. If anything, the tendency has been for the gap to grow. Despite some good intentions, many missional-church leaders regard the effort to engage and equip congregants for their working lives as something of a distraction from the real heart of mission.[21] They are more likely to try to steer these people into using their time and skills to support the gathered church community. Meanwhile, many missionally minded "faith at work" Christians tend to remove themselves from the life of the gathered church in reaction to the alienation they often experience from church culture.

This kind of mutual misunderstanding, suspicion, and antagonism is nothing short of a disaster for the health of the church in the West. It is

---

20. This includes the Lausanne movement itself, whose position papers on workplace ministry and business as mission explicitly acknowledge that these cannot be reduced to workplace evangelism. See, for example, Lausanne Committee for World Evangelization, "Business as Mission" and "Marketplace Ministry." I pick up the issue of the place of evangelism and what it really means to speak of the "kingdom coming" in chaps. 8 and 11.

21. A rare exception is Redeemer Presbyterian Church in New York City, under the leadership of Tim Keller, with its Center for Faith and Work, founded by tech-entrepreneur Katherine Leary Alsdorf.

something we must work not only to overcome but to move beyond by actively seeking synergies and integration between these movements.[22] Indeed, part of this book's purpose is to help bridge the communication gap between these two movements so that the full missional potential of the church—gathered and scattered—can be released. So I am writing as much for pastors, preachers, and mission workers as for businesspeople, professionals, and political activists.

Taking Stock

The church in the West has had over half a century to reflect on and respond to the changed missional context of postmodern culture. Most of the postwar theological conversations and more recent practical responses have contributed to the health of the church today. Some, however, either have ended up imitating the most problematic aspects of contemporary culture in an attempt to reach it (such as the church-growth movement and the emerging-church conversation) or have largely ignored change or been actively hostile toward it (such as the benign and toxic forms of retrenchment).

It would be easy at this point to leave it at that, agree that mistakes have been made, but be glad that there are plenty of positive signs of life around in the contemporary church. But the reality is that our review in this chapter has highlighted several ways in which the church in the West still clings to problematic aspects of the modern paradigm or has been compromised by the rapid changes in culture since the 1960s. It is important that we face this reality if we want to learn from experience and be faithful and fruitful in this generation. The following list summarizes

22. An excellent example of how to do this is the Made to Flourish network in the United States, which aims to support local churches in developing a fully integrated approach to mission in supporting the flourishing of local communities. Its president, Tom Nelson, speaks of his own past "pastoral malpractice" in failing to centralize and completely integrate the energy of the scattered church into his understanding of contemporary mission. See "Tom Nelson: Pastoral Malpractice," video, 4:35, *Christianity Today*, accessed August 28, 2019, https://www.christianitytoday.com/pastors/2014/december-online-only/tom-nelson-pastoral-malpractice.html.

eight hard truths about the contemporary church. Taken together they constitute a substantive (though partial) answer to the question we began this chapter with: How did we end up with the lack of missional effectiveness we experience today?

Eight Hard Truths about the Contemporary Church

1. A great deal of Protestant Christian culture and practice is still perpetuating a sacred-secular dualism.
2. Faithful, biblical, and relational whole-life discipleship is a rare experience, but a strong desire, for most young people.
3. The ministry and mission of the whole people of God continue to be marginalized by many church leaders and by theological training programs.
4. With few exceptions, the church has lost a clear, gracious, and intelligent public voice and tends to sound either shrill or unsure of itself.
5. Much of the energy of Christian public engagement is focused on changing or preventing changes to legislation that would affect Christians. It is a lobbying exercise, not a missional exercise.
6. Church leaders spend most of their time on matters of internal organization and practice rather than on the church's communal public works and witness.
7. Despite the lesson of World War II, much of the church is still vulnerable to ideological capture by the major narratives of Western culture.
8. Investment to ensure Bible confidence among Christians and church leaders is low.

I have indicated that these hard truths arise from one of two main causes: holding on to unhelpful elements of the modern paradigm or failing to adapt to the huge cultural changes that have occurred since modernity's collapse. Both of these causes concern the relationship between the church and the culture in which it works. The premise of this book is that the biblical experience and theology of "exile" are central to helping us understand this relationship so that we can function more faithfully in the contemporary world. But why focus on exile?

2

Are We in Exile?

Life in the contemporary world is not so bad. Isn't it rather counterintuitive to think of ourselves as being in "exile" when many of us live so comfortably? We are free to marry, have children, make friends, and associate with whom we like. We can work and earn enough to feed, shelter, and clothe ourselves based on wants, not just needs, and probably have something left over to pursue our interests and passions. We have a reasonable expectation of dying in old age, free from direct experience of war, famine, or plague. All these are undeniable goods.

Yet there remains a sense of unease. All this material abundance and relative security doesn't leave us feeling satisfied or deeply peaceful. True, it can distract us for a while, but underneath we want something more. We may be worried about any number of things that threaten the equilibrium of our world: global warming, the economy, international conflict and terrorism, family finances, relationship breakdown, ill health, or lack of job security—to name just a few. But even if we're not worried about these things, my experience is that most of us still feel a deep unease.

This book is written for Christians, so the sense of unease and restlessness I'm highlighting isn't about not having God in our lives. Saint Augustine is famous for the observation and prayer, "You have made us for your sake, [O Lord,] and our hearts are restless until they rest in you"[1]—but that

---

1. Augustine, *Confessions* 1.1, p. 1. The original Latin reads: *Fecisti nos ad te et inquietum est cor nostrum donec requiescat in te.*

kind of restlessness for God is not what I'm talking about, although it is related. Indeed, we may have great spiritual maturity and know and trust God's love, the forgiveness and friendship of the Lord Jesus Christ, and the presence of his Holy Spirit in our lives but still experience the unease of which I speak. We might even experience it more acutely than others who've known less spiritual growth.

For over a decade now I've traveled throughout the world teaching and speaking with Christians from a variety of backgrounds: businesspeople, professionals, college students, pastors, scholars, community leaders, and social activists. I've found that a handful of questions are repeatedly asked regardless of where I am or whom I'm speaking with. The language may differ, but the essential questions are the same:

- Why does the church seem so irrelevant to modern life?
- Should Christians try to change society or concentrate on personal holiness?
- How do I live out my faith in the workplace?
- Why do I feel embarrassed to bring my non-Christian friends to a typical church service?
- How can I share my faith in an environment that bans religious expression or is hostile to it?

At the heart of these questions are two quite basic concerns:

1. How do we make sense of the contemporary world?
2. How do we live a faithful Christian life in it?

The Complexity of Contemporary Life

My first proper job out of university in 1989 was with a small, niche economic consulting firm located between Oxford and London. In our office, with fifteen staff, there were five computers, four of which were used as word processors by the typing pool. On the fifth computer—an IBM PC with an Intel 8086 processor—I would use a modem to download our data sets from government and private statistical services before building our economic models using Lotus 1-2-3 spreadsheet software. The morning ritual included opening one's physical mail and reading the *Financial Times* over coffee. Cell phones were rare, as was evening and weekend work. Pretty much every night of the week I could enjoy the short commute home to dinner with my wife, Sarah, find out how her doctoral work was coming along, and then serve in some capacity or other with the local church. Most of the other staff had worked at the firm for over a decade. The directors owned beautiful homes in the countryside, and even the typists owned nice homes in the nearby suburbs. Everyone expected to retire around sixty or sixty-five on a reasonable pension.

This world was itself a radical change compared to the experience of the postwar generation. Dishwashers, second cars, and microwaves had become widespread during the 1970s and 1980s. Homeownership had increased rapidly, personal computers were commercially viable, and information and communication technology costs were falling rapidly. Equity ownership was no longer the domain of specialist investors or high-net-worth individuals; ordinary people looked forward to putting their savings into the next big IPO (which they quickly learned was short for "Initial Public Offering") on the stock market.

For some, though, even the 1980s were rather disorienting. I remember well the conversation with my great-aunt just a few years before I started my first job. I was on vacation from my studies at Oxford, and I had gotten my first set of contact lenses during the previous term. Aunty Mary, who was born in 1896, asked me where my glasses were. I tried to explain to her that I had just gotten contact lenses—small pieces of plastic that were sitting on my corneas. Aunty Mary drew herself back and, in a stern voice recalling her late-Victorian mannerisms, told me off for lying and threatened to box my ears!

All of this seems rather quaint now. Computers are everywhere, smartphones are ubiquitous, and instant messaging, email, Facebook, and Twitter are always on. We have to be reminded to disconnect ourselves from this technological network at the movie theater or during the sermon at church. Commute times have lengthened; job mobility has increased. In my last job in London, I could access vast amounts of data at my desk or on my laptop at the airport while waiting for a flight to take me to the next client meeting. Whether it's a good thing or not, somehow I led a team spread across five continents, thanks to the power of cheap information technology, video conferencing, and the organizational innovations that created first the matrix organization and then the network organization. I don't think we were sure which of those we were, but it was certainly complicated to figure out who was actually responsible for what! Change management went from being a coping strategy to being a profession.

Despite all this technological power and organizational efficiency at our disposal, somehow the workweek seems to have lengthened. The era of leisure, promised as the fruit of economic growth, seems further off now than it did in the 1950s and '60s when it became popularized—it is now instead a cruel joke. The productivity miracle of the last twenty years turns out to have been built on the use of . . . yes, our spare time! We may have maternity leave and paternity leave, but many people either don't have or don't take paid vacation because they don't feel they have the time or they're worried about the impact on their business or career if they take time away from work. Parents work hard to pay for all the latest labor-saving devices in the home but struggle to find moments of quality time that much of our family lives depend on.

We are awash with sophisticated communications technology, but according to the polls, most of us feel lonely.[2]

2. A 2011 poll by the Vancouver Foundation surprisingly discovered that city residents ranked loneliness higher than housing and poverty as issues they were concerned about (https://www.vancouverfoundation.ca/our-work/initiatives/connections-and-engagement); in 2017 the American Psychological Association heard evidence suggesting that loneliness is becoming an epidemic that threatens public health on par with obesity and heart disease (Julianne Hold-Lunstad, "So Lonely I Could Die," http://www.apa.org/news/press/releases/2017/08/lonely-die.aspx); and in 2018 the UK government appointed a minister for loneliness ("Minister for Loneliness Appointed to Continue Jo Cox's Work," http://www.bbc.co.uk/news/uk-42708507). Studies suggest that the elderly and the young are the most affected.

Globalization has impacted us all. In the team of forty people that I led in London, I counted over twenty nationalities. Over half the world's people now live in cities, and a good representation of world cultures and peoples can be found in most of those. Our globalized economy keeps getting more "productive," but most of us don't seem to be getting any better off. We're less confident than ever that we can repay our mortgages or get out of debt or that our children will inhabit a better world than the one we do.

The optimism that we enjoyed at the end of the Cold War has quickly turned to fear over international terrorism, financial instability, the unreliability of health and pension provisions, unemployment, global warming, and more.

Certainly the modern world has brought us much that we wouldn't want to do without. But it's also brought the challenge of complexity amid the fragmentation of many of the customs, institutions, and expectations that previous generations could take for granted and rely on. Increasingly, we're left as individuals to figure things out for ourselves, but it's harder and harder to make sense of it all. In the midst of this confusion, we're inundated with messages telling us what to do. Self-help publishing has become a growth industry; advertisements tell us to save more for our retirement—until, that is, the next ad tells us that we can buy the new car now on credit and pay nothing for six months: "Go on, you deserve it!" The institutions of government, science, and, most recently, finance have followed the church, parents, and teachers into the growing throng of leadership roles that we used to trust but now feel let down by and suspicious of. Part of the complexity of contemporary life is precisely the confusion—the babble of voices offering to help us navigate the surprisingly unpredictable terrain of early twenty-first-century life.

A Fragmented Life

What does Christian faith have to do with all of this? If we want to take the claims of Jesus Christ seriously, this is a question that we must answer.

Jesus said that he came to save and redeem the whole world, and he claimed the authority of God to do this. So *is* Christianity relevant for the whole of my life? Or is it simply something that provides a comfortable haven for my soul amid the turmoil that I experience much of the time? Was Marx (and Dawkins) right: is religion the opiate of the masses, a delusion we've made up to make ourselves feel better? Or is Jesus Christ of vital importance to my job, my family life, my community, my grandchildren?

It's crucial that Christianity is actually true, not just a convenient fairy tale to help us get by. The apostle Paul makes this point himself in 1 Corinthians 15:14: "If Christ has not been raised [from the dead], our preaching is useless and so is your faith." Whatever our individual stories, we Christians have become convinced that Jesus was raised from the dead and is alive and ruling the world. We've had life-changing encounters with God and seen our lives transformed by his love, word, and power. We desire to live our whole lives before God authentically, in ways that please him.

Yet Craig Gay, a colleague of mine at Regent College, is surely right when he observes that most of us Christians live like "practical atheists," getting on with the business of life *as if* God doesn't have anything to do with it.[3] Certainly I experienced real frustration in relating my faith to my work even in the relative simplicity of my first job. I'd trained as an economist. I was paid to do research, analyze evidence, and assess trends, and I was gradually promoted to give advice on public policy and corporate strategy. But as I began to give this advice, increasingly I asked myself, "How is the actual content of what I'm doing at work in any sense Christian?" The economic paradigms in which I'd been trained, and which clients assumed I would adopt, had some distant Christian influence to be sure but often seemed non-Christian and sometimes positively anti-Christian in their assumptions and impact on policy and behavior. Did Jesus care about that?

Of course, I could be sure to avoid cheating on my expense claims at work; I could aim to treat my coworkers well, live modestly, be a good husband (and later, father), and be sure to pay a tithe of my income to the

3. Gay, *The Way of the (Modern) World.*

local church. Somehow though, that didn't feel much like a truly integrated life if the thing that I spent most of my time doing wasn't really connected with my faith. Worse still, I couldn't see how to do anything about that. I couldn't see how I'd ever be able to integrate my faith into the way I worked without losing my job, and, even if I were able to, I wasn't sure how to go about integrating my faith with my work in any case.

Many Christians receive little help from the church in trying to answer these kinds of questions. It seems that for many church leaders, faith is about one's personal life, personal beliefs, personal values, and personal salvation—not about work, poverty, wealth creation, social welfare, technology, or any other of the issues that dominate our news media in any given week. On this view, if Christianity has anything at all to say about the many questions of contemporary life, big and small, they'll be answered, it seems, if and when everyone converts to Christianity. This line of thought leads us to the conclusion that the only way to be a faithful Christian is to evangelize all the time. At times, I wondered whether life would be easier if I became a pastor or an overseas missionary. Or alternatively, I wondered if I should stop worrying about the Christian content of my work and instead use my skills to make as much money as possible and then give it to churches and mission agencies who would do the evangelizing directly.

Christianity and Culture

These options, of course, are merely some of the many on offer in the often bewildering discussion concerning the right relationship between church and society. Much of the discussion of this relationship has been dominated in recent times by Richard Niebuhr's classic, *Christ and Culture*. Niebuhr identifies five distinct theological approaches to the relationship between faith and society. The first, "Christ against Culture," is exemplified by traditions stemming from the Radical Reformation, including groups such as the Anabaptists and the Mennonites, who responded to the corruption of Christianity they saw in the Constantinian model by seeking a pure church, refusing any allegiance with the world. A second approach, characterized by Niebuhr as "Christ of Culture," identifies changes in contemporary society *with* the advancement of the kingdom of God. An example would be the nineteenth-century liberal social-gospel movement, which believed that widening access to education and health care would advance the kingdom of God in society.

"Christ above Culture" is the label Niebuhr uses for the Constantinian model, in which secular power is subject to the church, such as occurred throughout much of the medieval period. A fourth response is that provided by Lutheran thought, characterized by Niebuhr as "Christ and Culture in Paradox." Christians are citizens of two kingdoms, one of which is irretrievably fallen. The Christian, therefore, cannot avoid living in tension, obeying God in the one kingdom but submitting to the secular authorities in the other. Finally, the Calvinist Reformed approach tends to resolve the paradox quite firmly in one direction, labeled "Christ Transforming Culture." This view sees culture as fallen but the gospel as having power to transform it. Society is progressively transformed as the kingdom of God advances on earth.

Niebuhr's framework has been widely debated yet remains influential. One approach to assessing the questions raised in the previous chapter would be to map the various positions outlined onto Niebuhr's framework. We could debate the extent to which the prophetic strand of postwar theological discourse is an instantiation of the "Christ against Culture" paradigm or whether elements of the emerging-church conversation have ended up as a contemporary version of the liberal social gospel ("Christ of Culture").

As helpful as Niebuhr's approach is, though, most honest readers find themselves seeing elements of truth in each paradigm and struggling to decide which to adopt. Different situations seem to call for different approaches. Deciding between approaches and when to adopt which one takes wisdom and scriptural study. We may find, therefore, that Niebuhr's paradigms serve as a more helpful framework if we place them alongside an alternative, and more explicitly biblical, one.

My approach in what follows is to use exemplar biblical stories as types, models, or paradigms for reflection. Using Scripture in this way flows naturally both from the belief that it is inspired revelation from God and from the genre of Scripture, which is dominated by story or narrative. Scripture gives us stories of how others have walked with God (well or badly) so that we learn holistically and inductively, not simply propositionally. We know well the experience of reading a familiar Bible story and suddenly discovering something new in it as we notice the perspective of a different character or an observation about a particular circumstance that the Holy Spirit uses to teach us in a new way. As this happens repeatedly and for people in different cultures and times, the Bible story itself becomes a "model story" or "type" of particular truths. So "Judas" has gone from being a character in a narrative to a "type" of betrayal. Scripture itself contains many examples. The story about Abraham, for instance, is treated by later New Testament writers not simply as a historical account but as a paradigm of trusting God despite the apparent evidence against doing so. This is the kind of approach I adopt in the next few paragraphs—to articulate a biblical framework for understanding how the people of God relate to the world.

From the outset of the biblical story, we can observe that the distinction between the people of God and the world is itself grounded in the fall, not in creation. God did not design a world in which only some human beings were to be in close relationship with him while others remained alienated. Prior to the fall, "the people of God" and "the world" were coterminous groups, because all people in the world were God's people. At the fall, there was a period when *all* human beings specified in the biblical story were alienated from God and expelled from his presence in the garden of Eden. A distinction soon emerged, however, between those who in humility continued to fear God and sought to please him and those who increasingly gave way to their own selfish desires (i.e., sin).

We see this in the Cain and Abel story and onward. This first biblical story of a distinction between the people of God and the world portrays the one mastered by sin becoming hostile toward the one offering an acceptable sacrifice—Cain murders Abel. The story of Noah provides a model in which God's people build an ark to escape judgment (a mind-set adopted, sometimes explicitly, in the contemporary Christian-schools movement). The exodus provides a powerful paradigm of God's deliverance of his people from slavery and oppression and has been used extensively in recent times by liberation theologians to sustain hope and mobilize action among the landless poor of Latin America. Joshua provides a model— easily abused—of how God led his people to invade and conquer a godless land in order to settle there and make a home after their years of wandering in the wilderness.

All these stories and more are biblical examples of the relationship between the people of God and the world. Most of them are explicitly referenced in the New Testament as in some sense fulfilled in Jesus Christ. What is fundamental to all of them, I suggest, is the theological motif of exile from God, from one another, and from creation, and the need for forgiveness, return, and restoration. The fall and the expulsion from Eden effectively place all of humanity in exile from God. After murdering Abel, Cain becomes a paradigm of exile from God as a "restless wanderer" in the land "east of Eden" (Gen. 4:12–16). Abraham is clearly one of the most important figures in biblical theology. With Abraham, God chooses one person to become the father of an entire nation and draws him into a covenantal relationship for the benefit of all the nations of the earth (Gen. 12:1–3). But Abraham is a pilgrim whose faithfulness to God is defined by his willingness to live in exile from his home country, always traveling in search of a home that God would provide (Heb. 11:8–10). The nation of Israel, the promised fruit of Abraham's obedience, is called not so that it alone could return from exile to God but so that it could be a light to the nations, enabling them also to return from exile (Deut. 4:5–8; Isa. 49:6).

In the Babylonian exile, God's people learn that their calling to bless the nations has not been revoked just because Jerusalem is captive—even in pagan Babylon they are to "seek the peace and prosperity of the city to which I have carried you" (Jer. 29:7). New Testament writers like Peter and Paul highlight how we are "exiles scattered throughout the provinces"

(1 Pet. 1:1) and our true citizenship is in heaven (Phil. 3:20). At one level then, the entire biblical story between Genesis 3 and Revelation 21 takes place in exile. It is the story of humanity's alienation from God and God's reconciling us to himself so that once again, as in the original intention of God in creation, "God's dwelling place is now among the people" (Rev. 21:3) and humanity's long exile is at last over. Our shame will have ended, and our longings will have been fulfilled.

In the exilic paradigm, the explicit role of the people of God in relation to the world is threefold: to be a model or example, to be a channel of God's blessing, and to actively seek to reconcile all aspects of life to God. In other words, exile is a context for God's people to exemplify faith that the condition of alienation from God can be overcome by God's grace. The condition of exile also presents significant challenges to faithfulness. God's people are repeatedly warned not to imitate the sinful behaviors of the surrounding nations. Being God's people amid a culture that is rejecting God is not easy or comfortable. This tension is also an important dimension of exile. It is the kind of tension we experience as God's people in the contemporary world, whether in our gathered communities as local churches or as individual Christians scattered throughout a vast range of workplaces, neighborhoods, and institutions. The legacy of modernity and the fragmentation of Western culture following its rejection of Christian faith as its unifying core have accentuated this tension in recent times.

The Experience of Exile

We need to attend to these feelings of tension and fragmentation. The loss of connection between our faith and every aspect of our lives—the sense that we're not able to be the same person in the varied communities and spheres of which we're a part—is a fracturing of integrity. It also leaves us ill-equipped to deal with the complexity of contemporary life and vulnerable to the same fear, confusion, and loneliness that many of our neighbors have. In dialogue with the biblical arguments presented above, I want to explore this state of affairs using the concept of exile as a sociological descriptor of our experience.

The *Oxford English Dictionary* defines an "exile" as "a person who lives away from their native country, either from choice or compulsion."[4] To be in exile is to be separated from one's home. This separation usually involves a sense of alienation, of not belonging where one is living, of not being at home.

As we will come to see in more detail in subsequent chapters, the theme of exile is extremely rich both in Scripture and in the contemporary world. Although I am writing this book while living in a country that is foreign to me, that is not the primary sense in which I want to use the word "exile." Instead, my concern in this book is with our sense of exile in "the world as we know it," of not being fully at home in the world as it is, of feeling that no matter how pleasant or good some of its features may be, we don't fully belong or fit in.

Maybe for some of us, this feeling may arise, as it did for the apostle Paul, as a positive yearning to be home with Christ: "We know that while we are at home in the body we are away from the Lord. . . . And we would rather be away from the body and at home with the Lord" (2 Cor. 5:6, 8 ESV).

For most of us, however, I suspect that this feeling of exile manifests itself to us also in more negative modes. The gap between our culture's stories and promises to itself and the lived experience of complexity, challenge, and confusion creates unease and dissatisfaction among more and more people. This generalized sense of exile from peace and happiness is magnified for groups, like Christians, who feel marginalized in some way from the dominant public culture. We live in a generation in which our elders at least can remember a time when Christianity was still a major force in our Western or Western-influenced societies. Thus we feel its declining influence more acutely. Our faith is increasingly marginalized and subjected to ridicule, mockery, and disdain. Our society is dominated by cultural stories and beliefs that seem impervious to Christian faith, even a threat to it. Our science and

---

4. *Oxford English Dictionary* online, s.v. "exile," accessed August 28, 2019, https://www .lexico.com/en/definition/exile.

technology, economic growth, and political processes all seem to exist and develop without need for God. Jesus seems an embarrassment to many of us in the corporate office, school, hospital, or café. Most of our neighbors seem ignorant of the gospel and uninterested in finding out more.

We gather on a Sunday to hear the good news, sing to Jesus as Lord, and confess our belief that he's the God who created the whole universe, but often we have no clear idea how Jesus makes any difference to how we respond to the six o'clock news, do our work on Tuesday afternoon, or engage in voting at election time. Increasingly we settle for a kind of split personality disorder—talking and living according to one story when we're with church family and friends but adopting a different language and lifestyle when we're not. This leaves us profoundly dissatisfied, because we're not living truly integrated lives. We can't seem to be a whole person, with all our beliefs, values, and passions, wherever we are.

Because of all this, some of us feel in exile *from* the church and may even have stopped attending church meetings. When we see the apparent disengagement of the church from society and the church's inability or unwillingness to help us live integrated and whole lives, we become disheartened and disillusioned and increasingly look for spiritual sustenance elsewhere, becoming spiritual refugees—perhaps with like-minded Christians, perhaps not.

The Reality of Exile

It's important that we understand these feelings of marginalization, alienation, and exile and what is causing them. There are two dimensions to the experience of exile I want to highlight.

The first dimension is that *all humanity is in exile*. We have been expelled from Eden. We were created for intimacy with God in his creation, a creation that he handed over to us to steward and make fruitful on his behalf. But ever since the fall we've been alienated as a race from God, from ourselves, and from the earth. Becoming a Christian has a huge impact, but it doesn't change everything. Believers are made alive to God in a new birth that awakens us to a heightened awareness of the reality that things are not right with the world, that God has come to save us all, that the problem is so bad that it requires God himself to die on a cross, and that things won't get properly sorted out until Jesus Christ returns. So although Christians experience something of a return from exile, beginning with a restored intimacy with God by the Spirit, the salvation we experience now is not the fullness of salvation that is promised. Sin remains our enemy, if not our master. We are still living in a creation that groans to be set free from the bondage of decay (Rom. 8:18–22). We still die.

To some extent becoming a Christian makes the problem seem worse. We become even more aware that humanity is in exile. We begin to grieve over sin and death in the world as God grieves over them. Yet also our hopes and expectations for change are aroused. Having experienced something of God's power, we know change is possible, we believe God's promises of salvation, and his Spirit within us groans inwardly for the redemption of all things. Yet in the present we continue to see and suffer the effects of humanity's bondage and exile from God. The gap between our hopes and our experience widens.

This first dimension of exile, then, is a reality for all people, but one that Christians living in the Spirit are especially aware of. We long for a world made right—for the kingdom come—and we can't feel entirely at home in the *world-as-it-is* because of that. In other words, there's probably something wrong with us if we don't feel exiled in this sense, a yearning for things to be better.

For Christians there is a second dimension to exile. Christians are those who've accepted God's invitation to become part of his solution to humanity's alienation in the world by humbly accepting the saving lordship of Jesus Christ and joining his mission to reconcile all things in himself. His mission is to subdue all the evil, mend all the brokenness, and remake the world as a place where God and humanity can be at home together. But following Jesus in this way *requires* a further separation from the *world-as-it-is*. It requires that we "not conform to the pattern of this world" but instead are "transformed by the renewing of [our] mind" (Rom. 12:2). What Paul in his Letter to the Romans teaches as an action at the center of discipleship, Jesus reveals as a spiritual fact of our Christian identity in his prayer for believers recorded in John 17. It is worth reading this prayer of Jesus in full, as it speaks of the relationship between Christians and the world. In the middle of Jesus' prayer are these words: "I have given them your word and *the world has hated them, for they are not of the world any more than I am of the world. My prayer is not that you take them out of the world but that you protect them from the evil one. They are not of the world, even as I am not of it.* Sanctify them by the truth; your word is truth. *As you sent me into the world, I have sent them into the world*" (John 17:14–18 [emphasis added]). From this prayer a few startling, and perhaps uncomfortable, truths are apparent:

1. Followers of Jesus are "not of the world" just as Jesus is not of the world. They have been taken by God from "out of the world" and given to Jesus (vv. 14, 16; and v. 6).
2. Jesus followers remain "in" the world and indeed have been "sent into the world" (vv. 11, 18).
3. The "world" is a hostile place for Jesus followers. They need protection because they are hated and have an evil opponent (vv. 11–12, 14, 15).

The conclusion is clear: in some sense, *by virtue of becoming Christians,* followers of Jesus have a relationship to the world such that they don't belong and are treated with hostility. In other words, *a heightened experience of exile is a reality of authentic Christian discipleship.* This is why becoming a Christian and growing in Christian maturity will likely make us feel more aware of our exile in the world even as we become more aware of belonging to God.

Exile Today

The reality of exile is clearly not new, even if our experience of it has taken a particular expression in the contemporary world. But there are particular reasons for emphasizing it, as I have, in the context of Christian mission in Western culture today.

So far I have discussed exile in this chapter without examining the most obvious biblical texts on the topic: the account of the siege and subsequent fall of Jerusalem; the stories of Daniel, Esther, Nehemiah, and Ezra; and the stern, mournful, and magnificent prophesies of Jeremiah, Ezekiel, and others. The exile of the Jews from Judea to Babylon was a devastating experience. Despite decades of prophetic warnings about impending judgment because of their idolatry and faithlessness, the Jews simply couldn't believe that God would allow pagan foreign nations to capture Jerusalem. Yet capture it and destroy it they did, to the horror of the watching exiles. Many, like Daniel and his friends, found themselves living and working in a pagan culture that was actively hostile to their home country.

In our own day we may not have been physically exiled, but Western culture has changed around us. Although the West was formed out of the rubble of the classical world by two thousand years of Christian influence, it has decisively thrown off that heritage and rejected the faith that brought it to birth. Many believers have still not come to terms with the fact that we live now in a post-Christian society. By this I mean not at all that Christ is no longer relevant but that society has turned away from Christ. Indeed, Lesslie Newbigin speaks of a post-Christian paganism, different from the pre-Christian kind because it is inoculated against Christianity, yet equally instrumental—and thus dehumanizing—in its inner life. We hark back to the days of greater Christian influence, and this nostalgia makes it all the harder to live faithfully in the present. Our culture may be godless, but it is also wealthy and comfortable. Comfort plus nostalgia for a half-remembered past form a dangerous emotional combination capable of numbing us to the reality of exile in our day and the missional challenges it presents.

Most of the Christian infrastructure of the West is organized around assumptions from a world that has almost completely disappeared. Our theological schools prepare church leaders to fill pastoral positions in churches that are assumed to exist and to preach to people who are already converted and who live in societies that are presumed culturally Christian. Our churches and mission agencies are almost all built to support overseas missions and domestic pastoral care. Yet we need to be equipped for pioneer church planting, we have a crisis of discipleship, cultural Christianity has largely gone, and Christianity is more vibrant in the Global South than it is in the West.

Our de facto mission strategy is woefully inadequate to the church's situation in the West, but decades of imbibing the toxic theology of the sacred-secular divide and the growing intimidation of contemporary public discourse have left us often confused, fearful, and timid. Exile ought to be expected, but perhaps we have become so used to a position of influential privilege that we think it our right. For those feeling somewhat traumatized by these changes, we need to ask ourselves some tough questions: Have we lost our nerve? Are we confident that the gospel is the very power of God for the salvation of all who believe? Is God sovereign in Babylon or only in Jerusalem? Is Jesus Lord in the world or only in the church? The condition of exile presents us with powerful temptations. Are we ready to meet these with faith and serve the purposes of God in our generation?

3

Two Temptations

All humanity is in exile from Eden—alienated from the tree of life by our own rebellion and unable to enter the place where God intended for us to dwell intimately with him, with one another, and with creation. Jesus came to restore us to the abundant life that God intended, but in following him, Christians find themselves in a second exile, one from "the world" that remains alienated from him and opposed to his lordship.

For Christians in the West, the full force of the second exile has been muted in recent generations. Centuries of Christian influence deposited an enormous store of Christian cultural capital at the heart of Western societies. Secular society has lived off the benefits of this capital for some time, believing that goods such as freedom of speech, the rule of law, family life, and business integrity can flourish without connection to any religious foundation. For a while it seemed this was true, and the church acquiesced to it, politely withdrawing from public life into a private realm. At the same time, a residue of nominal Christianity within the culture masked the underlying societal turn away from Christ. But in recent decades it has become obvious that this situation is not stable. The Christian cultural capital of the West is rapidly being consumed, and the cultural goods it supported are decaying. In subtle and less subtle ways, freedom of speech is being eroded, the rule of law undermined, marriage and family life corroded, health care and education instrumentalized, and enterprise and work increasingly subordinated to short-term profit making. The more militant secularists are busy dismantling the vestiges of the Christian architecture of society. Meanwhile, in most of the West, nominal Christianity has all but faded away, since identifying as a Christian is increasingly not a cultural asset but a disadvantage.

The rate at which these changes have occurred since the 1960s has been rapid. The church has suffered a kind of whiplash effect. By and large we've been dazed, reactive, and in denial—always responding to events with a backward-looking mind-set. Rather than explaining the gospel to a newly ignorant society, we've tended to criticize what we assume is deliberate rebellion. Many believers have found themselves deeply confused about the relationship of their faith to ordinary life and work, and they are deeply dismayed by the reactive and insular posture of church leaders.

The current context of exile for the church in the West is thus particularly problematic. Having grown too used to the assumptions of cultural Christianity, we are now acutely vulnerable to the temptations of exile. This chapter explores these temptations in dialogue with some of the biblical texts on exile.

The Root of Exilic Temptation

To be in exile is to be separated from one's place of belonging. This means more than merely traveling or feeling homesick. We can't be in exile as *visitors* but only as *residents*. For exile to occur, we must be *living* in a culture that is in some significant way at odds with our home culture. An experience of exile need not imply a physical separation from "home," but it does imply a cultural separation—a dissonance between the cultural story in which I feel "at home" and the cultural story I daily live in.

Sociologists and anthropologists have studied the ways that refugees, political exiles, immigrant families, and minority groups experience cultural dissonance. It can be defined as "an uncomfortable sense of discord, disharmony, confusion, or conflict experienced by people in the midst of change in their cultural environment."[1] This cultural dissonance is at the root of the various temptations we face as Christians living in exile. To understand why, we need to delve further into the notion of a cultural story.

If I asked you who you are and why you're doing what you're doing, pretty soon you'd start telling me your life story. You'd tell me about your childhood experiences; your parents, friends, and community; the most cherished beliefs and convictions that you hold and why you hold them; the choices you've made and why you made them; and the ups and downs that have created the dramatic tension in your life so far. You'd have some sense, however tentative, of how you hope the story of your life will end, your hopes and dreams for the future. We all have a personal story, but these stories are inevitably situated in and shaped by the larger stories of our culture, our geography, and our time in history. Growing up in postwar Europe under rationing, for example, shaped an entire generation to be frugal with resources. Growing up in early twenty-first-century America under conditions of easy credit shaped a good many of that generation to speculate on the housing market. How are we being shaped today? What stories are we living by?

The former chief rabbi of the United Kingdom, Jonathan Sacks, observed that "a culture is defined by its narratives."[2] That is, if we want to understand a culture, we should pay careful attention to the stories it tells about life, success, happiness, meaning, and purpose. Like it or not, we are surrounded by and immersed in cultural stories. We live by them because we are formed and shaped—our identities are defined—by the stories we tell one another. The moral philosopher Alasdair MacIntyre puts it like this: "I can only answer the question 'What am I to do?' if I can answer the prior question 'Of what story or stories do I find myself a part?'"[3] Cultural stories, personal identity, and meaningful action are deeply intertwined.

1. Farley, Smith, and Boyle, *Introduction to Social Work*.
2. Sacks, "In a World Run by MTV, Nobody Has Time to Think."
3. MacIntyre, *After Virtue*, 216.

There are several stories that are competing to try to define us. What is the cultural story that really shapes our identity? As Christians, we live in at least two storytelling communities: the community of the church and the community of the contemporary society in which we live. On the one hand, we have the story of the church—a story about repentance and salvation, loyalty to Jesus, and the gospel of the kingdom of God. It's a grand story about eternal life and the salvation of the world. On the other hand, we have the story of the contemporary world—primarily a story about individual choice, success, and achievement, and about loyalty to self and confidence in technological progress. It's a very alluring story. It seduces us constantly with the idea that here is the route to fulfillment, to happiness, to security. The media, advertising, and movies reinforce it. We can easily get the sense that there are huge forces driving this story, forces that are way beyond our control and our ability to influence: forces of advertising, large business, capitalism, globalization, and a political culture in which Christianity is not an accepted part of the discussion. These large forces that seem to be behind the story of the contemporary world can often make us—and the local church community—feel insignificant and irrelevant. They seem to reflect a kingdom that we have no part of and to which we don't belong, or alternatively they may highlight a sense that the church is out of touch.

There are many subcultures within contemporary society, each with its own version of the larger cultural story, but whichever subplot of the story we encounter, that is where we experience the discord, confusion, and conflict of the cultural dissonance between the Christian story and the story of the contemporary world.

This dissonance creates an enormous challenge, because all of us want to belong in community and to inhabit a story for our lives that makes our actions meaningful. Belonging-in-community is something we're made for as human beings. We want to fit in, to be liked, and to feel that we can contribute and that our work will be valued. So we may respond to this challenge in one of two ways.

One, we focus our lives on things that are obviously Christian: church activities, evangelism, missions trips, and the latest revival movement. We end up downgrading or withdrawing from our "secular" activities as somehow second best, and we may become church-paid youth workers, mission workers, or pastors as a result.

Two, we throw ourselves into social action, environmentalism, or fighting global injustice. We focus on our workplaces and "secular" communities, believing that by fitting in, we will set a better example. We often find ourselves increasingly impatient with a form of "churchianity" that doesn't seem to relate faith to any dimension of life except the personal and familial.

Of course these descriptions are caricatures, but they represent tendencies with which we are all too familiar. Both types of response risk missing God's purposes for the church; both fall short of faithfulness and obedience to his call; both may be adapting unhealthily to cultural dissonance, seeking to avoid a life of constant conflict. It is so much easier to find a way to avoid the tension of living in both stories. It is so much easier to give in to the temptation either to assimilate or to withdraw.

The Temptation to Assimilate

The temptation to assimilate is essentially a temptation to compromise on essentials in order to fit in with the dominant culture. While there is an entirely good and right way for Christians to be in dialogue with the cultural stories that surround them, assimilation often leads to an unhealthy loss of community identity and ideals. By attempting to fit in, the community often loses itself. In the sociological literature on cultural dissonance, this temptation corresponds to two well-documented "patterns of adjustment": to try to synthesize the minority cultural story with the dominant one and to try to pass as a member of the dominant group.[4] These two patterns show us the two forms assimilation often takes.

The first route to assimilation is one that attempts to blur the differences between cultural stories; to minimize difficult beliefs, doctrines,

---

4. See Suárez-Orozco and Suárez-Orozco, *Children of Immigration*, 84.

or practices; and to adopt and "baptize" central cultural practices from the dominant story. What results is a syncretistic religion. Biblical Israel exemplifies this kind of assimilation. Under the gathering military and cultural pressure of the surrounding nations, and with leaders motivated to achieve political influence or popular support, both Israel and Judah began to worship the Canaanite, Egyptian, Assyrian, and Babylonian gods alongside Yahweh. Second Kings 17 describes religious syncretism as a major reason for the fall of Samaria and the final defeat of the Northern Kingdom of Israel at the hands of the Assyrian empire around 722 BC: "They imitated the nations around them" (2 Kings 17:15). The surrender and subsequent destruction of Jerusalem some 125 years later was also attributed by the prophets to syncretistic religion. Ezekiel 8–10 describes these practices before the prophet declares God's summary judgment on the Southern Kingdom of Judah: "You have not followed my decrees or kept my laws but have conformed to the standards of the nations around you" (Ezek. 11:12).

In our day, orthodox believers have tended to identify cultural assimilation and syncretistic religion with the misguided attempt of the liberal church to achieve acceptance and influence. Liberal Christianity has tended to jettison all or most of the miraculous elements of the biblical story, import a version of the scientific method into theological reasoning, and reduce conversion and discipleship to education and societal progress. These forms of syncretism tend to lead to empty churches, though they may seem very "relevant" for a while. We should also ask whether evangelicals might have uncritically assimilated to the individualistic, therapeutic, and consumerist ideology of contemporary capitalism or to the political populism and Marxist versions of theology that have arisen in response.

Syncretism effectively undermines the identity of the community. In fact, empires in the ancient world often used this technique deliberately, adopting explicit policies of assimilation to subdue defeated nations. The Assyrians deliberately transplanted defeated communities into other geographies, mixed them with other defeated groups, destroyed their powerful cultural symbols such as temples and shrines, and enforced outward worship to the Assyrian religion. Similarly, we see the Babylonian model of enculturation in the treatment of the Jewish exiles recorded in the book of Daniel. Daniel and his friends Hananiah, Mishael, and Azariah are representative of the Jewish noble families carried off to Babylon following the first defeat of Jerusalem by King Nebuchadnezzar. They are given Babylonian names and ordered to learn the Babylonian culture in order to serve the very king who has defeated and annexed Jerusalem. They are also commanded to eat the pagan delicacies from the king's table.

Daniel and friends resolve not to compromise. Whereas being called by different names or being made to study would not threaten their identity as Jews, defiling themselves by breaking the Israelite food laws would. Sunday school lessons often tell the story of how these four find favor with the court officials because, despite their leaner diet, they somehow prove to be healthier than those who complied and ate the rich food. As a result, they are given permission to decline the rich food. This courageous stand on what may seem a relatively minor matter sets the stage for their response to later temptations to compromise, most notably the command to bow down before the image of the king or face the threat of the fiery furnace. Jeremiah's account of the exile implies that around three thousand of the leading citizens of Jerusalem were exiled at this point (Jer. 52:28–30). The text of Daniel is silent on the matter of how many other Jewish exiles of noble birth were ordered to serve in Nebuchadnezzar's court. It seems unlikely that only four of the three thousand found themselves in this position. What happened to the others? Did they eat the pagan food and defile themselves? Did they think perhaps that it was better to survive to live another day rather than risk angering the king? Did they later bow down to the image of Nebuchadnezzar rather than risk the fiery furnace?

If one of the routes to assimilation is syncretistic religion, a second is the attempt to hide one's identity and pass as an adherent of the dominant cultural story. In his careful study of newly influential evangelical leaders in America, D. Michael Lindsay highlights the troubling trend of successful "cosmopolitan" evangelicals who disengage from the local church. One interviewee sums it up: "I've become kind of a floating Christian. . . . I'm not a member of any [particular] church."[5] How many of us seek to hide our Christian identity while pursuing a successful secular career and increasingly view the local church as an embarrassing irrelevance? Perhaps we imagine that keeping a low profile now will enable us to gain more influence later. While there may be some extreme situations in which hidden faith is necessary (e.g., some "tent-making" missionaries functioning in jurisdictions where Christianity is illegal), the lesson of Daniel highlights the need for open identity in community to keep us accountable and help us avoid compromise.

The Temptation to Withdraw

Fear of assimilation tends to be one factor leading us to a second common reaction to cultural dissonance: withdrawal. Instead of trying to fit in, a community can try to cope by withdrawing into the presumed safety of a community defined by the story of faith. This temptation responds to the tension of living in two cultural stories by adopting a defensive identity, one that tries to live completely inside a form of the "home" story. Examples of this in the sociological literature on cultural dissonance include gang membership and other forms of community defined with very strong boundaries on the basis of insider-outsider status. One writer describes such a typical defensive identity in the following terms: "Gangs offer their members a sense of belonging, solidarity, support, discipline and warmth. Gangs also structure rage."[6]

"Rage" is a good word to capture the feeling of the Babylonian exiles portrayed in Scripture. Psalm 137 gives us a graphic picture of the mood in the Jewish ghetto. The exiles are down by the rivers of Babylon, weeping and wailing. They have their harps, but they won't play them. Their entire

5. Lindsay, *Faith in the Halls of Power*, 222–23.
6. Suárez-Orozco and Suárez-Orozco, *Migration, Family Life, and Achievement Motivation among Latino Adolescents*, 69.

focus is on what they've lost, on how they were betrayed by the Edomites, and on their hatred toward their "captors" and "tormentors." "Happy is the one who seizes your infants and dashes them against the rocks" (v. 9) is their prayer. Such a community was very open to listening to the false prophets who rose up both back in Judah and in Babylon itself. We learn about these false prophets in Jeremiah 27–29. Their basic message is a popular one: God will break the power of the Babylonians in only a few years and bring the exiles back to Jerusalem. These false prophecies encouraged open rebellion against King Nebuchadnezzar.

Do we see ourselves at all in this depiction?

Are we prone at times to adopt an angry posture toward our culture? Do we sometimes enjoy the chance of using our pulpits (or Bible studies) to denounce its sins and announce its imminent judgment? Are our engagements in public discourse limited to criticism and complaint around a narrow range of topics (such as abortion, euthanasia, and sexuality); rarely concerned with broader issues of social justice such as inequality, creation care, unemployment, or debt; and even less likely to involve affirmations of what is good alongside concern for what is deficient?

When we invest energy, creativity, and resources in new ventures, are they aimed at the common good of society or at ourselves? Many churches prioritize new buildings and educational institutions in their spending decisions. In the design and ethos of these, are we seeking a place of retreat from the world or protection from the culture? Do we design and invest with the needs and interests of those outside the church in mind? When it becomes not only possible but actually quite routine for the children of Christian families to be educated at home or in Christian primary and secondary (high) schools, go to Bible college, and then train to be a pastor, overseas missionary, or Christian school teacher without at any point being exposed to the majority secular culture except when they shop, have we not created a cultural Christian ghetto?

Equally, is the sacred-secular divide not itself a device for protecting the church within the Christian ghetto? Do we imagine that by reducing the gospel to the personal and private dimensions of life (the "sacred") we can insulate Christian community and culture from the messy realities of the economy, politics, and society (the "secular")? Judging by the average church service, we believe that what we do as workers, citizens, consumers, and investors is of no real concern to Christ, so long as we're having our daily quiet time, reading our Bible, and taking part in the occasional mission trip or Sunday school teaching rotation. Certainly, we can't easily avoid work, spending money, and the involvement with nonbelievers that comes from being a citizen in a modern society, but it appears we think those things don't really matter in any ultimate sense. We may see them as unavoidable arenas that contaminate us and from which we need cleansing via the ablutions of the weekly church meeting. Is there so much difference between us and the Babylonian exiles who realized they had to make a living but basically wanted to opt out of the society that had taken them captive and huddle together to bemoan their fate?

The sacred-secular divide shapes us as both communities and individuals. While some individuals respond to such a ghettoized community by abandoning it and risking assimilation, others spiritualize their own avoidance of a challenging commission to work in a "secular" job. In his book *Under the Unpredictable Plant* (1992), Eugene Peterson writes powerfully about this tendency to opt for the apparent purity of an idealized spiritual career (Jonah's preference for Tarshish) against the clear command to risk a messy missional engagement with nonbelievers (Jonah's actual commission to Nineveh). Many of us struggle to see how our work as accountants, IT specialists, marketers, or administrators has anything to do with God. What leads us to leave a secular job to work for an overseas mission agency and then do the same accounting, IT support, and communications work in another country while seeking financial and prayer support from our friends and churches because we're now "missionaries"? Is it working for a Christian mission agency that makes our work significant? Were we not able to function as missionaries in the former job? If not, where does that leave Daniel and friends, employing their gifts for the pagan Nebuchadnezzar? Were they falling short of God's best use of their time?

Avoiding Temptation?

The growing cultural dissonance that many Christians experience makes us particularly vulnerable to these two primary temptations of exile: assimilating or withdrawing.

Fear and anger are the powerful emotions at the center of these temptations. We fear the shame, embarrassment, and cultural disadvantage involved in living out a biblical faith. We're angry at the deceit, mockery, and degeneracy we see in parts of contemporary life. Often these emotions are then taken out on one another. We critique other believers for "selling out" as they get involved or for being "super spiritual" in their pietistic disengagement. What did the exiles gathered by the waters of Babylon think of those like Daniel who were working every day in the courts of King Nebuchadnezzar? How are today's "Daniels," who seek to work faithfully in difficult secular contexts, viewed by church leaders? Do we see them as good tithe payers, as people who would be better employed in church programs, or as those needing extra support and prayer?

We shouldn't assume that these temptations are mutually exclusive, or that they cannot coexist in the very same congregation. Indeed, the public-private split in contemporary life aligns with the sacred-secular divide to make it easy for us to succumb to both temptations at the same time. We can withdraw into doctrinal purity while pursuing secular careers in which our faith has little influence.

So what do we do with these temptations? Can they be avoided? Are the pressure of temptation and the compromise of exile unavoidable? One perspective on this question, which perhaps finds deeper resonance in Christian thinking than we might imagine, comes from contemporary Judaism.

In his book *Gold from the Land of Israel* (2006), Chanan Morrison translates and summarizes some of the teachings on exile from the celebrated first chief rabbi of pre-state Israel, Rabbi Abraham Isaac Kook. Rabbi Kook's reflection on the nature of exile is based on the story of Joseph being thrown into the pit by his brothers and subsequently sold into slavery in Egypt. For Rabbi Kook, the pit is a metaphor for exile. He identifies three different kinds of pits: those filled with water that, while potentially threatening (due to the possibility of drowning), nevertheless are useful in supporting life; those that are empty and useless but with effort can be filled with water and made useful; and finally, those that are empty of water but contain snakes and scorpions and are simply dangerous. According to the Talmud, Joseph's pit belongs to this third category. For Rabbi Kook, this is the true nature of exile—a dangerous pit of snakes who bite intentionally with the head (such as the Crusaders, Cossacks, and Nazis) and scorpions who sting instinctively with the tail (such as cultural dissonance, intermarriage, and assimilation). Summarizing Rabbi Kook, Morrison concludes: "The afflictions of Exile are by heavenly decree, lest we confuse a temporary resting place in the Diaspora for a permanent home for the Jewish people. The only true remedy for these snakebites and scorpion-stings is to rescue the Jews from the pit, and restore them to their proper homeland."[7]

Is Rabbi Kook right? Are the "afflictions of Exile" essentially a divine judgment designed to keep God's people restless while they await rescue and the full restoration of the coming kingdom? Are the temptation and missional compromise that it leads to unavoidable facts of exile? Even more fundamentally, is the exilic experience of the church in the contemporary world a form of judgment, just as the exile of the Jews in the sixth century BC was an expression of judgment on them?

---

7. Morrison, "Vayeishev: The Nature of Exile," in *Gold from the Land of Israel*, 81–82.

4

Judgment and Mission

The reality of exile and the growing tension of cultural dissonance leave Christians acutely vulnerable to two main temptations: assimilation and withdrawal.

The fear and anger that animate these temptations are directed outward toward the world around us and, sometimes, also at one another as we feel threatened or critical when other Christians are tempted in different ways than we are.

The question we consider in this chapter is whether these negative effects of exile can be avoided. If Israel's exile was the result of God's judgment on the nation, is that also true of the exilic experience of the contemporary church? Can we learn from the posture of some modern Jews and see the difficulties of exile as a kind of unavoidable, purifying judgment of God on his people as we await Christ's return and the fullness of his salvation? How *should* we respond to being in exile?

Is All Exile Judgment?

All humanity is in exile from Eden, excluded from full fellowship with God and access to eternal life. This state of exile clearly reflects the consequences of human sin and thus God's judgment on all humanity. Yet this is not the whole of our story. The church is also witness to God's merciful intervention in human history, most fully in Jesus Christ, to reverse the effects of the fall and restore humanity to right relationship with God, others, and creation. For those who receive Christ, many, though not all, of the effects of this fundamental exile are reversed. Judgment turns into grace for the church. While the church is full of sinners, the church witnesses to God's incredible mercy and grace in making a way for our forgiveness and salvation.

So for Christians, the effect of God's judgment on humanity is diminished. However, another kind of exile is amplified. To the extent that we identify with Christ, we experience the broken relationship between God and his creation from his perspective. Like Jesus, we are "not of this world" (John 17:14, 16). Because of this identification with him, Jesus told us to expect hostility and persecution, a reality to which the apostolic writers of the New Testament give further witness. As the early church suffered repeated persecution under different Roman emperors, various New Testament writers aim to encourage believers to stand up under persecution. The writer to the Hebrews likens such suffering to a battle of faith in which persecution generates a powerful temptation to compromise (Heb. 10:32–39). Similarly, the apostle Peter encourages believers that suffering for being a Christian should not surprise us but rather should encourage us that we bear God's name (1 Pet. 4:12–16). Thus, Peter can argue that "it is better, if it is God's will, to suffer for doing good than for doing evil" (1 Pet. 3:17). This suffering is not arising because the individual Christian is being judged. Rather, part of Christians' call is to share in God's judgment on sin, in this case through persecution. Just as Jesus took God's judgment on himself in his ultimate exile on the cross, we too must carry our cross. Similarly, the writer to the Hebrews argues that though we are not exempt from the consequences of sin, God can use hardship to do us good and purify our lives (Heb. 12:7–11). In this sense, we could agree with Rabbi Kook: God does intend to use the persecution and suffering of believers as a blessing.

We have not yet accounted for the kind of exile that Israel experienced during the Babylonian captivity. Wasn't that because of judgment? Couldn't that kind of exile be what the church is experiencing now?

Israel's exile in Babylon arises from God's judgment on the nation for its persistent apostasy. Jeremiah summarizes for the people the many years of prophetic warnings they have received to turn from their evil ways, stop following other gods, and heed God's call to repent: "'But you did not listen to me,' declares the LORD, 'and you have aroused my anger with what your hands have made, and you have brought harm to yourselves.' Therefore the LORD Almighty says this: 'Because you have not listened to my words, I will summon all the peoples of the north and my servant Nebuchadnezzar king of Babylon,' declares the LORD, 'and I will bring them against this land and its inhabitants and against all the surrounding nations'" (Jer. 25:7–9).

How does this relate to us today? Clearly there is a huge gap between the contemporary church and ancient Israel. Yet the biblical accounts of Israel's judgment and exile from the land are also instructive for the church (2 Tim. 3:16). As God's own people, privileged to have received the covenant promises and revelation of God's character and will, Israel is judged more severely: for its idolatry, for its trusting in other gods, and for its injustice and oppression that is comparable to, or worse than, the behavior of the surrounding nations. Jesus' words to the seven churches in Revelation underline the truth that God's people will also be judged on the basis of what we know of God's grace and will. We are expected, like Israel, to be a light and a blessing to the peoples around us. This calling requires that our personal and corporate lives be distinctive in the degree to which we manifest God's holiness and love. It is how we live and how we treat one another that is our primary witness: "By this everyone will know that you are my disciples" (John 13:34–35). Our calling, while a blessing, also comes with greater responsibility and the potential for greater judgment.

In chapter 1, we reviewed how Western culture has shifted away from its Christian foundations, evidenced by the sustained rejection of faith throughout society in general. While this has undoubtedly occurred, does that mean that atheists and non-Christians should receive all the blame? Might there be ways that the church has failed to witness fully to the Lord? Have these failures hastened the rejection of Christian faith? One of the most challenging sayings of the late John Stott is this:

> If meat goes bad and becomes inedible, there is no sense in blaming the meat; that is what happens when bacteria are left alone to breed. The question to ask is "Where is the salt?" Just so, if society deteriorates and its standards decline, till it becomes like a dark night or stinking fish, there is no sense in blaming society; that is what happens when fallen men and women are left to themselves, and human selfishness is unchecked. The question to ask is "Where is the church? Why are the salt and light of Jesus Christ not permeating and changing our society?" It is sheer hypocrisy on our part to raise our eyebrows, shrug our shoulders or wring our hands. The Lord Jesus told *us* to be the world's salt and light.[1]

The sacred-secular divide is toxic in part because it has given generations of believers the sense that we can best maintain Christian distinctiveness by keeping separate from larger social, political, and economic activities. Evangelicals, in particular, largely withdrew from public life as an arena of discipleship and mission for much of the twentieth century.[2] Stott is resolute in opposing this attitude. Salt must be salty, but it must also be used—it must be rubbed into the meat if it is to have any preservative effect. Similarly, the "light" of the church is of no use in a dark world if it is hidden. These reflections are subtly different in emphasis to those of Rabbi Kook concerning the afflictions of exile. For Stott, the temptations of withdrawal and assimilation are not part of God's blessings to keep us focused on our true home. The "true remedy" for these afflictions is not that we be removed from the "pit" of exile but rather

1. Stott, *New Issues Facing Christians Today*, 75.
2. George Marsden traces the shift within evangelicalism from an assumed integration of evangelism and social justice in the early nineteenth century, to an assumed separation by the early twentieth (Marsden, *Fundamentalism and American Culture*, 12, 86). Attitudes began to change during the 1970s, but in many ways the church is still grappling with this issue. See also Bosch, *Transforming Mission*, 403–8.

that we overcome these temptations and thereby purify the surrounding culture by our witness.

Stott's reflections come, of course, from part of Jesus' Sermon on the Mount: "You are the salt of the earth. But if the salt loses its saltiness, how can it be made salty again? It is no longer good for anything, except to be thrown out and trampled underfoot. You are the light of the world. . . . In the same way, let your light shine before others, that they may see your good deeds and glorify your Father in heaven" (Matt. 5:13–14, 16).

There is here then a double call—with accompanying warnings—for God's people. We must not lose our saltiness or we risk being "thrown out and trampled underfoot," and we must not hide our light. Israel, as we saw earlier, was also called as a light to the nations and to permeate surrounding nations with God's wisdom and laws. But they failed to take seriously God's expectation that they had been called for the sake of others, not simply for themselves. Rather than being a light and blessing to the nations around them, they were condemned for behaving exactly like them. Their light was hidden and eventually they were thrown out of the land and trampled by the Babylonians.

Is Exile Mercy?

In addition to being a consequence both of humanity's sin and of the people of God's holy life in a fallen world, exile was also a specific judgment on Israel that contains lessons for the contemporary church. But the way in which Christians "share" in God's general judgment on sin, through their suffering for doing good, points to a further perspective. Does God's judgment on the nation of Israel equate to a judgment on the exiles in particular?

Strictly speaking, the exiles are the *survivors* of God's judgment on Judah and Jerusalem, carried off to Babylon in several waves of deportation. A small group, including Daniel and friends, is taken in 604 BC when King Jehoiakim is forced to become a vassal of Nebuchadnezzar. When Jehoiakim later rebels against Nebuchadnezzar, a further group of captives—among them, the prophet Ezekiel—is taken off to Babylon when Jerusalem surrenders in 597 BC.

Up until this point, God's judgment has not fully registered on the exiles. There is a false confidence that the presence of God's temple in Jerusalem makes the nation immune to final defeat. Rebellion against Babylon is still in the air, among both the exiles and those left in Judah under the vassal kingship of Zedekiah. Much of Jeremiah's and Ezekiel's prophetic oracles are aimed at quelling this rebellious attitude toward the Babylonians (see esp. Jer. 27–29; Ezek. 11:1–15). However, Judah, under Zedekiah, does rebel yet again, and this time, in 587 BC, Nebuchadnezzar's armies reduce the city, including the temple, to rubble and take a further group of traumatized survivors to Babylon.

What is overwhelming for these exiles now is that the seemingly unthinkable has occurred: God's holy temple has been destroyed. Has God completely abandoned them? Or was Israel's God overpowered by stronger Babylonian gods? Either way, the national dream now lies in ruins. They are now not simply prisoners of war but aliens and captives in a foreign land with no home to return to and no hope for the future. God's judgment has left them utterly devastated.

They might well have thought of themselves as "thrown out and trampled underfoot," but surprisingly, both Jeremiah and Ezekiel prophesy that God sees things differently. In Jeremiah 24, God likens the exiles to "good figs" that he will watch over and plant back in the land, in comparison to the "bad figs" of the remaining inhabitants of Judah whom God intends to destroy. Those who are not exiled but remain in the land, presuming themselves to be saved, are the very ones whom God declares he will punish and destroy. Similarly, in Ezekiel 11 we find God describing himself as a sanctuary for the exiles and promising to bring them back to the land (Ezek. 11:16–21). It seems, then, that the exiles are those whom God has mercifully spared from the full onslaught of judgment. Certainly they have suffered because of the sin of the nation, and certainly they are admonished to heed the obvious lessons. But rather than abandoning them, as God clearly has abandoned the temple in Jerusalem, God promises to "watch over" and be a "sanctuary" to them, *even while* they are in Babylon.

In sum, the exiles are separated from the land of God's *promise*, but they are not separated from God's *presence*. Similarly for the church today, because of God's judgment on the whole of humanity, we are (still) separated from the land of God's promise—the new heavens and the new earth that we will enjoy when Christ returns—but we are not separated from God's presence. Indeed, his presence and the land of his promise are in some sense collapsed into our relationship with and participation in Christ. It is in Christ that all the promises of God are "Yes" and "Amen" (2 Cor. 1:20). It is in Christ that we will experience a growing sense of dwelling with God in God's world. It is in Christ that the future fullness of the kingdom of God begins to enter our lived experience now.

Many of the stories of the exilic characters that we know so well—like Esther and Daniel—give us a sense of what it meant for God's people to respond to a situation of presence without fullness, *in faith*.

Esther finds herself part of the harem of King Xerxes during a period when the Jews have been in exile for many years. Political power plays had led to the imminent persecution of the Jews throughout the empire. Esther is challenged, via her godly uncle Mordecai, to speak up to the king on behalf of her people. The pivotal piece of dialogue in the account occurs when Esther is wavering about the risks involved to her in speaking to the king. Mordecai encourages her with these well-known words: "Who knows but that you have come to your royal position for such a time as this" (Esther 4:14). Esther responds in faith, prays, and takes the risk of speaking to the king on behalf of her people. At first the power politics appear to overwhelm all hope and threaten Esther's life, but as she acts with faith she experiences God's deliverance of the Jewish people and her own deliverance and honor before the king. The very understated point of this story is that God was at work, even during the exile and even among the pagan kings, watching over his people.

Daniel, as we have seen, is one of the first Jews to be taken into exile in Babylon. He's been trained and schooled to serve God in the sacred city of Jerusalem. This was the future hope that was crushed when he was taken captive, transported to Babylon, and told to serve the pagan king Nebuchadnezzar. He has to learn the Babylonians' language and culture, including their astrology and their gods. He is told to eat their food and was called by a Babylonian name. He is forcefully enculturated.

He could easily have accepted the luxuries that life in the royal court offered in exchange for what seemed like a failed Jewish identity. Maybe there were other Jewish exiles at the king's table who compromised and assimilated. But Daniel and his friends are willing to risk their lives by refusing the food that would have defiled their Jewish identity. They trust God, and he delivers them. They won't compromise over who they are or who, fundamentally, they serve.

Daniel had thought he would serve God in Jerusalem, but he believes and learns that *God is still king in Babylon*, even if Jerusalem is in ruins. He can stand in his identity as God's servant because he is confident in God's character and power. Are we confident that God is as much king in our workplace, home, or community as he is in our church? Do we trust God "out there" in the world as much as we trust him "in here" in the church?

The confidence exhibited by Daniel and his friends in God's sovereignty and presence, even in Babylon, leads to some extraordinary outcomes. Not only are they permitted not to eat the royal food; they also are delivered from the fiery furnace and the lions' den. Facing a death sentence from an angry Nebuchadnezzar, a lengthy prayer meeting results in Daniel being given the details and interpretation of Nebuchadnezzar's dream. These revelations save the lives of all of the court advisors. Moreover, in this incident and subsequent ones, God speaks through Daniel to the Babylonian kings in direction, discipline, judgment, and revelation, leading to extraordinary statements of confession and faith from the mouths of these pagan kings.

The story of Daniel should lead us to ask: What if God is working and present in our world yet we missed him because, in our exiled state, we ceased looking?

Is Exile Mission?

The accounts of the Jewish exiles in Babylon also raise the question of whether there is a missional element to exile. Israel has always been called to be a blessing to the nations. Part of the judgment God brings on both the Northern Kingdom of Israel and the Southern Kingdom of Judah is because of their failure in this calling. In their exile, they are not released from their calling; instead, they are just given another opportunity. God's call on his people remains unchanged. Again, he uses them to reveal his power to the pagan kings and to bring blessing to the pagan people.

God tells the Jewish exiles to bless their Babylonian captors. Jeremiah 29 contains a copy of a letter from Jeremiah to the exiles in Babylon. In it, God rebukes the false prophets who are cursing the Babylonians and prophesying imminent judgment on them. Instead of withdrawing in resentment and anger, God tells the people to adopt a quite different attitude:

> This is what the LORD Almighty, the God of Israel, says to all those I carried into exile from Jerusalem to Babylon. "Build houses and settle down; plant gardens and eat what they produce. Marry and have sons and daughters; find wives for your sons and give your daughters in marriage, so that they too may have sons and daughters. Increase in number there; do not decrease. Also seek the peace and prosperity of the city to which I have carried you into exile. Pray to the LORD for it, because if it prospers, you too will prosper. . . . For I know the plans I have for you," declares the LORD, "plans to prosper you and not to harm you, plans to give you hope and a future." (Jer. 29:4–7, 11)

Later in the same passage, God promises to eventually gather the exiles home—but for now, they are to do what Israel was always meant to do: be a blessing to the nations, be agents of peace and reconciliation.

In the New Testament, the connection between exile and mission becomes even more explicit. Peter puts it like this at the opening of his first letter: "Peter, an apostle of Jesus Christ. To God's elect, *exiles scattered throughout* the provinces of Pontus, Galatia . . ." (and we might add our own city names, whether in Asia, Australasia, Africa, Europe, or the Americas; 1 Pet. 1:1). In chapter 2 he continues: "Dear friends, I urge you, as *foreigners and exiles*, to abstain from sinful desires, which wage war against your soul. Live such good lives among the pagans that, though they accuse you of doing wrong, they may see your good deeds and glorify God on the day he visits us" (1 Pet. 2:11–12).

Peter understands that the church is in exile among the pagans. We are exiled from our true home, from the fullness of the kingdom that we long to see. But solely acknowledging this is not the end goal. Peter sees this exile as an opportunity for us to witness through our lives so that those around us will encounter and glorify God.

The apostle Paul adds to this picture in chapter 1 of his letter to the Philippians: "Whatever happens, conduct yourselves in a manner worthy of the gospel of Christ" (Phil. 1:27). Later in the same letter Paul reveals the ground of this and other admonitions, when he asserts that "our citizenship is in heaven" (Phil 3:20). Paul underlines the point in Jesus' prayer in John 17 that the church is "not of the world" (vv. 14, 16). It's important to recognize that we feel a sense of exile not simply because we're scattered among the world but also because our true citizenship is in heaven. We are not primarily Canadian, British, American, Chinese, Korean, New Zealander, Kenyan, or Brazilian. Nor are we primarily pastors, businesspeople, professionals, homemakers, farmers, or factory workers. We are fundamentally citizens of the kingdom of God. We belong to and with Jesus Christ, and our ultimate allegiance is to him. This makes us foreigners and strangers in the world.

But notice that neither of these New Testament writers ends the discussion here. They're not content simply to explain and validate the feeling of exile, as important as that is for those receiving their words in the context of persecution by Rome. Instead, both go on to urge the church that this sense of exile is the impetus for doing good, for living in a manner worthy of the gospel, for blessing the world as God's image bearers. We are to be agents of reconciliation, promoting right-relatedness with God, each other, and creation.

Different Types of Stranger

We've seen that for Christians, then, exile is not merely an expression of God's judgment on human sin. Exile is also an aspect of our identity and calling. Just as Abraham was chosen out of all the peoples of the earth and called to go wherever God sent him, so the church has been called out of the world in order to be sent back into it. Just as Abraham's offspring acquired a new identity and citizenship in Israel, so Christians are given a new identity and citizenship in the kingdom of God. Just as Israel was called to be a blessing to the nations, so also the church is called to be a blessing of salt and light to the world.

But this will not happen automatically. We will certainly experience exile, but how will we choose respond to it?

There are several different ways of being a stranger in a foreign land. You can be a stranger and understand yourself as an *alien*. You can resent all the differences between the culture you're in and the one where you belong. You can feel permanently isolated and trapped—almost like a captive in a foreign land. The alien feels that they are in a foreign place against their will. The story of the foreign culture dominates and stifles them. They feel stuck and unable to live out of who they really are. They are overcome and overwhelmed by the foreign culture and prone to the anger and fear arising from cultural dissonance.

A second way to live in a strange land is as a *visitor*. One way of dealing with cultural alienation that is worth noting here is to live in a kind of denial and treat the whole experience as if it is temporary. We are "just visiting." This enables people to live in permanent transience; they remain strangers in a foreign culture, always believing that "soon" they will return home. Adopting this "visiting" mentality gives us the excuse to remain disengaged. We don't have to fit in or form community because we will soon be leaving. As long as it doesn't personally impact us, we are not concerned with understanding the cultural story or social, political, and economic life of our neighbors. Ultimately, this "just visiting" mentality has allowed Christians to avoid their calling. In the "just visiting" mentality, we focus on texts that tell us our citizenship is in heaven, that we are not "of this world," but conveniently forget the requirements of that citizenship— namely, to be God's representatives for and in the world.

But a third way of living as a stranger in a foreign land is to live as an *ambassador*. An ambassador is still a stranger who still might miss home, but they're not resentful, and they don't feel trapped. Neither are they disengaged, because they know they're living in a strange land *on purpose*. They've been sent there. They have a job to do. They try to understand the dominant cultural story in their new country, but they are completely secure in their own. They know they can expect all the help that they need from their home country. God's call on Christians is to this third way. We are to be ambassadors of Christ, sent into the world *on purpose*, in all of the places that God has put us, knowing that God is with us and for us because we are on his mission. This is the image that the apostle Paul uses to reframe the experience of exile into a call to enter into God's mission in the world. In 2 Corinthians he writes: "[God] has committed to us the message of reconciliation. We are therefore Christ's ambassadors, as though God were making his appeal through us" (2 Cor. 5:19c–20a).

This then is the ministry and posture of the church in the world: to function as Christ's ambassadors; to make God's appeal to the world. Ambassadors are those who represent a sovereign power. They have an aspect, then, of being kings: they are regents who function to represent the authority of another. They're also there to mediate relationships, to broker reconciliation, to be diplomats, to be "priestly." That is the way in which ambassadors function. They know that they're sent with authority. They are there on purpose with a mission to accomplish. They're there to mediate and do the work of diplomacy. How different from the experience of an alien or a visitor, and yet they're also strangers.

An "alien" feels resentment, fear, and anger toward the dominant culture. A "visitor" is disengaged and curious—they have no real investment in it. An "ambassador" is focused on positive engagement. So which kind of stranger are you?

PART TWO

FOSTERING HOPE

From Alien to Ambassador

5

Learning to Lament

In the previous chapter, we saw how both the Old and New Testaments reframe exile from a paradigm of judgment and oppression to one of mission and opportunity. We may be strangers in a foreign land, but we need not understand ourselves as captive aliens or transient visitors. Instead, we can assume the role of purposeful ambassadors.

The remainder of this book is premised on the assumption that such a shift in self-understanding and identity is biblical, desirable, and possible. But a vital question arises from the discussion of the last chapter: *How* do we make the shift from alien or visitor to ambassador?

Much of the evangelical tradition conditions Christians to assume that if we know the right thing to do, we simply need to do it; if we see or understand something, this information will be enough to effect change. To put this starkly, it is perhaps obvious that this assumption is not so much wrong as inadequate in its understanding of human nature and God's character. This is so in two main respects.

First, ambassadorship is not something you can decide to inhabit. Ambassadors are appointed, not self-appointed.

Second, we cannot simply shift our identity based on our cognitive understanding, because exile is an *experience*, not merely an idea. Although

I have argued that exile is (for the most part) not an expression of God's specific judgment against us, this does not mean that exile is thereby rendered innocuous. On the contrary, it is deeply troubling, complex, and disorienting. Exile may not be an expression of specific judgment, but it still produces real suffering. Cultural dissonance is a jarring experience to live with, one that generates powerful emotions, especially of anger and fear. The temptations to assimilate or withdraw are potent; resisting them requires more than just correct thinking. We need to foster hope. Ideas must be accompanied with emotional maturity, character formed and sustained in community, and a willingness to take risks. Before we can truly function as ambassadors, these temptations, and the difficulties and emotions that make them so tempting, need to be faced and overcome in the power of the Holy Spirit. Facing our fears, controlling our anger, and overcoming temptation require honesty and vulnerability in the presence of God. Before we can experience fresh hope, we need to learn to lament.

Honest Lament

Perhaps the biblical book that you are least likely to hear preached is Lamentations.

We prefer to hear sermons that are edifying and encouraging rather than those that speak of grief, suffering, and the absence of God. Our culture encourages us to believe that wisdom can be gained without bothering with the tiresome need to reflect carefully on lived experience, that knowing the truth can substitute for doing it, and that resurrection power can come without having to carry a cross. In real life, however, there are no shortcuts. If we will attend to the suffering of exile, we will gain a much deeper understanding of Christ's suffering on the cross and the resurrection that followed it. We also put ourselves in a place to be empowered for Christ's mission in our exilic context.

Scripture does not encourage us to skim over our grief and anger at the suffering we experience. This is true throughout the Bible, and a survey of its contents reveals a nuanced, sensitive, and brutally honest engagement with suffering. Over a third of the psalms are individual or corporate laments. Whereas the book of Job is an extended window on God's relationship with us in the context of personal suffering, Lamentations focuses on the suffering of a whole people. These examples—along with other passages in the exilic literature of Scripture[1]—serve as a powerful testimony to the fact that God hears our laments and encourages us to voice our suffering.

If you have any lingering doubt over the spirituality of openly expressing raw anger, grief, and fear before God, I recommend reading Lamentations in one sitting. It is five chapters long and remarkably bereft of the kind of easy answers that we Christians sometimes give to one another in hard times. Its five chapters contain five "dirges" describing the utter devastation felt by the survivors of the destruction of Jerusalem. God is described as "like an enemy" (2:5) who has treated his people worse than anyone else (2:20), ignores prayer (3:8), and attacks his people (3:11–12). The book ends by asking if God has rejected his people for good (5:22).

Although Lamentations does not censor itself in describing the full horror of the destruction of the city, it is nuanced in its understanding of who is to blame and what can be done. On the one hand, the human attackers are blamed, and God is expected to punish them for their behavior (e.g., 1:21–22; 3:64–66; 4:21–22). On the other hand, the suffering of the people is acknowledged as coming from God's hand as a just response to their own sin and disobedience (e.g., 1:5, 8, 14, 18, 20). The literary center of the book (3:22–42) is a clear expression of hope in God's love, a call to confession and repentance, and a cry to God to forgive, relent, and rescue.

What would it look like for us to lament today?

To find examples of Christians suffering deliberate and violent destruction of their communities today, we would have to look to countries like Somalia, Syria, and Iraq. Christians in states like China, North Korea, and Iran have also suffered state censure, imprisonment, confiscation of

---

1. See, e.g., Ezra 9:5–15; Neh. 1:3–2:3; 9:1–37; Jer. 12:1–17; 20:7–18; Dan. 9:1–28; Hab. 1:2–2:20.

property, and other forms of persecution.[2] We may feel that any difficulty or suffering we experience in the West is not worth mentioning. This sounds like a spiritual attitude, but really it is not.

One of the most basic things we can do for our brothers and sisters suffering violent persecution elsewhere is to allow their witness to inspire us to maintain a pure and faithful witness to Jesus Christ in our own context.[3] Maintaining that witness, however, requires both facing the grief, anger, fear, and sense of failure that we have and also allowing God to cleanse and soften our hearts so that we can bear witness to him more fully where we are.

The truth is, we also experience being forgotten and forsaken by God (Lam. 5:20) in the midst of our own cultural context. We have good reason to feel this way: many secularists seem increasingly intolerant of any expression of faith in public life. We've seen the impact of this attitude on believing employees in a wide range of sectors, but especially in state-funded jobs, where people have been disciplined or dismissed because of some minor expression of faith, such as praying for a medical patient who asked for prayer or wearing a cross as a piece of jewelry. The last few decades have seen people arrested or brought to public trial for speaking openly about Christian faith and the claims of Scripture and for trying to live out their beliefs faithfully in their own businesses and workplaces. A growing pressure to stay silent about one's beliefs is coupled with a growing feeling of shame about being a Christian as public denunciations, criticisms, and mockery of Christian faith become more common. While all this carries on, we watch—or sometimes try and fail to prevent—the kinds of choices our societies have been making in terms of the sanctity

2. The Open Doors organization maintains an international World Watch List of countries in which Christians face persecution and works to support believers in such contexts. See http://www.opendoors.org for more information.

3. My views on this have been informed by recent experience. Over the last few years I've had the privilege of meeting many Christian leaders around the Middle East—including from Syria, Iraq, Jordan, Lebanon, Egypt, and Palestine—as I've traveled on behalf of the British and Foreign Bible Society. I've made a point of asking them what their message is for the church in the West. The two themes that stand out in their answers are these: "Don't compromise your witness" and "Don't forget us—pray and speak up."

of life, the treatment of the poor, the value of marriage, the erosion of civic and community life, and the apparent obsession with individualism, choice, and materialism.

We likely feel angry toward those initiating and championing these changes, as well as toward the various governments and courts that appear happy to dilute long-held freedoms of religion, speech, and conscience.

In my experience, many of us also feel a great deal of anger toward other Christians. Depending on which political wing of faith we identify with most, the content of that anger may differ. We may feel angry with weak church leaders and liberal believers who don't speak out clearly to defend the essentials of the faith, allowing, by their silence or prevarication, appalling legal and policy developments on vital issues to go unchallenged. By their compromise and accommodation to secularism, we feel the witness of the gospel is undermined. Alternatively, we may be furious with ignorant and critical Christians who crash around in public like bulls in a china shop, always sounding judgmental and shrill, damaging the credibility of the faith, and accommodating themselves to the insidious individualism and materialism of contemporary capitalism.

I expect most readers will identify with some of these woes. Perhaps you feel embarrassed in some way at your own emotions about the state of the church in the contemporary world. I suggest that we would have cause for much greater concern if these examples failed to arouse grief or anger in us. Lament about the state of things when things are, in fact, bad is a sign of health, showing that God's Holy Spirit is still getting through to us. In Ezekiel's vision of the appalling wickedness and idolatry taking place back in Jerusalem, it was those who lamented the state of the nation and the temple who were marked out for protection from the judgment to come: "Then the LORD called to the man clothed in linen who had the writing kit at his side and said to him, 'Go throughout the city of Jerusalem and put a mark on the foreheads of those who grieve and lament over all the detestable things that are done in it'" (Ezek. 9:3–4).

However, honest lament must go beyond identifying what grieves us, what we're angry about, and who we blame. We must also ask ourselves to what extent we are at fault. We must move to confession. A healthy posture for Western churches for a while would be one of grief and lament over the state of our culture and our complicity in it.

We need to invite God to reveal the heart attitudes that underlie our grief and anger. Are we sharing in his own grief in—and then also his grace for—the state of the world? Are we angry at the persecution and suffering we've experienced because of our faithful witness to Christ (in which case, we need to forgive)? Or are we resenting the loss of influence and status that the cultural Christianity of the recent past has afforded us (in which case, we need to repent)? It is crucial that we shed all traces of the sense of privilege that cultural Christianity has given us if we are to escape the snares of temptation and move from an identity of alienation toward one of ambassadorship.

As we do this, we may be ashamed of the compromise and assimilation we see in our own life. We may feel that we have failed God and are disqualified from serving him. Equally, we may be repulsed by the consequences of our ghetto mentality. We no longer want to stay in the fearful and reactive "us and them" mentality we've adopted toward non-Christians. With respect to our own part in the growing antipathy toward faith in our own societies, we can ask: Have we truly been distinctive in our lifestyles so that we function as "salt" in all our relationships? Have we been clear and confident in the gospel, able to shed Christ's light and "give the reason for the hope that [we] have" to whoever questions us (cf. 1 Pet. 3:15)? Have we treated other believers with the love and grace of Christ? Are we able to truly love our enemies in our attitudes and actions? Is our trust truly in God, or is it in our favorite interpretation of the Bible or our intellectual grasp of theology?

The point of asking these questions is not to condemn. Feelings of failure and shame are more likely to make us vulnerable to the temptations of exile than to help us move into a more faithful and missional mode. Instead, the point of honest anger, grief, and confession is to exercise humility before God, admitting to ourselves and one another before him what he already knows but we often dare not acknowledge. The chief sin for us all is the pride of autonomy—thinking we can work things out for ourselves, that we alone are the "faithful remnant" that God has preserved and is relying on, that we alone understand the signs of the times and know what to do, or that we alone are beyond Christ's power to forgive, heal, and transform.

Active Listening

Simply expressing our anger and grief will not achieve a great deal. It may be cathartic, but without a response from God, it is a lonely cry in the darkness. Honest lament for Christians, however, presupposes a loving God who hears, understands, and cares. It presupposes a living God who speaks, blesses, and acts. This is why Christian lament must be followed by active listening—an expectant waiting for God to respond to us.

Lamentations encourages us to adopt this posture of attentive waiting. The core of the book's message is to be found in the heart of Lamentations 3, where amid all the grief, wailing, and lament, we find these words: "I say to myself, 'The LORD is my portion; therefore I will wait for him.' The LORD is good to those whose hope is in him, to the one who seeks him. It is good to wait quietly for the salvation of the LORD" (3:24–26).

This attentive stillness of spirit allows God to show us our hearts and help us consider our actions. The same passage goes on to urge: "Let us examine our ways and test them, and let us return to the LORD" (Lam. 3:40). Seeking God, testing our ways, and returning to him obviously assumes that God will allow himself to be found by us and will forgive us and answer us. Notice, too, that the pronouns in these verses are both singular and plural. It is important to be able to cry out to God alone from the depths of our hearts. It is equally important to share our grief and confess our sins with others. This is not merely wise human advice. There is a powerful anointing of God that is released for our healing when we come together as believers and humble ourselves before one another with a focus on "return[ing] to the LORD." Often it is in such a context that we will encounter God through the words, care, and prayers of other believers.

To say that we should expect the living God to respond to us is theologically true and basic. Yet it is precisely on this point that many contemporary Christians struggle. Indeed, it is perhaps in this that the existential reality of exilic alienation is most keenly known: the feeling that God is absent. For many Western believers, it is a sad truth that a personal encounter with the living God—in which I know in my heart that I have been addressed directly by the Maker of heaven and earth—is either a distant memory or a fading hope.

Our tendency to "practical atheism"—to carry out our work and daily decisions *as if* God is uninterested—contributes greatly to a sense of God's absence. If I don't believe that God is relevant to or interested in a part of my life, then I'm not likely to pray about it in any serious manner. If I don't pray, I'm not going to have any answered prayers. Nor am I likely to be attuned to God's presence and activity. When the only things I pray about are either crisis situations for family and friends or what, for me, are abstract situations affecting largely anonymous people overseas (which, I suggest, is indeed the typical makeup of many Christians' prayer lives), then there is little scope to see the kind of specific answers to prayer that build our faith and confidence that God is present and at work in the world. Moreover, if I am not praying about the detail of my daily life, I'm implicitly assuming that God is not interested in it except perhaps in some spiritualized or highly generalized sense. Any difficulties that I then experience become obstacles for me to deal with alone while God watches to see if I'll screw up. This is hardly a spirituality of hope!

By contrast, Scripture presents God to us as one intimately engaged with the detail of our lives, one inviting us into dialogue and relationship with him at every level. We find a God who desired to walk with Adam and Eve in the cool of the day; who accepted hospitality from Abraham and Sarah, asked why Sarah laughed at his promise, and allowed Abraham to shape his judgment of Sodom and Gomorrah; who answered the specific prayer of Abraham's servant in his search for a wife for Isaac; who saw the suffering of his people in Egypt and came to deliver them; who gave detailed instructions about health and safety, land management, economic exchange, and the impartiality of the courts in the promised land; who taught Solomon wisdom through observation of ant colonies and wild animals; who noticed the faithfulness of the obscure Rekabite family[4] and used them as an example for the rest of Israel; and who persisted in teaching the grumpy and heartless Jonah that he cared about the pagan citizens of Nineveh.

The exilic prophets record God's extended response to the Jewish lament over the destruction of Jerusalem. In Isaiah 49:14–15, God hears and answers the specific cry of Lamentations 5:20–22:

> But Zion said, "The LORD has forsaken me,
>   the Lord has forgotten me."
>
> "Can a mother forget the baby at her breast
>   and have no compassion on the child she has borne?
> Though she may forget,
>   I will not forget you!"[5]

Jeremiah 29:10 records God's promise to rescue the people from Babylon ("When seventy years are completed for Babylon, I will come for you"), and Isaiah 44:28 specifies that it will be Cyrus, king of Persia, through whom God will deliver his people and return them to the land. The famous passage in Isaiah 52:7 is the prophetic announcement of a military messenger that this deliverance is at hand: "How beautiful on the mountains are the feet of those who bring good news, who proclaim peace, who bring good tidings, who proclaim salvation, who say to Zion 'Your God reigns!'"

These prophetic promises were realized when, in 539 BC, King Cyrus of Persia did indeed defeat the Babylonian army, occupy Babylon itself, and subsequently issue a decree allowing the Jewish exiles to return to Jerusalem and rebuild the temple (see 2 Chron. 36:20–23; Ezra 1:1–4).

There are three important lessons for us here in the nature of God's responses to Israel.

4. See Jer. 35.
5. The consensus of modern scholarship is that Isa. 40–66 was written much later than the first part of the book and that the prophecies of Isa. 40–55 were written during the Babylonian exile.

First, God cares and is present to his people. He engages with the detail of our lives. He sees our situation, and he listens to our cry. He speaks a specific reply. God does not leave us in our suffering but remains very present to us.

Second, God oversees history. God is sovereign over all nations and peoples, whether they acknowledge him or not, and is able to accomplish his purposes even through the actions of those who serve other gods (such as Nebuchadnezzar and Cyrus). This is no less true of the modern empires and ideologies that appear to overwhelm and intimidate us today. God is bigger than secularism, capitalism, environmentalism, Marxism, and globalization. He is King in the world, not just in the church.

Third, and perhaps most important, God has a vision for us that is good. Although God *can* direct world history and major events toward his ends and *does* punish sin and unfaithfulness in the process, that is *not* God's delight. "For he does not willingly bring affliction or grief to anyone" (Lam. 3:33). Rather, what God wants is a people whom he can dwell with and who honor his name and character through their actions. Israel's prophets addressed this directly because it was obvious that, despite the ending of the Babylonian exile, sin would quickly lead to repeated failure and further judgment. Jeremiah foretold of a new covenant in which the law would be written on the hearts of God's people (Jer. 31:31–34), and Ezekiel prophesied that it would be God's own Spirit that would be poured out on each person to effect this (Ezek. 36:26–27). God's intent for people is not that they simply repeat a cycle of sin, failure, confession, and forgiveness. While true repentance and forgiveness are crucial, what God wants for us is life, fruitfulness, blessing, and stability. God wants to see us break out of the cycle of failure and sin and enter a cycle of fruitfulness and life. God wants us to flourish, not merely survive.

These examples of active listening, and the promise of God's response that they convey, are repeated and developed in the New Testament. As Jesus prepared for his death and resurrection, he knew that the disciples would feel forgotten and forsaken. Thus, he promised the Holy Spirit as his presence with them while he is bodily absent: "I will ask the Father, and he will give you another advocate to help you and be with you forever—the Spirit of truth. The world cannot accept him, because it neither sees him nor knows him. But you know him, for he lives with you and will be in you. I will not leave you as orphans; I will come to you" (John 14:16–18).

Jesus knew that he was about to experience absolute exile from God as he took the entirety of humanity's sin upon himself on the cross. Having resisted the many temptations to assimilate or withdraw that challenged his own faithfulness, he then endured shame, mockery, and injustice at the hands of the religious and secular powers of his day. He entered into our exile with us. Jesus' longing for a redeemed people was more powerful than the shame of mockery and injustice. He received the full consequences of our sin and the horror of separation from the Father. He absorbed into himself all that the powers of evil could throw at him and, in doing so, exhausted their power. This is how Christ overcame the world and how we are freed from the cycle of sin, judgment, and exile. In Christ, the sins that would justly lead to our judgment and alienation from God are forgiven. In Christ, the powers of evil that would attack and destroy our life in God have been defeated and the promises of a new covenant and the outpouring of God's spirit are fulfilled; we inherit them in and through Jesus Christ.

Anticipating both his victory over all the powers of evil on the cross and the persecution of his followers that would ensue (Rev. 12:17), Jesus also encouraged his disciples concerning their suffering and his victory: "I have told you these things, so that in me you may have peace. In this world you will have trouble. But take heart! I have overcome the world" (John 16:33).

True Worship

As Jesus' words penetrate our hearts, we will find an authentic spirit of worship beginning to bubble up within us. "If God is for us, who can be against us?" (Rom. 8:31). If, knowing the worst about our heart attitudes, anger, and sin, God is still for us, then we can take great comfort in his presence. And if Jesus truly has overcome all the powers of evil and death, is King of kings and Lord of lords, and is establishing a kingdom that cannot be shaken, then his presence is also empowering. We need not fear the "isms" and ideologies of our own day or the trials of persecution and suffering that are beginning to reemerge in the West. Our hope has a firm anchor in God's promises: "Who shall separate us from the love of Christ? Shall trouble or hardship or persecution or famine or nakedness or danger or sword? . . . No, in all these things we are more than conquerors through him who loved us. For I am convinced that neither death nor life, neither angels nor demons, neither the present nor the future, nor any powers, neither height nor depth, nor anything else in all creation, will be able to separate us from the love of God that is in Christ Jesus our Lord" (Rom. 8:35, 37–39).

Becoming aware that God knows us thoroughly and is nevertheless for us gives us great confidence. It is this confidence that enables us to move into the spirit of praise that is the foundation of ambassadorial living. A spirit of praise and worship is what enables us to "sing the songs of the LORD while in a foreign land" (cf. Ps. 137:4). A spirit of praise arises from and builds up our confidence in God and in the gospel. A spirit of praise in others is the goal of the ambassadorial ministry of reconciliation—that people will see and experience the goodness of God and praise him for it.

Psalm 138 captures well this spirit of praise and worship as a response to God's answer and presence in a time of real trouble. The psalm is part of the last book (section) of Psalms (starting at Ps. 107) that many commentators believe was collected together for use in the postexilic period. It is placed directly after Psalm 137, the psalm we considered in chapter 3 that exemplifies the weeping and anger of the Babylonian exiles.

Psalm 138 speaks of God's deliverance from the midst of troubles, his answer to a cry for help, and the confidence that comes as a result. The praise of the psalmist is directed toward God, but the hope of the psalm is oriented outward, toward the nations. The psalmist wants to praise God publicly; wants to proclaim all other gods, ideologies, and creeds as false objects of worship; and yearns for the nations to also sing and praise when they hear God's words and see his ways made visible to them. May this psalm also be our prayer.

Of David.

I will praise you, Lord, with all my heart;
  before the "gods" I will sing your praise.
I will bow down toward your holy temple
    and will praise your name
    for your unfailing love and your faithfulness,
for you have so exalted your solemn decree
    that it surpasses your fame.
When I called, you answered me;
    you greatly emboldened me.

May all the kings of the earth praise you, Lord,
    when they hear what you have decreed.
May they sing of the ways of the Lord,
    for the glory of the Lord is great.

Though the Lord is exalted, he looks kindly on the lowly;
    though lofty, he sees them from afar.

Though I walk in the midst of trouble,
    you preserve my life.
You stretch out your hand against the anger of my foes;
    with your right hand you save me.
The Lord will vindicate me;
    your love, Lord, endures forever—
    do not abandon the works of your hands.

6

Calling, Citizenship, and Commission

Ambassadors are those who are sent to represent a sovereign power. They are living in a foreign land on purpose. As we move away from the identity of captive aliens or visitors through lament, active listening, and worship, there are three important steps to being established in our identity as Christ's ambassadors in the world. To be sent requires, first, that we have been called into service by that sovereign power; second, that we have been trained for our role as citizens and servants; and, finally, that we have been appointed and commissioned to a particular post. In this chapter, we will examine each of these steps—what it means to be *called*, *discipled*, and *commissioned* as ambassadors.

All the Gospels attest to the pattern in which Jesus called various people to follow him and how those disciples then lived with Jesus, were taught by him, and subsequently were sent out by Jesus on mission. Matthew 4:19 and Mark 1:17 contain the most succinct statement of all three elements: "Come, follow me, . . . and I will send you out to fish for people." We find the same basic pattern at the end of John's Gospel. After all the disciples have abandoned Jesus in alarm and dismay at his crucifixion, a group of them are out fishing when Jesus says, "Come and have breakfast" (John 21:12). In this simple invitation, Jesus calls them again into relationship with him through an act of friendship and hospitality. Their previous commission is assumed by Jesus when he asks Peter, "Do you love me?" and then tells him, "Feed my sheep" (21:15–18). In other words, "I still want you to do the job I gave you to do." But Jesus does remind all of them how to do it by closing the conversation with the command, "Follow me" (21:19).

Calling, *discipleship*, and *commission* are thus familiar steps for us as Christians. They are the steps that every believer has to repeat, often several times, in their lives.

Calling: A Summons to Follow Jesus

Our usual way of talking about calling is distorted by many aspects of the historic mind-set of Christendom and the identity of alienation that has developed in us. In my experience, vocational uncertainty and confusion are rife in the church.

Our usual way of talking connects "calling" or "vocation"[1] language to some sort of task. "God called me to this local church," we might say, or "I'm called to be a pastor," or "I'm called to be a businessperson."

Yet you'll be hard-pressed to find in the New Testament any use of "call" language that is connected to a task in this sense. Rather, the overwhelming witness of Scripture is that "calling" is essentially a salvation word, a conversion word, an identity word. So in Matthew 9:13 we learn that Christ came to call sinners to repentance. The apostle Paul tells us that God calls us into his kingdom and glory (1 Thess. 2:12) and that we are called to a holy life (2 Tim. 1:9). We are called out of darkness into light (1 Pet. 2:9), and we are called to be conformed to Christ (Rom. 8:29).

In other words, "call" language in Scripture is about the transfer of allegiance and the adoption of a new identity that occurs when we encounter Jesus Christ. When Jesus calls us, he is a King calling us into his kingdom.

1. "Vocation" is simply the Latin translation of the Greek *kaleo*, from which we get the English word "calling." In modern usage, though, especially outside the Christian community, the popular meanings of these words have diverged such that "vocation" often has connotations of less-academic "vocational" training, while "calling" retains the Reformation sense of work that has meaning and purpose.

If we respond to his invitation, we will grow in intimate relationship with him, be discipled by him, and be sent into the world to work for and with him. He calls us to himself, to embrace our true identity as children of God and citizens of heaven. *Our calling is not to a new task but to a new identity.* Again, our call is not primarily to *do* anything, but rather it is *to* Christ. Christ himself is our calling. The *language* of calling hints at this: for there to be "calling" there must be a Call*er*. Calling is what takes place when Jesus says, "Come to me, all you who are weary and burdened, and I will give you rest. Take my yoke upon you and learn from me, for I am gentle and humble in heart, and you will find rest for your souls. For my yoke is easy and my burden is light" (Matt. 11:28–30).

As Hendrik Kraemer summarizes, "*All* members of the ekklèsia have in principle the same calling."[2] We're not called to be pastors, missionaries, businesspeople, nurses, or teachers. We're all called to Christ—to know him, to follow him, to lay everything down before him.

Our willingness to maintain our allegiance to Christ is fundamentally challenged in the context of exile. The feeling of being captive aliens, trapped in a culture that is rejecting our values, generates fear that we don't belong, that our identity is being overwhelmed, and that we will be rejected if we don't fit in.

Daniel and his fellow Hebrews were overwhelmed by a foreign culture, reinforced by having their names changed to Babylonian names and being forced to learn the Babylonian language and study its astrology and culture. They were completely immersed in this alien culture, and the pressure to compromise on their identity as *God's* people was immense. Our culture also attempts to rename us and overwhelm us with its cultural stories. Christians are often given pejorative names such as "intolerant," "bigoted," and "homophobic," which convey a sense of shame and alienation. We are overwhelmed with constant advertising designed to reinforce our acceptance of the name "individualist consumer" as constitutive of our identity. Our culture foists an identity on us and does not accept or recognize the

---

2. Kraemer, *A Theology of the Laity*, 160, emphasis original. *Ekklesia* is the Greek term generally translated "church." I discuss its meaning and usage more fully in chap. 7.

legitimacy of our identity in Christ. These cultural namings induce in us a sense that we do not fit in and that our identity is under threat. They induce a primal fear of losing our identity—of a kind of death.

Fear makes us vulnerable to assimilate, withdraw, or be aggressive toward those we blame or who threaten us. Fear is the first emotion expressed after the fall (Gen. 3:10). Having disobeyed God by eating of the "tree of the knowledge of good and evil" (Gen. 2:9), Adam and Eve were self-named "naked" because of that sin. They felt fear and shame for the first time and hid from God. The naming that comes from the sinful aspects of our culture has the same effect on people today. It is no wonder that the command "Do not be afraid" is one of the most repeated in the Bible. Always this command comes with a reminder that God is for us, or a promise of what God will do for us, to help us not give way to fear and hide from God again. We need to hear this command afresh and to be reminded by Jesus of our *allegiance* to him and our *acceptance* by him. *His* voice and *his* naming need to cut across the voices and naming of our culture, calling us back to him. Being named and loved by God is the only thing that will give us the confidence to push back the fear and live freely in our identity as Christians. We need again to hear words like the following, spoken originally by God to the Babylonian exiles:

> But now, this is what the LORD says—
>   he who created you, Jacob,
>   he who formed you, Israel:
> "Do not fear, for I have redeemed you;
>   *I have summoned you by name; you are mine.*"
>   (Isa. 43:1, emphasis added)

Fear is at the heart of exilic temptation. But its counterpoint, hope, is at the heart of joyful missional living. Hope comes when we attend to the voice of God calling us by name, telling us that we belong. When Jesus wants to encourage and restore the disciples who failed him after his crucifixion, he addresses them with intimacy as "children," recalling the affection with which he explicitly named them "friends" back in John

83

15:15: "I no longer call you servants, because a servant does not know his master's business. Instead, I have called you friends." Family members and friends belong to one another. They have an identity formed by their mutual relationship that goes beyond any transaction or contractual exchange. Jesus establishes the belonging of intimate covenant relationship, and that relationship is sustained by the indwelling Holy Spirit in our lives. It is by the Spirit, according to Romans 8:15, that we can say "*Abba*, Father" to God, that we can use an intimate personal name and do so *knowing* that we belong.

Baptism is the public declaration of this reality—the culmination of our calling to Christ. According to Romans 6, we are baptized into Christ's death. Our "old self"—the sinful self that belongs to the "world" and is named by it—is crucified with Christ. It is put to death and buried with Christ. It goes down, into death, under the waters of baptism, from which we rise to a new life and a new citizenship. Baptism is thus an intensely political act. It is the spiritual equivalent of burning the flag of a nation along with our passport and identity papers and then embracing a new citizenship, under a new authority, and with an entirely new set of rights and responsibilities. We are transferred from the dominion of darkness into the kingdom of light (Col. 1:12–13). Henceforth, our citizenship is in heaven (Phil. 3:20) and our names are written in the Lamb's book of life (Rev. 3:5).

This positive affirmation of a new identity in Christ necessarily subordinates all other claims to allegiance. For the early Christians suffering persecution from Rome, baptism entailed a refusal to recognize the emperor's claims to worship. Rather than offer incense and utter the words "Caesar is Lord," Christians insisted that ultimate allegiance was due only to Jesus Christ. In our context we similarly need to resist any claim whatsoever, whether religious, political, national, or economic, that would take precedence over our allegiance to Christ.

In addition to being a *public* declaration of our allegiance, baptism also involves an intensely *personal* encounter with God in which God identifies himself with us. Jesus, though sinless, was publicly baptized, identifying himself with his Father and with us. The Holy Spirit came upon him in the form of a dove and a voice from heaven saying, "This is my Son, whom I love; with him I am well pleased" (Matt. 3:17). In baptism we are united with Jesus Christ—by the Holy Spirit his death becomes our death and his resurrection life becomes available to us. He gives his life for us, and we give our lives to him. The sinful self is put to death and a new self is "born from above" by the Holy Spirit (John 3:3 NRSV). Again, through baptism we drink of the one cup of the Spirit (1 Cor. 12:13). Scripture speaks of baptism in water and in the Holy Spirit. Our theological disputes over exactly how to baptize, or exactly how the baptism of the Holy Spirit happens, distract us from the central point: our old identity is put to death. We are filled with God's Holy Spirit as a marker of our new identity and to bring us into intimate relationship with the living God. We now hear the astounding words spoken over us: "You are my beloved child. In you I am well pleased." This intimate relational connection imparts to us the empowering love to live a new life. Scripture uses numerous images to reinforce this point. We are "born again" (John 3:3), made a "new creation" (Col. 3:9–10; 2 Cor. 5:17), and "adopted into God's family" (John 1:12–13; Rom. 8:14–16). The exchange is radical and encompasses the entire person. God claims us as his own. He is where we belong.

We cannot expect to represent God as an ambassador for Christ in the world if we do not encounter God at this level; if we do not hear God's voice for ourselves, addressing us personally, by name; and if we do not know deep within our spirit that we are loved by God, that he has forgiven, cleansed, and claimed us for himself. We can't expect to communicate God's love if we are still bound by fear. We can't expect to overcome the alienation in the world if we ourselves are still alienated from God.[3]

I began this section by saying that our usual way of talking about calling is distorted by the mind-set of Christendom. It may be argued that the basic understanding of Christian calling and identity that I have sketched here is *assumed* in our popular way of speaking about calling. After all

3. For further reading on this theme, see Dallas Willard's classic, *The Divine Conspiracy*.

(one might argue), having called us to himself, Jesus does in the end commission us to some task. I agree that this is so and that in theory, at least, our distorted use of the term may be benign.

However, our tendency to center the language of calling on tasks makes it easier to skip the previous two vital stages that are supposed to ground truly *Christian* activity—namely, encountering God in Christ such that I am transformed in my identity, and growing in that identity in a disciple-making community. I do not know of many churches where disciple making is really taken seriously. If the typical Christian student at theological schools in the West is anything to go by, we have something of a crisis of discipleship in the church today, and as a result, large numbers of Christians lack hope for the future because they lack confidence in the gospel, have shallow roots in their identity in Christ, and struggle to know how to pray, hear God, and be led by him in the world. In this context, our common language is at odds with Scripture in ways that may not be so benign.

What might it do in our Christian culture—and indeed in our hearts—if we stopped using "call" language with reference to *what we will do* and instead spoke to one another of our calling to *intimate relationship with Christ*?

Discipleship: Becoming Fellow Citizens with God's People

When God calls us, our attention turns toward his person. We look upon his face and see our Lord Jesus and our loving heavenly Father. In discipleship, our attention shifts further. Indeed, one could say that discipleship itself can be defined as a radical shift in our attention in which we focus our whole being on Christ. Like the first disciples, we now "follow him," and our gaze is on him. Discipleship involves becoming imitators of God so that we mature in his likeness.

This discipleship pattern takes place for us not only as individuals but also in the context of intergenerational community. All communities are disciple-making communities to some extent. As we saw in chapter 3, communities are bearers of cultural stories, and these stories shape and form meaning, purpose, and behavior. The new identity arising from our calling to Christ means that we "are no longer foreigners and strangers, but fellow citizens with God's people and also members of his household" (Eph. 2:19). Our fundamental place of belonging has shifted, but like everyone else, we have been formed by the various cultural stories of the contemporary world. Discipleship is the process of learning what the rights and responsibilities of our new citizenship mean and involve and how to live in our new adopted family in the light of our new identity. Helped by other believers, we can progressively detach from the influence of contemporary cultural stories and become fully embedded within God's story of the world. Discipleship is the crucible of faithful exilic living. It is where the clash of cultures, ideologies, and temptations becomes concrete and particular in our own lives.

Scripture provides two powerful accounts of this discipleship process: the exodus from Egypt and the Babylonian exile. The people of Israel had a particularly formative experience of discipleship during the exodus from Egypt and the giving of the law that followed as they journeyed together in the desert of Sinai. After the exodus, Israel had to shed the identity of slavery and adopt its identity as a people belonging to God. The familiar (though oppressive) routines and "comforts" of Egypt were gone in the open expanse of the desert. Some of the people grumbled about the loss of the predictable food that slave labor required (Exod. 16:2–3). They had to learn to let God guide them and to trust him for provision. They had left the "gods" of Egypt behind, defeated under the waters of the Red Sea, but the allure of those gods remained. Israel was out of Egypt, but the powerful cultural stories of Egypt were still in the consciousness of Israel. Through Moses, God gave them the law—God's wisdom for flourishing in freedom and avoiding a return to slavery. If they lived by it, they would be a light to the surrounding nations (Deut. 4:5–8). If they trusted God, they could enter the promised land.

Many biblical scholars have drawn attention to the parallels between this wilderness experience of Israel and the Babylonian exile. The experience of exile threw the community back into a mentality of slavery—of captivity by a foreign power. Figures like Daniel and Jeremiah were unusual in their conviction that God was as much king in Babylon as he was in Jerusalem. The people had to learn again to find hope in their covenant relationship with God, not in their attachment to a particular piece of land and a physical temple. The first step was to stop listening to the false prophets and to pay attention to God's voice. They had to learn obedience by settling down, resisting the temptation either to give up on their covenant identity (assimilate to Babylonian culture) or to plot against the Babylonians (withdraw into an oppositional ghetto), and instead do what they were always meant to do—namely, be a blessing to the surrounding nations who were now their captors (see Jer. 29).

These stories capture two central aspects of discipleship: learning to hear and follow God's voice (rather than any of the other voices that compete for our attention) and learning to love the things that God loves (rather than those that our culture or our sinful nature draw us toward). Discipleship is about attending to God's voice and having our attachments and loves reordered.

Jesus, the good shepherd, tells us that "his sheep follow him because they know his voice" (John 10:4). Disciples are likened to sheep who have become familiar with the voice of the shepherd and so are willing to move from one place to another only when they hear that voice—and that voice alone—speaking to them. A friend of mine who served in the Royal Marines gave me a modern example of this. Soldiers are taught to obey the voice of only their company commanding officer amid the terrifying noise and confusion of battle. As we study the Scripture and apply it obediently in our lives, we will become increasingly familiar with the voice of Jesus and become able to discern it amid the cacophony and storms of life. There are, of course, many situations that the Bible does not directly address. It tells us to work but not which job to take. It tells us that both married life and single life are honorable but not which is for us. It tells us to love God and neighbor but not how to deal with a particular conflict in the workplace. We are not led in these matters by a cloud and pillar of fire. We have something much better: the presence of the Holy Spirit within us. As we pray specific prayers and ask for the Spirit to lead us in line with Scripture, we will learn to hear Jesus in the detail of our lives, especially if we do this in accountable relationships with other mature believers. We will learn to discern the true prophets from the false prophets. We will grow in wisdom and confidence that God is able to lead us in the most complex situations. Even more important, our trust in and love for God will grow as we listen and hear his voice.

The second aspect of discipleship follows from this growing attentiveness to the voice of Jesus. Our desires are changed as we come closer to the heart of God. When the Babylonian exiles finally made it back to Jerusalem after seventy years of captivity, they devoted themselves to hearing the Scripture taught by Ezra (see the book of Ezra and Nehemiah 8–10). They were shocked by how far they had departed from it and knew they needed repentance. In numerous ways their faith had become syncretistic, accommodating to the "gods" of their exilic environment. They had made all kinds of social, marital, and economic alliances contrary to God's commands, reflecting an ambivalence about whether they could trust God for community flourishing. Their response to hearing Scripture read and realizing the gap between God's desires and their actual lives was to weep and grieve and repent and reorient their hearts and practices toward God.

Like the Babylonian exiles, our attachments to aspects of Western society—and to our central place of power and influence within them—need to be reordered. We too need a deep heart change as we realize how far we are from God's desire for us and from God's extraordinary love for his world, for all that he has made, for every person and every creature.

When I was working as an economic consultant, I developed a habit of driving a short way from the office each lunch break and spending an hour in Bible reading and prayer. One summer day, as I prayed earnestly to know God's heart, I was surprised to sense that the Holy Spirit was drawing my attention to a car parked behind me and prompting me to move my own vehicle. After a bit of rationalizing and grappling with the question of whether this was God speaking or my imagination, I moved my car. It became clear to me that God cared about the old woman in the car behind me, who needed the shade of the tree in the heat of the day much more than I did. That God should see such a tiny detail and show it to me as important had a profound impact on me—focused as I was on grand plans to change the world. Yet in this seemingly insignificant detail, God was expanding and reorienting my heart. As we attend to his voice and obey his word, at first we will find trust and obedience very difficult because of the conflict with other competing voices around us and with our own desires and loves. But gradually we will be surprised by how much the Holy Spirit works within us to transform and change our desires.

Together, these two main aspects of discipleship—attending to God's voice and drawing near to God's heart—inculcate in us the prime characteristic of all citizens of God's kingdom: being in an intimate, loving relationship with the King. This extraordinary privilege is the reason Christ died for us. God wants to draw us to himself. It is the antithesis of alienation and exile. An ever-closer union with God is the goal of our existence. It fosters hope, joy, and love in our hearts. It is the basis for our unity with one another and our ability to bring reconciliation in the world. It is the foundation for living as ambassadors.

This is a prize so great that it should be no surprise that it comes only with a struggle. For Israel in the desert and for the exiles in Babylon, discipleship takes place in suffering and opposition. Israel's experience in Egypt is brutal, and following their stunning deliverance by God from slavery, he offers them a land "flowing with milk and honey" where they will be free to serve him. But to enter it, the entire community must cross the Sinai desert, follow God's guidance in the form of a cloud and a pillar of fire, trust God for food and shelter, fight off marauding armies, and then fight to possess the land. They are so intimidated by the "giants" in the land that they lose hope, stop trusting God, and are afraid to enter, so they end up wandering around in the desert for forty years, until they are given the chance to try again. When they do enter the land under Joshua's leadership, God allows some of Israel's enemies to remain undefeated to test the faith of subsequent generations (Judg. 3:4). Many years later, the

Babylonian exiles find themselves back in captivity, away from the land, because of Israel's unfaithfulness. Though they are the "good figs" that God keeps from judgment, they must experience the humiliation and difficulty of foreign captivity. When, after seventy years, God does finally send them back to Jerusalem under King Cyrus, they face local officials' opposition to the rebuilding of the temple and the city.

If these stories are instructive examples of our discipleship (and I believe they are), then this quick sketch makes for rather uncomfortable reading. Our society does all it can to avoid suffering and hardship. Advertising and media lead us to believe we can live comfortable, happy, peaceful, and healthy lives if only we make the right lifestyle choices. It is very easy for our view of discipleship to become infected by this therapeutic culture so that instead of challenging our attachment to comfort and security over obedience and truth, we tacitly condone it. Inviting people to become Christians and then to start training to stand in battle as a test of their faith does not seem like a good selling point! We are tempted to reduce discipleship to positive aspects of pastoral ministry, such as healing and pastoral care, alongside serving in various church programs and community projects. Our attention to Scripture is often woefully superficial. Though we have a vast array of Bible translations and versions, reading aids, commentaries, devotional guides, and Bible apps, the actual situation of many churches is not that different from the situation described by the writer of Hebrews: "Though by this time you ought to be teachers, you need someone to teach you the elementary truths of God's word all over again. You need milk, not solid food!" (Heb. 5:12). As communities we need our "Ezra moment"—a "scriptural reset" that leads to revelation, grief, and deep heart change. As individuals, we may avoid any discipleship relationships that truly challenge us. We may hear lots of teaching but be lazy in applying it because it's too difficult. In short, contemporary discipleship can easily fall into helping people feel good and do good rather than helping them learn to trust God when they feel bad and to suffer for doing good.[4]

---

4. A classic resource to help us rise to the challenge of discipleship is Richard Foster's *Celebration of Discipline*.

From beginning to end, Scripture teaches that abundant human life involves challenge and overcoming adversity. God's creation is described as "very good" but not perfect. Although God provides a garden for Adam and Eve, they are commanded to subdue and cultivate the rest of the planet. Their environment contains an enemy, evil in the form of the snake, who seeks to persuade them not to trust God. From the outset, they are told to "guard and protect" as well as to "work and cultivate" the land if they are to see the fruitful abundance that God desires.[5] The fall of humanity, in which Adam and Eve fail to trust God and guard against evil, makes this goal harder to achieve. Only God's intervention can put things back on track.

The uphill battle for human beings is more intense for Christians because of the devil's hatred of Jesus (Rev. 12:17), though Christians are given the empowering and authority of Jesus to enable them to stand. In other words, the context for human life is one of spiritual battle, at least until Jesus returns. We are either spiritually captive to the devil or we have been freed and aligned with his enemy, Jesus Christ. There is no comfortable neutral territory to inhabit, no spiritual "Switzerland," though a great tactic of the enemy is to persuade us that there is. The ministry of reconciliation at the heart of our ambassadorial commission as a community also involves at the same time intense spiritual battle, because reconciliation with God is opposed by the devil, resisted by our proud fallen human nature, and mocked by an unbelieving culture.

We must learn to trust God amid powerful temptations that make us doubt his word, and during adversity and suffering that make us doubt his heart. We must learn to trust when it seems foolish and to do good when it hurts. The foundation of all our responsibilities as Christian citizens is summarized by Jesus in Matthew 16:24: "If anyone would come after me, let him deny himself and take up his cross and follow me" (ESV). It is important to understand—and not underestimate—the cost of discipleship. Although the rights of Christian citizenship are incredible, the cost of obtaining them is absolute. I must be willing to put Jesus first, to make God God, in every

5. These are the essential meanings of the Hebrew words in Genesis 2:15 translated variously as "work," "keep," and "care" for the land.

aspect of my life, to the point that I am willing to give up everything I have and value for his sake. Jesus makes the point starkly in Luke 14:26: "If anyone comes to me and does not hate his own father and mother and wife and children and brothers and sisters, yes, even his own life, he cannot be my disciple" (ESV). As verse 33 of the same chapter makes clear, this is not a literal command to "hate" (Jesus repeatedly commands us to love) but rather a command to put everything, even the closest of human bonds, as secondary to our allegiance to him. Even so, this is an outrageous claim that coming from any other person would be monstrous. Coming from Jesus it is not. He is simply saying that only God can be God in your life. There is room for only one king in the kingdom of God in which we hold citizenship—and that King is Jesus, not us nor anything else that he has given us, however good it may be. Being absolutely clear on Christ's lordship as our primary allegiance and our heavenly citizenship as our core identity is the starting point for a right ordering of our relationships, attachments, and desires in all areas of life, including our posture toward contemporary society.[6]

Rising to the challenge of discipleship will make us more truly ourselves. It will bring maturity, strength, and compassion into every aspect of our lives. It will fill us with hope as the character of Jesus will be formed within us. Failing to rise to the challenges we face in life leaves us feeling diminished, subjugated, and overcome. This is not God's heart for us. He wants us to enter into all the rights of Christian citizenship. These rights are extraordinary. As God's children, we inherit the kingdom. We receive the gift of the Holy Spirit. We are promised a resurrection body in a transformed new creation. Our sins are forgiven and cleansed. All the resources of heaven are available to us. Our identity, provision, and security are sure. We share in God's authority over the world. We are sent into the world to represent Jesus with the authority to drive out demons, heal the sick, and disciple the nations.[7]

---

6. For an excellent study on the right ordering of our desires amid the challenges of contemporary society, see Smith, *Desiring the Kingdom*. I discuss this book further in chap. 9.

7. This short paragraph is a summary of just a few of the many Scriptures that tell us what God has promised and prepared for us. The main ones I have drawn from here are Matt. 10:1; 28:19; Luke 9:1; 12:22–34; Rom. 8:17, 22–23; Gal. 4:7; 2 Tim. 2:12; 1 Pet. 1:4; 2 Pet. 3:13; 1 John 1:8–9; Rev. 20:4. But there are many more.

God wants us to enter fully into our inheritance. He expects us to use the resources and authority he has given us. As disciples, we follow the One who also had to overcome temptation, opposition, and spiritual battle. But God empowers us with his Holy Spirit and the authority of Jesus to overcome. He wants us to succeed.

Commission: Being Anointed and Authorized to Serve

As disciples who attend carefully to what Jesus is doing as we follow him, it becomes obvious to us that Jesus *works*. He knows that he is about his Father's business. He only does what he sees the Father doing. His Father, he tells us, is working. Scripture relentlessly portrays God as a worker—constantly active to create, organize, evaluate, and nurture the world—a God who is likened to a builder, a shepherd, a teacher, a gardener, a king, and a servant. Jesus came not as an adult to deliver some messages and leave but as a baby who grew, learned, studied, and worked in the family trade. The Holy Spirit works as a helper, counselor, and enabler. Scripture presents work as an essential attribute of God.

Human beings, created in God's image, are also workers. Our image bearing is itself a commission to rule and to work—to act as God's authoritative representatives on earth and steward it on his behalf. Genesis presents work as central to the human commission. In dialogue with other competing ancient Near Eastern cosmologies, the whole creation is presented as a temple in which worshipful work is offered up to God. Work in the garden of Eden is described with the same words used to describe the work of the Levitical priests in the tabernacle. Human beings have been designed to work in partnership with God, in all spheres of life, to cultivate and care for creation, as an act of worship to him. Work is the foundational human commission.

As ambassadors of Christ we have a "ministry" (literally, a work of service) of reconciliation to collaborate with God in bringing every part of creation back into right relationship with him. Whether in the foundational human commission to work found in Genesis or in the New Testament commissioning of ambassadors for Christ, no part of God's creation is outside the scope of these responsibilities. There is no hierarchy of vocations or occupations that makes a pastor or missionary more important to God than a plumber or a marketing executive. Nor is God's focus simply on getting tasks done. Instead, our commission to work with God in the world is an intensely relational appointment. We are treated not as servants but as friends. What matters is not what we do but that we do everything responding to and participating with God. God's purpose is to reconcile all things to himself in Christ. We should expect the Holy Spirit to anoint and commission ambassadors for service in every sphere of society.

If the scope is so wide, how do we know what to do? Jesus calls us to himself and leads us to the Father, that we might know him and his heart for the world and find the source of our life in him (John 17:3). As we mature as disciples, our hearts become progressively *detached* from the fallen aspects of this world and progressively *attached* to those things that God loves and desires. At some point in the course of our discipleship, and in the context of a growing intimate relationship with Jesus, we will find ourselves drawn to a particular part of God's work in the world. Each of us has been created in God's image and likeness, and each of us is unique in reflecting some particular combination of personality, skills, desires, and strengths. Increasingly we will find that the new life of God within us begins to bring life to every part of our personhood, and there is a deepening resonance between who we are, how God has made us, and some aspect of God's mission to reconcile and renew all things in Christ (Eph. 1:10). We may find that through prayer, preaching, Scripture reading, the counsel of fellow Christians, and the circumstances of our lives, we begin to notice this resonance and can put words to it. We may have memorable encounters with God that accelerate and deepen this process of discovery. At some point we will know that Jesus' words to his disciples "As the Father has sent me, I am sending you" (John 20:21) apply very directly and specifically to us in a particular context.

When this process becomes public and is shared and recognized by others in the body of Christ, we can speak of a *commissioning* for service.

95

Although it is rare, some churches have begun to commission Christians into all spheres of life, just as they might lay hands on and ordain pastors and missionaries. In London, a collaboration between the London Institute for Contemporary Christianity and the bishop of London has led to a citywide movement to commission ten thousand workplace ambassadors for Christ. But in most churches, recognizing, consecrating, and praying for the anointing of the Holy Spirit over individuals for works of service is confined to a narrow range of activities.

There are several reasons for this, but one I want to highlight is the problematic nature of modern vocation theology. Christians should understand that God is a God who *speaks* (through Scripture but also through other means attested by Scripture, including the continual witness of the Holy Spirit) and speaks *to us* (such that we know we are being personally addressed). That is not to say that we should remain naive about how we can deceive ourselves, abuse others, or contradict the clear teaching of Scripture by invoking the authority of "God speaking." But it does mean that we cannot afford to rationalize away the extraordinary biblical witness to God's regular direct speech and encounter with individual human beings or to theologize these into the witness of circumstances such that we reduce God's voice to what the late Klaus Bockmuehl describes as "the mute voice of Providence."[8] If it is truly Christian at all, Christian living is a response to God's initiative in our lives. To say or believe this last statement as a theoretical truth without expecting some experiential corollary of it is theological sophistry.

Sadly, however, for all its benefits (and there are many), the theology of vocation that Protestants have inherited from the Reformers has contributed to a truncated modern view of calling and commission that largely eliminates the personal, relational dimension. Both Luther and Calvin opposed the Anabaptist emphasis on the direct guidance of the Holy Spirit in helping believers discern their part in the church's cross-cultural mission. Instead, these Magisterial Reformers emphasized the providential

---

8. See Bockmuehl, "Recovering Vocation Today," 31, and his *Listening to the God Who Speaks*.

ordering of circumstances as the best guidance for discerning the place or station in the existing social order that God was calling a person to serve in. There are of course historical reasons for this rationalistic and conservative posture,[9] but historians and sociologists conclude that reducing guidance to Scripture plus Providence is the main source of the secularizing tendency that developed within Protestantism in the late seventeenth century and onward.[10] Protestant vocation theology extended the holiness of the monastic call to all of life but then theologically disconnected the individual believer from the direct leading of and dependence on the Holy Spirit. It became very easy for ordinary life, now largely rid of the magical and superstitious, to become even more profoundly secularized than it was before. A truncated vocation theology has contributed to the secularization of Western culture.

In my experience, these developments have also left many believers confused about how to hear God or unable to connect their faith with ordinary life in the world and thus experiencing a protracted vocational crisis. This tragedy is fundamentally a failure of discipleship that we must not repeat in this generation.

Scripture tells us that ordination, the anointing of the Holy Spirit, and the consecration of people as sacred is intended for all believers, not just a spiritual elite. The trajectory of the Old Testament is one in which God promises to pour out the Holy Spirit on all people. The Old Testament vision of the new creation does not involve some kind of sacred-secular divide, but instead even the cooking pots in Jerusalem will be considered holy and sacred (Zech. 14:21). These promises are realized and reinforced in the New Testament, when the promised Holy Spirit is given and believers

9. On the one hand, the Reformers were responding to the prevalence of superstition in Catholicism and a wide variety of magical beliefs in popular culture. On the other hand, the rising threat of militant Islam to European Christendom made them resistant to any impetus that might disrupt the social order.

10. See esp. Thomas, *Religion and the Decline of Magic*, and Tawney, *Religion and the Rise of Capitalism*. In dialogue with Max Weber's celebrated work *The Protestant Ethic and the Spirit of Capitalism*, Tawney highlights how the *character* of Puritanism, rather than wealth per se, was the primary secularizing force and that this character arose from a false theological dualism between spirit and matter.

are exhorted that whatever we do, we should do it for the glory of God (1 Cor. 10:21; Col. 3:23–24).

If the Reformation led to a democratization of calling, what we need today is a democratization of mission. Every believer is sent by Jesus into all the world. Every believer is a missionary, and mission involves the reconciliation of every person and every sphere of life and work. All God's people constitute a "royal priesthood"—a people belonging to God for the sake of the world (1 Pet. 2:9–12). Each one of us is invited by Jesus to follow him and be sent by him into the world. Each one of us is offered the anointing of the Holy Spirit for the intimacy, wisdom, and empowering that we will need.

When the Jewish exiles finally returned from Babylon to Jerusalem, they found the city in ruins. Under the leadership of Nehemiah they began the task of rebuilding the walls, gates, and, later, houses of the city. Each family and occupational group had a specific part of the city wall to rebuild (Neh. 3–4). Western society is in a state of spiritual disrepair. Its walls are broken down. God's heart is to see it reconciled to him in Christ. Which part of the wall is God sending you to rebuild?

7

Establish an Embassy

Sovereign Territory

A few years back, I was in Washington, DC, and decided to visit the British embassy there. I'd been living in North America for several years, and I was feeling a bit homesick. It was heartening to arrive at the embassy and find a large statue of Winston Churchill outside. Beneath his outstretched foot was a line along the sidewalk. On Churchill's side of the line were the words "United Kingdom," and on the other side, "United States." Here was a real piece of home! Inside, the decor and furnishings were elegant, welcoming, and classically English—designed for comfort, conversation, and conviviality. You could totally imagine having a cup of tea and cucumber sandwiches at four o'clock on the veranda before settling some important matter of state—or simply getting your passport renewed! Alas, this was not to be my experience. The embassy was closed to visitors, and I left somewhat forlorn.

Under international law, modern embassies are considered the sovereign territory of the home country rather than part of the host country where they are located. There is a spiritual analogy to this. The sixth-century Celtic Christians adopted a pattern of mission known as *peregrinatio*— a journey from their home community that was a voluntary "exile for

Christ,"[1] sometimes involving new lands in which the gospel would be proclaimed. On arriving at some foreign coast in their small but seaworthy boats, they would walk ashore and proclaim, "The kingdom of God is here!"[2]

This is the spirit of the ambassador. It should not be mistaken for a conquering arrogance. It has nothing to do with a coercive use of force. Rather, it is an acknowledgment that the Holy Spirit within us, who has also already gone ahead of us, is the very presence of God in our midst. The kingdom of God is righteousness, peace, and joy in the Holy Spirit. It conquers by love, and the only coercion involved is the forceful subduing of the spiritual powers of darkness that seek to deceive and enslave human beings and prevent them from being restored as full image bearers of God. As God's people we are also the temple of the Holy Spirit, both individually and, even more so, corporately. To declare "The kingdom of God is here" is to acknowledge that Jesus is Lord over everything in our influence and agency. This might be a church building, a business, a house, or a vehicle. It might be any area of leadership responsibility and influence that we have. We acknowledge his lordship in our home, at our workstation, and, of course, wherever we gather as believers in his name. Jesus Christ lays claim to every square inch of creation,[3] but an embassy is a place where that claim is acknowledged.

Just as there may be numerous consulates and trade missions as well as a primary embassy in a given host country, believers form many types of diplomatic community when they gather in neighborhoods, workplaces, and homes. The primary embassy, though, on which all these others depend, is the local church, described by Paul in Ephesians 1:23 as "the fullness of him who fills everything in every way." This phrase comes at the end of a passage in which Paul has set out the purpose of God to "bring unity

1. A common translation of the motto *peregrinatio pro Christi*.
2. See the description of St. Illtud in *The Life of St. Samson of Dol*. See also Robinson, *Rediscovering the Celts*.
3. Abraham Kuyper is famous for his statement, "There is not a square inch in the whole domain of our human existence over which Christ, who is Sovereign over all, does not cry: 'Mine!'" See Kuyper, "Sphere Sovereignty," 488.

to all things in heaven and on earth under Christ" (Eph. 1:10). In verses 20–21 he describes how Christ has been raised far above every name, rule, authority, and dominion that could be invoked, not only now but also in the age to come. Jesus is Lord of lords and King of kings. The punch line of the passage is that all of this is *for* the church. Somehow, in the mystery and grace of God, the church as the body of Christ gets to participate in Christ's headship and glory—*we* are to become the fullness of him who fills everything in every way.

One of the ways this happens is embedded in the New Testament word for church. *Ekklesia* is a word borrowed from the realm of politics and government. It refers to a gathering of citizens to form a political council. Just as Caesar might call together an *ekklesia* to make decisions, so God has called together citizens of his kingdom to exercise spiritual authority in a particular place. The authority of the king that is *recognized* in the embassy is to be projected beyond it by *inviting* others to reconciliation. Reconciliation cannot be imposed. The gathered community is scattered into the world, and both the church gathered and church scattered are to carry the authority of the kingdom in their communal and individual witness. The church is absolutely at the center of God's purposes and mission in the world.

I make the point about the centrality of the church in God's purposes in part because there are many ways in which the church falls short of our expectations. Some of the movements and voices critical of the institutional church in modern times, while expressing some important truths, have fallen into articulating these truths in ways that are not redemptive. Some Christians even imagine that the failings of the gathered church justify abandoning it and following Jesus as "lone ranger" Christians. There is no biblical warrant for such a practice, any more than there is political warrant for "lone ranger" diplomats. A vital aspect of the witness of the gathered church is that we demonstrate unity and love for one another as the family of God. Like a natural family, that may mean getting on with people we don't particularly like but nonetheless are committed to love. We are exhorted to "not [give] up meeting together, as some are in the habit of doing, but [encourage] one another" (Heb. 10:25).

Modern embassies often aim to project something of the culture of their home country. If you wander into the Canadian high commission in London, you'll be greeted not by pictures of Winston Churchill but by images of maple syrup and tree-covered ski mountains. What is the kingdom culture that Jesus wants us to project? Despite the fact that believers are ordinary sinners, we have treasure in these "jars of clay" (2 Cor. 4:7). This treasure is what the outside world is meant to "taste and see" (Ps. 34:8). This is why it is not only aspirational but also possible that Christian communities function as embassies that project something of the culture of the kingdom of God. Whenever an outsider comes into our "embassy"—our church community or our spheres of influence as believers in workplaces, governments, neighborhoods, and homes—they should experience something of the presence of God in us. Our life together should be a fragrance and foretaste of heaven, not because of anything special about us, but because we are sufficiently open to allow God within us to shine through. "By this everyone will know that you are my disciples, if you love one another" (John 13:35). It is important that we understand this projection of the culture of the kingdom of God *not* as a projection of a derivative imitation of it. If I had managed to gain entry to the British embassy in Washington, DC, there's little chance I'd have met Her Majesty Queen Elizabeth II. Yet any outsider encountering Christian hospitality and community should be able to encounter the King of kings in person, because we are "built together to become a dwelling in which God lives by his Spirit" (Eph. 2:22). God's presence is the amazing distinctive we have and the only one we need.

God's sovereign presence within us is what turns a diverse gathering, an association of people with certain ideas and practices, into an embassy of the kingdom of God—a royal priesthood with a ministry of reconciliation. We should expect to encounter God's presence and be aware of his presence with us. Knowing that God is for us, with us, and able to speak and act by his Holy Spirit gives us confidence, hope, and authority. When we go out from the local church and into our town or city, workplace, home, or neighborhood, we are confident that God is as much King in those places as he is in the church meeting.

This was Daniel's conviction. He and his friends gathered together to pray in that pagan palace with the expectation that God was King over the Babylonians just as he was over the Israelites in Jerusalem. They thought God was just as able to speak and intervene with Nebuchadnezzar as he was with David or Hezekiah. They understood that "the kingdom of God is not a matter of talk but of power" (1 Cor. 4:20). This power includes the spiritual power to overcome evil. "The God of peace will soon crush Satan under your feet" (Rom. 16:20). Where the historic Christendom model tends to make us rely on temporal and political power to effect change, the exilic paradigm places the emphasis on prayer—our spiritual battle with the principalities and powers that hold our societies, institutions, and neighbors in bondage (Eph. 6:12)—and good works (Matt. 5:16; 1 Pet. 2:12).

Resourcing and Communications

International embassies today are economically supported by the home country, and the embassy must have ongoing communications with the home country to function well. The same is true in the spiritual realm. The embassy is fundamentally dependent on God's providing and empowering presence and on prayer. For an ambassadorial community operating in spiritually foreign territory, a vital devotional and prayer life are not "nice to have" but mission critical. Individually and corporately the ambassadorial community has a model in the lives of Daniel and his friends in Babylon. Daniel has the habit of praying three times a day (Dan. 6:10) and gathering to pray with his friends. His prayer life shows broad concern: daily thanksgiving, intercession for the whole people of Israel in exile (Dan. 9), and specific prayer for challenging situations (Dan. 2:18). He expects God to speak, give wisdom, and answer specific prayers. His focus is not only on his own safety but also on doing good to the (sometimes hostile) pagans around him (Dan. 2:24). His regular habits of prayer mean that in an emergency situation, his instinct is to pray and expect God's help. We can imagine him being summoned to the court orgy of Belshazzar (Dan. 5:12–16) and then walking through the palace firing "arrow prayers" to

God concerning what he will encounter. He has learned to listen and so is confident in an incredibly hostile context and able to hear God and interpret the writing on the wall.

This is the kind of prayer and devotional life that needs to be normal for the ambassadorial community. This life of communal attentiveness to God is part of a decision-making culture that is highly participatory. It relies on strong friendship, high degrees of trust, and regular exchange of information and resources within a rich web of relationships. The flow of energy and information in this kind of high-trust, prayerful culture is also what is communicated by the image of the church as the body of Christ. In a healthy body, every part is in direct communication with the head via the nervous system and the brain's complex hormonal regulation of body function. There are also highly complex interrelationships between the various parts of the body.

In contrast with this participatory culture, many "Christendom" churches have a top-down performance culture. Church leaders often function as one-man superministries (rather than having the team leadership that is taught and modeled in the New Testament)[4] and feel pressured to provide high-quality performances to meet the congregation's style preference. Whether this takes place via the rarefied beauty of sung evensong and a ten-minute homily or the rock-concert atmosphere of Pentecostal worship bands accompanied by a one-hour motivational speech, the effect is the same: the worshipers are reduced to passive consumers of an experience. They either can't sing or can't hear themselves sing. They are not expected or taught to participate actively in the gathered meeting (contra 1 Cor. 14:26–33). Direction for the church is rarely discerned corporately but is rather imposed from above. God is expected to speak to the community not through congregants but only through the leader. Relationships within the church are often developed centrally, with the leader, but not actively cultivated horizontally, with one another. Small groups—crucial places for nurturing

4. Paul always traveled and ministered with others. Ephesians 4:11, for instance, speaks of apostles, prophets, and evangelists (APEs) as well as pastors and teachers. For an extended discussion of the missional-leadership paradigm of this text and the problem of missing "APEs" in contemporary church leadership, see Hirsch and Frost, *The Shaping of Things to Come*, chap. 10; and Hirsch, *The Forgotten Ways*, 169.

deep relationship—are routinely disrupted, not to enhance relational life, but in pursuit of the latest church-growth fad.

My point here is not to say that we should do away with choral music or contemporary worship; I see value in both. Rather, I want to draw attention to the way in which the pedagogies of our gathered services—what is implicitly taught by the structure of our gatherings—often shape us as passive consumers. Whatever relational and devotional culture we have then extends to and is embodied in other aspects of our daily lives, such as the way we handle money.

When the church is scattered into the world, we rightly engage in the economy of our city, suburb, or countryside. From this economy we earn a living. To function truly as ambassadors in these places—to be ministers of reconciliation in these economies—we must be able to transcend them, to relativize and even suspend our dependence on these economies. We must look to God as our ultimate provider, not to our employer, our paycheck, or our skill sets. What marked Daniel's life as an ambassador for God in the court of the Babylonians was his willingness to risk everything to remain faithful. In many things, he was willing to compromise, but not over his faithfulness to God. Ultimately, he didn't see Nebuchadnezzar or the other Babylonian kings as the source of life. Because of that, he could be a source of life to them.

The same is true for the gathered church. It too must be dependent on God for its economic life, even as it is also enmeshed in the economy of a particular place. In this regard, nowhere is the historic mind-set of Christendom more obviously visible than in the persistent teaching that congregants should tithe their income. In some European countries, this tithe is still collected by the state, but the legalistic overtones are present elsewhere. Church leaders might blush when they reflect on the self-serving nature of teaching on giving by quoting sections of the Old Testament (Mal. 3:10 is a favorite) while ignoring or marginalizing Old Testament passages on, for instance, keeping the Sabbath (often on the basis that "we are not under law"). In many cases, church leaders can't imagine anyone giving to the church unless they convince congregants that they have a strong biblical duty to do so. Not only is tithing an unbiblical way to teach Christians about giving; by confusing the issue of motivation, it also obstructs the godly giving that most Christians want to undertake. Giving is supposed to be a generous response of the heart to God, not an obligation or duty we perform. Although many people who teach and practice tithing do so because they genuinely believe they are being obedient to God, the doctrine itself tends toward an attitude of legalism ("I've paid my 10 percent, now the rest is mine") rather than generosity ("100 percent is God's generosity to me, and I want to give generously"). Giving 10 percent of my income is a helpful rule of thumb as a minimal level of giving, but giving is supposed to flow from my relationship with God, not be mediated by a rule, and is supposed to be based on my means and ability. For some families, 10 percent is beyond their means; for others, 20 percent is well below it.

Christians are encouraged to give generously, to give to the local church (and beyond), and to give regularly. But the spirit and motivation of giving in the New Testament is radically different from that of tithing (2 Cor. 8:4; 9:7). Not only does tithing undermine the New Testament motivation for giving, it also conceives of the church as an organization needing support rather than as an enterprise seeking to embody and serve God's mission in the world. Western congregations are typically presented with a budget for the church at strategic points in the year and asked to help meet those budgets. Most of the budget will involve expenditure on the church building (or the next building) and on staff paid to preach and lead congregational worship. These spending priorities are predetermined and almost never opened for serious discussion. Congregants are implicitly treated as recipients of a service or members of a club who ought to contribute to the costs of those services. Few churches gather their members together to discern how they ought to spend their money. Many churches emphasize the inward life of the Christian "club," not its witness and outward mission. Rather than challenging the consumerist mind-set of contemporary capitalism, church budgeting and financing tends to reinforce it.

All this is a long way from the example of the apostle Paul, who sometimes refused support and worked with his hands to pay his own way and whose primary teaching on giving was in the context of gathering funds not for himself or his coworkers or even for local teachers and preachers but rather to support the poor in other cities. Passages such as Acts 2:44 and Acts 4:32–35 show Christians giving freely to meet the needs of fellow believers.[5] Giving was an extension and embodiment of their love for one another and their witness to the gospel. The Greek word used in these passages, often translated as "sharing" or "fellowship" in modern Bibles, is *koinonia*. Typically this word has been understood either as some form of early Christian communism or a rather tame "fellowship over coffee and cake." Recent scholarship suggests it carries a much more dynamic meaning, drawn from the business world. A *koinonia* was a form of business partnership in which members voluntarily invested resources in support of an agreed-upon mission or objective. The objective did not have to be solely profit, and it appears that Paul is creatively using the term in Philippians (1:5) to form a business partnership with the Philippian Christians to extend the gospel.[6]

What would it be like if believers gathered as the local embassy of the kingdom of God in a given place and under the guidance of the Holy Spirit agreed together to pursue a particular mission strategy in their locale? What if they committed to support one another economically to do so and formed an enterprise together in pursuit of that objective? What if they all contributed what they could in finance, time, and skills and worked to ensure the achievement of the agreed-upon objectives?[7]

5. These texts also represent a continuation of the ideals of the biblical jubilee, the year of the Lord's favor announced by Jesus as a paradigm of his own ministry in Luke 4:16–21. The original jubilee of Leviticus 25 is, in essence, a market-based economic structure designed to resist the debt slavery of Egypt. It is a paradigm with enormous relevance for us today in the context of the debt slavery of contemporary capitalism at local, national, and international levels. See Williams, "Christianity and the Global Economic Order."

6. See Ogereau, "The Jerusalem Collection as κοινωνία"; and Ogereau, "Paul's κοινωνία with the Philippians." Bruce Winter has also shown how Paul seeks to actively undermine the patron-client dependency culture of Greco-Roman society by encouraging all believers to work to support themselves so that they are able to help others both within and outside the Christian community as part of their Christian witness; see *Seek the Welfare of the City*, chap. 3.

7. More could be said here about the assumption we make of the church being structured as a registered charity so that it pays no tax and that individual giving to the church is incentivized through tax credits of some kind (depending on the jurisdiction). This is a

An Equipping Community

Given the historic mind-set of Christendom and the assumptions of modernity, even the metaphor of "embassy" for the local church makes little sense. If we assume cultural Christianity as the norm in the civic realm, then church is primarily about congregants' ritual piety. Many local churches have struggled to move beyond this mind-set. Today, coming into church can be like being in the Middle East when war or revolution breaks out, rushing to the American or Australian embassy to seek refuge, only to find that no guards are posted and everyone is watching the World Series or the Ashes as if nothing is going on outside. Many highly committed lay Christians find local-church gatherings to be nearly irrelevant to the missional challenges they face on a daily basis.

During the second half of the twentieth century and the beginning of the twenty-first, a number of lay renewal movements have sought to recover an authentic vital connection between Christian faith and daily life and work. As I reviewed in chapter 1, these movements, though at times encouraged by some church leaders, have repeatedly ended up marginalized. Their energy has been co-opted by a narrow clerical agenda in order to build up church programs and "ministries" within the gathered congregation. This pattern must change if the church is to be biblically faithful and missionally effective in the contemporary world.

Ephesians 4:12 makes it clear that the leadership gifts that Christ gives to the church are for equipping believers for works of service. Each of us has been created to do good works that God has prepared in advance for us to do (2:10). Repeatedly the New Testament writers emphasize how these good works include the public witness of Christians in ordinary life, even in the face of hostility (Phil. 1:27; Col. 3:23; 1 Pet. 2:12; etc.). The

cozy relationship between church and state—and perhaps justified—but the possibility of receiving a tax credit can distort the pattern of our giving, and the organizational form itself alters our engagement from active investors (the business enterprise) to passive donors (the registered charity). Increasingly today, donors do not want to be passive, and this is one reason why many charities are increasingly behaving like, or reconstituting themselves as, social enterprises.

socioeconomic realm of work and business is a major theme of New Testament ethical teaching, as is conduct in the civic realm. Teaching on how Christian faith ought to be manifest in the wider culture is given alongside teaching on how it should be manifest in the relational life of the gathered community. In other words, Christian faithfulness and missional witness relate not to some subset of especially pious or sacred duties but to all of life. Both the gathered and the scattered life of the church constitute modes of missional witness.

The frontline of mission in the West today is both the church gathered in its embodied gospel witness *and* the church scattered in a multitude of neighborhoods, workplaces, schools, and homes. Until we focus our attention on this reality, additional programs and ministries, however worthy, are a distraction. As Lesslie Newbigin has said, "The only hermeneutic of the gospel is a congregation of men and women who believe it and live by it."[8]

In light of this, we need to radically overhaul how we form leaders. We need to orient church leaders toward the communal witness of the gathered community within its surrounding city or town and toward fostering a disciple-making culture that equips believers for whole-life mission. Disciple making is inherently relational and time-consuming. It cannot be achieved through a twenty-minute sermon once a week. We are tempted to assimilate or withdraw in light of the cultural dissonance of exile because all cultures are disciple-making cultures, whether they intend to be or not. The contemporary culture of late-modern capitalism is most certainly a disciple-making culture, and intentionally so. Every moment we are bombarded with messages designed to support and stimulate a cultural story of happiness, security, and health achieved through individual consumerist choices about what we have, invest, wear, do, and eat. Moreover, our very status as a worthy human is presented as our responsibility and choice to secure as part of the culture's encouragement that we endlessly reinvent our self-identity. These stories and behaviors are reinforced powerfully through the media, the shopping mall, the debt-based consumer financial system,

8. Newbigin, *The Gospel in a Pluralist Society*, 227.

the internet, and virtual reality. All of this and much more is a massive and powerful disciple-making system that seeks to shape not only what we do but also what we desire and imagine.

Effective Christian discipleship requires that everything about our ambassadorial communities deliberately and thoughtfully engages the stories of our surrounding culture. In subsequent chapters I discuss some specific responses to the dominant cultural stories we encounter, but the absolute base minimum for a healthy discipleship culture involves a proactive personal mentoring to bring encouragement, application, and accountability. If we want to avoid our young people being discipled into the culture of Western individualism, we need to raise our expectations of discipleship. Don't we want all believers to have a fundamental grasp of the overall shape of the biblical story, of where we are in it, and of how it differs from the dominant narratives of our society? We want them to be confident in their ability to relate faith to the details of daily life and work, to pray and hear God for themselves, and to live in accountable relationship with other believers. We want them to put what they have learned into practice and to grow in an understanding and discernment of their passions, skills, and gifts in the context of service to others and an awareness of God's leading in their lives. For many people, the crucible of growth and sanctification in these matters will be their workplace and their actual relationships with other people in the local Christian community.

This discipling culture should not be thought of in individual terms only. Effective communal mission requires that our gathered life embodies meaningful alternatives to the options and lifestyles encouraged by the surrounding culture both to help believers live faithful lives and for outsiders to see and experience. The church needs to imagine itself again as a microcosm of what society could be rather than as a religious club within it. Hope is birthed in others when the church lives in a way that embodies the gospel. We need a complete rethink concerning the common practice of focusing almost solely on age- and stage-specific discipleship programs, which undermine the important place for intergenerational discipleship and mentoring. By living all of life—familial, social, economic, and political—under a different kingdom, we can demonstrate a different way, a path of life that can draw people to Christ.

Equipping Leadership

Any meaningful response to what I have set out thus far in this chapter requires leadership. Yet when church leaders hear arguments like this, many respond, "I haven't got enough time." This is typically not presented as an excuse but rather is a genuine heart cry. In my experience, many pastors are instinctively aware of the kinds of problems I am raising and seeking to address in this book, and they want to do something about them. But many feel trapped in the model of leadership they have inherited and by the expectations of their congregations and denominational hierarchies. To the extent that congregations have consumerist expectations of the local church, we must look precisely to church leaders for energy to make disciples so that "the body of Christ may be built up until we all reach unity in the faith and in the knowledge of the Son of God and become mature" (Eph. 4:12–13). As I have indicated, however, I think that congregational expectations may not be entirely as consumerist as many pastors imagine, and pastors might be pleasantly surprised if, as church leaders, they articulated a clear vision in a missional direction. Be that as it may, we must nevertheless focus our attention on the nature of church leadership and on how such leaders are formed.

The scholar-priest model of the one-man pastor-teacher has its origins in the nineteenth-century response to Enlightenment skepticism. Today, especially with the inward turn toward religious experience as an escape from the nihilism of the contemporary world, pastors are increasingly seen as managers of a religious social service, not as leaders of a missionary community. In the Christendom mind-set that assumes cultural Christianity, church leaders focus on congregants' personal piety, involving at best the teaching of orthodox doctrine and at worst faith as a form of therapy toward the goal of (religious) self-realization. There are numerous variants of this model; one visible marker of success is the megachurch pastor as business executive, presiding over a large congregation of contented religious consumers.

In such a model, leaders are expected to be able to preach, oversee congregational worship, and undertake pastoral care. The latter bears little resemblance to the kind of discipleship discussed earlier in this chapter; instead it focuses largely on the important care for individuals facing crisis moments or transitions such as job loss, sickness, marriage, divorce, birth, and death. These qualities are also likely to be the only ones in which church leaders will have received practical training as part of their theological education. In the West, the curriculum for pastors-in-training (note that it is never apostles-, prophets-, or evangelists-in-training) is dominated by biblical studies, systematic theology, and church history. Together, these account for around 70 percent of most programs. Almost none of this content will develop any sustained reflection on mission, contemporary culture, or the workplace (though it could). Almost all of it, at least in Protestant schools, is substantially biased toward the theological agenda of the Reformation. This is particularly ironic given the Reformers' recovery of vocation theology for all arenas of work, set against the persistent marginalization of a theology of work in the seminary curriculum. A further 10 to 15 percent of courses focus on the specific applied areas of preaching, worship, and pastoral care, and another 10 percent of courses are designed to give direct experience of church-based practice and to test whether a candidate is ready to be "called."[9] This leaves precious little space for courses focused on the missional challenges of the West, on equipping for cross-cultural mission, or on developing the leadership skills needed to communicate vision, think strategically, make disciples, delegate responsibility, and organize and build effective teams. Worse still, many church leaders are being formed with little to no experience in a work context outside the church. A frightening proportion undertake this seminary education as the culmination of a sustained experience within a "Christian bubble" of secondary

9. Information on the typical Western seminary curriculum comes from program information I gathered while academic dean at Regent College in the early 2010s.

schools, Bible colleges, Christian liberal arts universities, and parachurch institutions.

For Christians working in business and professional environments, the previous paragraph will come as no surprise. Many find that leaders in most workplace environments are far more competent as leaders than are their local pastors. Many Christians find that church leaders are hopelessly out of touch with their daily realities. Training church leaders is a highly expensive process. It is professionally akin to the training we expect of a lawyer or an accountant. It takes three to four years of full-time study beyond an initial undergraduate degree and costs on average at least $30,000 in tuition fees, on top of living costs. Despite this costly investment, for most people attending most seminaries, it is a broken model.

It remains to be seen whether seminaries can adapt. Higher education is not known for being entrepreneurial, and seminaries are typically on the conservative end of higher-educational innovation. Most of them have deep roots in the modern era of the church, and even those that don't are vulnerable to the powerful tendencies toward an assumption of clerical superiority and insular, rarefied scholarship in the theological academy. This mission drift at the heart of theological education is already driving the more-innovative churches to eschew formal theological education in favor of less-clerical and less-scholastic on-the-job training. Enrollments at theological schools are falling, and the sector is in financial crisis, yet there is little sense of a strategic crisis among seminary leaders. The primary instinct is to retreat to the traditional core curriculum and try to sell more courses via cheaper online delivery modes. It may be that today, as in other periods of church history when the institutional church has been moribund, God is raising up a lay renewal movement.

However change occurs, we must hope for a radical shift in how Christian leaders are formed. A good example of innovation in the right direction is provided by the Church of England, which now requires ordinands to work for several years in nonchurch workplaces prior to commencing their training. In the political arena, ambassadors are rotated between postings. Part of the solution to our current problems might be to end the division between clergy and laypeople so that trained Christian leaders can move more easily between church and societal roles.

We will likely see immediate fruit by returning to the practice of the early apostles, who all had work experience in ordinary life and continued to practice their trades from time to time. Let current church leaders work part-time in a societal role and finance additional leadership training for existing clergy from Christian business and professional leadership training organizations, ideally in partnership with mission-training colleges. Much of the church's expertise in cross-cultural mission is to be found in our missionary-training colleges and in those based in non-Western countries. While Christians preparing for mission work overseas are effectively trained in missiology and cross-cultural communication, those preparing for mission work in the West usually are not.

In the former paragraph, and elsewhere in this book thus far, I have used the words and phrases "mission," "missionary," "mission work," and "missionary training" without trying to define them. Such definition is important and necessary. Any ambassador, and any ambassadorial community, must know what they are sent *for* and what they are supposed to do. They have to know the mission.

8

Know the Mission

An ambassadorial community, or embassy, is a group representing the interest of another—namely, the home country. "Mission" is a way of speaking about that interest. A mission is a special assignment or task that someone or some group is given to do. It is clearly a vital matter that Christians know the mission they have been given.

This apparently simple statement leads us, though, into a rather problematic zone. At the beginning of the last century, the unequivocal answer to the question of the mission of the church was overseas evangelism. European and North American mission focused on reaching the adherents of other religions, especially in Africa and Asia. The role of laypeople back home was either to volunteer and train as missionaries or to support the activities financially. Some churches might add a ministry for serving the urban poor or disadvantaged youth to the list of activities deserving of the terminology of "mission work" or "missions."

Two world wars and the retreat of European empires began to change this emphasis in several ways. First, the colonial nature of foreign missions came under scrutiny, as it seemed like what many missionaries taught to be Christianity was often mixed up with the values of white European civilization. Second, the success of foreign missions—and the explosive growth of Christianity outside Europe and North America—also brought new perspectives from the resulting churches and Christian communities. Often, these challenged the perceived Western reduction of the gospel to matters of personal piety and private life, and they generated new voices from contexts where the biblical witness concerning a just society had all-too-relevant application to the immediate surroundings of the new believing communities.

As these non-Western Christian communities became increasingly self-confident in articulating a more public and social gospel, Western Christians became confused and less confident in what they were doing. In chapter 1, I outlined the kind of arguments about the relative priority of evangelism and social action that preoccupied evangelicals for much of the postwar period. Once it became evident that secularism was opening a new missionary frontier in the West, the primary instinct was to adapt the previous focus on evangelism overseas to the domestic context. While this has had some success, a new generation of Westerners finds the emphasis in many churches on personal piety and personal evangelism to be narrow, hypocritical (because public and social behavior can be left untouched by such a faith), and irrelevant to the issues facing them in daily life. Thus, in many quarters, our responses to the new missionary challenges in the West have prolonged or reigninited the debate about the relative primacy of evangelism and social action in Christian mission.

This brief sketch has touched on only some of the major issues that arise when we try to discuss the mission of the church. How do we begin to untangle this? A good place to start is with some definitions.

A Basic Definition

Our English word "mission" derives from the Latin *missio*, meaning "sent." It is not itself a biblical word, though the concept clearly is: Jesus sends out the seventy, for instance, and tells his disciples to "go" into all the world. The *Oxford English Dictionary* defines "mission" as "an important assignment given to a person or group."[1] The sense of givenness, of being sent, implies of course that there is a sender. The primary characteristics of the sender are those of intentionality, or purpose, and the authority to accomplish the purpose and send others to achieve it. Both intent and authority are necessary characteristics of the sender. Thus, when giving the Great Commission to his disciples, Jesus begins with the words, "All authority in heaven and on earth has been given to me. Therefore go and make disciples of all nations" (Matt. 28:18–19).

Much of the contemporary church's loss of confidence arises because we are confused about our purpose in the world and unsure of the authority God has given us. Our use of the word "mission" to refer to a certain group of activities contributes to our confusion. What these activities are may vary depending on which particular Christian group we are part of, but typically the core activities involve evangelism, church planting, and relief activities to alleviate poverty, largely in developing countries. This reduction of the meaning of "mission" to a particular range of activities suffers from the same kind of problems as the similar reduction in the meaning of the word "vocation" discussed in chapter 6: it tends toward an activism that is disconnected from the very intimate personal relationship with God that ought to characterize our lives (and from which we gain confidence in our authority as believers). Further, it distorts our reading of Scripture in ways that also narrow the scope of the gospel (and thereby confuse us about what mission is for). So when we talk about mission, we must begin by asking, "Whose mission?" and "To what end?" before fixating on particular activities.

Noninstinctive human action always arises from intent or purpose. Sometimes people engage others in helping them achieve their purpose or even establish entire organizations to do this. More often, we carry out our own intentions because we don't have servants, because we lack the funds to employ someone else, or simply because it's more convenient to carry out our purpose ourselves. Our own existence as purposeful agents

1. *Oxford English Dictionary* online, s.v. "exile," accessed August 28, 2019, https://www.lexico.com/en/definition/exile.

also arises from the deliberate activity of our parents. Although human intentions are sometimes frustrated, and human actions sometimes give rise to unintended consequences, we can nevertheless recognize that all human activity ultimately arises from the intention of God in creation, even those activities that stand in opposition to God—because God intended the freedom that made such rebellion possible.

We see therefore that all activity, including whatever Christians call mission, finds its source and origin in the purpose and intention of God. This does not mean that everything that happens is mission. It does mean that a minimal criterion for a Christian understanding of mission is that the activity in question is in fact *aligned* with God's purpose and intent and *submitted* to God's authority. What follows immediately is that we need to be as clear as possible in understanding both what God's purpose and intentions are and how, precisely, we are authorized by God to carry out those intentions.

God's Purpose

We clearly need to be very careful as human beings when talking of God's purpose and intentions, since we do not have direct access to them. Scripture says that God's ways and thoughts are not ours. The immediate empathy we have with other human beings that helps us judge their intentions cannot be relied on when it comes to God. Our evidence must be confined to God's self-revelation of his own intentions through words and actions recorded in Scripture and understood in the context of the Christian tradition. With these qualifiers, a number of things can be said.

First, God did *not* create the world or human beings because he needed to. This point is made explicitly by Paul in Acts 17:24–25, but it is also apparent in the Genesis account of creation. The first few chapters of Genesis are in dialogue with the contemporary ancient Near Eastern cosmologies that would have competed for the hearts and minds of God's people, particularly during the period after the exodus from Egypt. In most of these cosmologies, humanity was created as an afterthought, to supply the gods with food, but in the Genesis account humanity is the pinnacle of creation and God supplies a whole garden of food for them. The Genesis account thus deliberately counters the idea that human beings exist to meet God's needs and instead presents God as meeting human needs (purposeful work, a place to live, food to eat, companionship and community, and [postfall] clothes to wear).

Second, God's purpose for human beings is revealed in Genesis as one in which they have a place of great honor and dignity in the created order. In the competing cosmologies of the ancient Near East, kings were often understood as a god's representative on the earth. Only those kings bore the image of the god. An idol would be placed in a pagan temple and was believed to be representative of the god being worshiped and, indeed, to be somehow animated by that god. In similar fashion, some of the pagan kings were understood to be the representative of the god and animated by the spirit of the god. What the Genesis account does with this cultural background is quite remarkable. First, the garden of Eden is depicted as "an archetypal sanctuary, prefiguring the later tabernacle and temples."[2] Humanity is placed in this temple-garden, each is created in the image of God, each is animated by God's Spirit, and each is given authority to rule. Work is the way that this rule is activated, and the words for work in Genesis 2—variously translated as "cultivate" (GNT) or "dress" (KJV) and "keep" (ESV), "guard" (GNT), or "care" (NIV) for the earth—are the very same Hebrew words used later of the priestly work in the tabernacle. Each human being is then commissioned to be fruitful, to multiply, and to extend the worshipful work of cultivating and keeping the earth into the rest of creation. Genesis thus radically democratizes an exalted view of human dignity and portrays the whole of creation as a temple in which humanity honors and serves God by cultivating (drawing out its bounty) and caring (protecting its integrity) in cooperation with one another and with God himself. God's intent is that human beings govern the earth as his representatives.

Third, the Genesis account reveals the *delight* of God in his creation. He declares the created world to be "good" in its own right, prior to the

2. Wenham, *Genesis 1–15*, 61.

account of the creation of human beings, and declares the whole creation including humanity to be "very good." The depiction of God as a creator who delights in the work of his hands likens God to an artist creating something delightful out of his imagination. This sense of delight is reinforced in Proverbs 8, in which personified wisdom speaks of the delight and rejoicing involved in the act of creation and its result.

The dutiful care for human needs, the dignity given to human beings, and God's delight over us as a parent with a newborn child leads the psalmist to wonder:

> When I consider your heavens,
> > the work of your fingers,
> the moon and the stars,
> > which you have set in place,
> what is mankind that you are mindful of them,
> > human beings that you care for them?

> You have made them a little lower than the angels
> > and crowned them with glory and honor.
> You made them rulers over the works of your hands;
> > you put everything under their feet. (Ps. 8:3–6)

We learn a lot about a person's intentions by seeing what happens when things go wrong. What goes wrong is that Adam and Eve disobey God's command not to eat of one of the trees in the garden. They are persuaded by the crafty serpent to disbelieve God and trust the snake concerning what will happen if they eat of this particular tree. The very first effect of this disobedience is that they feel naked and ashamed, cover themselves from each other, and hide from God's presence when they hear him coming to see them while "walking in the garden in the cool of the day" (Gen. 3:8). God's questions to them are revealing: "Where are you?" "Why are you hiding?"[3]

---

3. This second question is my gloss of Gen. 3:10–11. Adam replies to the first question by saying that he hid because he was afraid, and he was afraid because of his nakedness. God then asks Adam how he knows he is naked. An expansion of this exchange might be, "You say you are hiding because you are naked, but how do you know you are naked? Why

"What is this you have done?" (3:9, 13). These are deeply relational questions, so we are not surprised when, a few chapters later, the narrator tells us that God's "heart was deeply troubled" (Gen. 6:6) over the disobedience of humanity and the wickedness, violence, and corruption of creation that followed (Gen. 6:5–6, 11–12).

God does not scrap the whole project and start again, though he could have and clearly thinks about it (Gen. 6:7, 13). That God does not simply destroy the earth reveals something remarkable about God's intentions. While God certainly *sees* wickedness and violence and is grieved by it, he *looks* for what is good and delights in it. Many people imagine God to be always looking out for what they have done wrong, like a perfectionist parent or teacher. But Genesis, and the Bible as a whole, instead reveals God as one who looks for reasons to limit his judgment, to show mercy, to bless. These reasons always involve delight in, or favor for, specific human beings.

Progressively from this point, Scripture reveals God as deciding to preserve creation in partnership with Noah (Gen. 8:21), to limit judgment in council with Abraham (Gen. 18:20–33), and ultimately to come himself (in partnership with many people and generations, but especially Mary) to overcome human violence and wickedness by absorbing it into himself on the cross (Col. 2:13–15; Heb. 2:14–15). Moreover, God reaffirms to Noah humanity's commission to cultivate and fill the earth (Gen. 9:1); promises Abraham that he and his descendants will be made fruitful and become a blessing to all the nations (Gen. 12:1–3); tells Moses how, after years of slavery in Egypt, Israel can sustain the possibility of worshipful work in the promised land (Lev. 25); and ultimately delivers us all from the futility of our own sin and failure by making us anew: "For we are God's handiwork, created in Christ Jesus to do good works, which God prepared in advance for us to do" (Eph. 2:10).

God neither destroys his creation when it falls nor wavers in his purpose. His care, commissioning, and delight continue. He restores, saves, and

---

are you really hiding? Did someone tell you that you were naked or to hide? Did you disobey my command?"

renews. In a world that has become alienated and fragmented as a result of the fall, his purpose is "to bring unity to all things in heaven and on earth under Christ" (Eph. 1:10).

We might still ask why. Why does God do all this? Although the story has hinted at an answer, we need to keep reading to the end for it to be spelled out. The answer is love. Jesus famously told Nicodemus that "God loved the world so much that he gave his only Son so that every one who believes in him shall not be lost, but should have eternal life" (John 3:16, J. B. Phillips). We get a further amazing glimpse into God's heart intentions in the prayer of Jesus recorded in John 17:21–23: "Just as you, Father, live in me and I live in you, I am asking that [all those who believe in me] may live in us, that the world may believe that you did send me. I have given them the honor that you gave me, that they may be one, as we are one—I in them and you in me, that they may grow complete into one, so that the world may realize that you sent me and *have loved them as you loved me*" (J. B. Phillips, emphasis added).

The final chapters of the Bible reveal what God intends in the future. There is a new heaven and a new earth. The new Jerusalem comes down from heaven to earth. The announcement from God's throne describes this scene: "Look! God's dwelling place is now among the people, and he will dwell with them" (Rev. 21:3). The verses that follow describe a restored and developed Eden, a garden-city. Humanity's exile is over, and there is access to the tree of life. There is no more death or pain, but there is work and service. There are still nations, but they are healed; there is still rulership, but it is God-honoring. All human culture, the glory and honor of the nations—the product of good work—has been reconciled and reoriented toward God and is offered as worship before his throne (Rev. 21:24–26). And God is present in a completely unmediated way. We will see him face-to-face.

Scripture reveals God as one who created an amazing cosmos and a beautiful world so that he could share both it and his life with human beings. The picture of God's intimate presence among his people in the garden-city of Jerusalem at the end of the Bible is a fulfillment of what

God intended when he walked with Adam and Eve in the garden. Moreover, this is not simply a reset. Amazingly, all the things that God did to rescue humanity from the effects of our own disobedience—the redemptive history of Israel and the church—also find a place in this future. The history of fallen humanity is not discarded but is purified and honored in the basic architecture of the city (see Rev. 21:9–27).

The Drama of Scripture

Understanding God's purpose in the world unlocks the whole story of the Bible and, with it, an enormous amount of hope for the future. Literally everything finds its place in this story, because everything finds its place in God's purposes. The Bible's story is all about everything that has been in exile from God being fully reconciled to him. Everything that he created good, that has been alienated and damaged by the fall—human beings, our relationships with each other, creation itself—is being renewed and restored to right relationship again, as God originally intended in the garden. The result is peace—God's peace as captured in the Hebrew word *shalom*—the abundance of life that Jesus said he came to give us.

Without a clear sense of God's purpose in our minds, many of us lapse into reading the Bible as if it starts in Genesis 3 (the fall) and ends in Revelation 20 (the final judgment). That is, we become so focused on sin and the need to be saved that we forget why. We then easily start to think, or communicate, that Christianity is all about stopping people from sinning, avoiding punishment, and escaping the wrath of God. While these things certainly have a *part* in the story, they are not the whole. We end up preaching truths, but the gospel we preach is narrowed and thereby less powerful. The first and last two chapters of the Bible are crucial in helping us get the whole story. Without them we are stuck in the middle of the story and don't have a firm view of how it started or where it is headed.

In recent years, this danger has led scholars to emphasize the overall story or narrative shape of the Bible. In a classic study, Hans Frei showed how Enlightenment rationalism led the church to focus on propositional truth and to gradually detach those truths from their context in the story of God recorded in the Bible.[4] Being a Christian increasingly became a matter of adherence to a set of belief statements rather than having one's whole life and imagination redefined by and caught up in God's story about the world. Scholars have begun to pay more attention to the literary genres of Scripture and the way that Scripture is intended to communicate. N. T. Wright powerfully presented the narrative structure of the Bible by likening it to an unfinished Shakespearean play in which we have five acts but are missing details of the final act.[5] The power of this metaphor is that the actors (Christians) are challenged to know the previous acts (creation, fall, Israel, and Jesus) and then to improvise the current act (church) in ways that will make sense of the ending (new creation).[6] Other scholars have built on and refined this dramatic metaphor. One of the clearest and most accessible presentations is provided by Mike Goheen and Craig Bartholomew in their book *The Drama of Scripture*.[7] Table 1 provides a shortened summary of this dramatic story, as retold by the authors, alongside the major stages of biblical history.

Table 1. The Dramatic Story of Scripture

	Descriptor	Shorthand Label
Act 1	God Establishes His Kingdom	Creation
Act 2	Rebellion in the Kingdom	Fall
Act 3	Redemption Initiated	Israel
Interlude	*Intertestamental Period*	*Awaiting Messiah*
Act 4	The Coming of the King	Jesus
Act 5	Spreading the News of the King	Church
Act 6	The Return of the King	New Creation

Source: Adapted from Bartholomew and Goheen, *Drama of Scripture*, 22–23.

4. Frei, *The Eclipse of Biblical Narrative*.

5. Wright, *The New Testament and the People of God*, 140. Wright's use of the metaphor at this point is to show how biblical authority can function through narrative.

6. This metaphor of mission as dramatic improvisation is one we will return to in chap. 10.

7. Bartholomew and Goheen, *The Drama of Scripture*.

The Mission of God

We will return to the dramatic structure of the biblical story in the next chapter, but this brief summary demonstrates the point that God's purpose and agency shape the form of the biblical story as a whole. Both these emphases (God's purpose and God's agency) tend to centralize God's initiative and God's kingdom in the way we read Scripture. To talk about God's intent and purpose in creation and redemption is another way of speaking about God's rule and reign. To say that God intends to reconcile all things in heaven and on earth under Christ, and to recognize that God is a God who doesn't just have "good intentions" but acts on them, is to speak of the kingdom of God. The vision in Revelation previously summarized is the vision of God's kingship (at least, it's the bit of God's kingly vision that we know about; who knows what amazing plans God has beyond this). At the center of the garden-city is a throne. God's kingly mission is to make this vision a reality.

From this, we see that the scope of God's mission is larger than the scope of the church's mission; or alternatively we could say that the kingdom of God is greater than the church. We should not simply equate the two, but we do need to ask what the relationship between them is. This is another way of asking about the relationship between the mission of God and the mission of the church. Theologians traditionally understood the *missio Dei* (the mission of God) in fundamentally trinitarian categories. God the Father sends the Son, and God the Father and Son send the Spirit. By contrast, the *missiones ecclesiae* (the missionary activities of the church) involved church planting, evangelism, conversion, and church growth. In this rendering, there is a disconnect between the two, but during the postwar period it became increasingly clear to missiologists that the missionary activities of the church had to serve the wider mission of God in the world. The importance of this is only underlined when we realize that the church itself is an expression of the Triune God's mission to the whole of creation.

In love, God moved out (sent himself) to create. He sent his Word and his Spirit to bring the cosmos into being. In love he sent humanity into the world to cultivate and rule it before him. He sent Abraham on a journey and blessed him to become a nation that would bless the world. Israel's very existence is thus an expression of God's mission. The same is true of the Scripture. God sent his word, he sent his Son, he sent the Spirit, and he sent the church. All of these embody God's mission, most fully expressed, of course, in Jesus Christ. The church is thus an *expression* of God's mission and an *agent* of God's mission. The church constitutes those who have acknowledged God's kingship, but God's kingship extends beyond the church into the whole world, though it is not acknowledged there.

Understanding mission as the outward impulse of love, and thus central to God's character and nature, brings unity to many things that we often find difficult or confusing to reconcile. For instance, the Creation Mandate (to fill, cultivate, and rule the earth), the Great Commandments (to love God and neighbor), the Great Commission (to scatter, be witnesses, and make disciples), and the New Commandment (to "love one another as I have loved you" [John 15:12 ESV]) all serve the mission of God in the world. We often focus heavily on the third of these, but it is worth noting that the Great Commission is the only temporary command on this list. The other three are permanent. In the vision of the garden-city there is still work and rulership in a renewed earth. There is still love for God and neighbor. There is still love for one another modeled on that of Jesus. But there is no need of evangelism. Scripture tells us this quite explicitly: "No longer will they teach their neighbor, or say to one another, 'Know the Lord,' because they will all know me, from the least of them to the greatest" (Heb. 8:11; cf. Jer. 31:32).

This in no way means that the Great Commission is unimportant, but its importance lies in its relationship to the other three. The Great Commission matters *because* God wants everyone to know of his love and forgiveness (witness), he wants everyone to be restored into relationship with him in Christ (evangelism and conversion), and he wants everyone to live their whole lives worshipfully under Christ's lordship (discipleship). If the church's missionary activity is to serve the wider mission of God, then the Great Commission must be understood and conducted in a way that reinforces these other commands. This is another way of saying that the church must have a kingdom vision in all that it does. It must be kingdom-minded and not focused only on itself. This was Israel's mistake. They relished the fact that they were "chosen" by God but ignored the fact that they'd been chosen to bless the nations.

Once we detach the Great Commission from these other commands in Scripture, we begin to distort the gospel. We can begin to sound as if the fall means that God's original plan has failed so now Christ has come with plan B, in which our sins will be forgiven and we will escape judgment but the rest of the world will be destroyed and God will start again. Against this view we must say that the gospel is not God's no to the world but God's yes to it. It's not a plan B—a kind of spiritual evacuation from a war zone—but a profound commitment on God's part to plan A. In the gospel, God does not announce that an escape route to heaven is being provided. Rather, he announces that the kingdom of God is here. Heaven is coming to earth because God is committed to plan A—his original purpose for the world. The gospel is good news precisely because, in Jesus, God is drawing near to put things right, to sort out the mess we've gotten ourselves into, to save us from our sin, to restore us to relationship with himself, to recommission us as his representatives on earth, and ultimately to renew creation itself. That's good news!

God's mission is to unite everything in all creation under the lordship of Jesus Christ. This "uniting of everything under Christ's lordship" is the kingdom coming. The gospel is the announcement of this, and the church is the bearer of this message. We are ambassadors of the gospel of the kingdom.

The Church *as* Mission

The church, in its very existence, is missional because it expresses God's mission in the world. Christians are ordinary human beings who, having encountered and responded to God, are given a new nature that is alive to and empowered by God's Spirit, are given a new identity as citizens of

God's kingdom, and are formed into a new community under Christ's lordship. God calls this new community into existence by the gospel and then sends it back into the world as part of his purpose. It is this "calling out" and "being sent back" that gives the church its fundamental exilic and missional character. The exile of the church in the world arises from God's missional *intent*. The local church communicates the gospel just by existing as an ambassadorial community.

This is not simply a matter of semantics. A foreign embassy both witnesses to the existence of another sovereign nation and also partially embodies the culture of that nation. Likewise, the local church witnesses to God's kingdom and embodies something of its culture. This was a major point of the previous chapter. The local church is both a sign and a foretaste of the kingdom of God. How does this happen?

The church projects the culture of the kingdom to the extent that it truly embodies in its life God's intent that we dwell together in him in a unity of love. Jesus explicitly connects the quality of our love for one another with our witness in the world: "A new command I give you: Love one another. As I have loved you, so you must love one another. By this everyone will know that you are my disciples, if you love one another" (John 13:34–35). To love as Jesus loved us is to serve, to look out for one another's interests and not just our own, to have the same attitude as Christ Jesus, who humbled himself even to death on a cross (Phil. 2:1–11). This kind of love is completely countercultural. It cannot fail to communicate God's nature and instill hope in others. Despite our finitude and failure, if we give ourselves to living like this in the power of the Holy Spirit, the treasure of Christ will shine forth through the broken clay jars of our lives. This love is infectious. It is not that we love one another while acting selfishly toward those outside the ambassadorial community. It is rather that God's love permeates through our lives and our Christian community out to all those around us in our workplaces, homes, schools, and neighborhoods.

It is this love that will also undergird the *authority* of God that we carry as a community. Paul reminds Timothy to "fan into flame" (2 Tim. 1:6) the gifting of God that he has been given to serve God's purposes in the world. He encourages Timothy to be full of confidence, "for the Spirit of God does not make us timid, but gives us power, love and self-discipline" (2 Tim. 1:7). The church is not sent into the world empty-handed. We have been sent with authority and the empowering of the Holy Spirit. Our authority rests on the resurrected Christ, to whom "all authority in heaven and on earth" (Matt. 28:18) has been given. We have been raised up and seated with Christ (Eph. 2:6; Col. 3:1). He has given the church the keys of the kingdom of God. We have been promised that the gates of hell cannot stand against us (Matt. 16:17–20), that if we resist the devil he will flee (James 4:7), that we have spiritual armor that can withstand enemy attack (Eph. 6:10–18), that God will soon crush Satan under our feet (Rom. 16:20), and that we can overcome evil with good (Rom. 12:21).

We shouldn't confuse embodying Christ's humble love with timidity, or gentleness with weakness. The love of Christ is not timid or weak. It is a passionate commitment to give everything to overcome the evil that imprisons people.

The church *as* mission is a community that is missional because of its changed identity and new life. It is missional in its being and identity not because of anything that it does. Confidence in God's authority is not a feeling that we work up to but a natural outcome of having encountered God in Christ and of having seen God's saving power at work. Love for others is not a duty that we have to perform but a natural outcome of experiencing God's love in our own lives and of having our hearts expanded and enlivened by that love.[8]

One might ask, "If it is a natural outcome, is there anything for us to do?" There are many voices and temptations in our culture that seek to persuade us to abandon our identity in Christ and live out of our old nature, to leave the identity of the "foreign embassy" of the local church and go native in the host culture of the surrounding society. If we listen

---

8. I have seen the reality of the church *as* mission more clearly since a professional colleague of mine described his experience of entering a London church as a nonbeliever. What struck him powerfully was seeing an ethnically, socially, politically, class-, and gender-diverse congregation all equal before God as they knelt to say the confession and pray the Lord's Prayer. He has since come to faith.

to these voices and give way to these temptations, we will lose hope and our love will wane.

Christ calls us to remain in him (John 15). He is like a vine, and we are like branches that can only draw sap by being connected to the vine. If we remain in him, his life will flow through us and we cannot fail to be fruitful. If we don't remain, we cannot do anything at all, but if we do remain, we will have great confidence. We can "ask whatever [we] wish, and it will be done" (v. 7); we are called friends, not servants, because we share in the governance of God's work in the world (v. 15).

The vine is an organic image in which small branches and twigs bear fruit by being connected to the vine and the root that brings life. It is an image of community in which Christians draw life not simply by having a private relationship with Jesus but by being deeply connected to other believers in love. The life of the Holy Spirit flows to us in our relationships with other believers, not just in our relationship with God. It is precisely in the context of this passage that Jesus gives his disciples the new commandment to love one another (v. 12). As the apostle John puts it in his first letter, "We know that we have passed from death to life, because we love each other. Anyone who does not love remains in death" (1 John 3:14).

If we needed any further confirmation that the church is missional just by existing, John 15 also tells us that we can expect to be hated, persecuted— though sometimes heard—as Jesus was, simply by virtue of the fact that we no longer belong to the world but instead belong to Christ and have been sent into the world in his name (vv. 18–21).

Everything that has been said in this section about the church *as* mission applies to every believer and every church. There is no hierarchy here of some who are missionaries and others who support, some churches who are running successful programs and others whose techniques lag behind. Christians are either part of the church and therefore a part of God's mission in the world or have cut themselves off from the life of God and will be unable to bear fruit. Every local church is either connected to Christ the vine and growing in love and authority or is a branch in danger of being cut off and discarded.

The Church *on* Mission

The position set forth in the previous section is foundational to our understanding of mission. It corrects activist theologies of mission that ignore the quality and character of Christian community and relationships or measure success in terms of numbers alone. It also counters triumphalist theologies of mission that envision taking over political power or transforming culture by imposing Christian morality. We should be grateful, therefore, to thinkers such as Stanley Hauerwas, whose writings have highlighted the missional character of the church and brought a much-needed correction to the debate in recent decades.[9]

Nevertheless, there is more to be said. The church is missional in its existence and identity, but it also has been commissioned to act in particular ways in the world. Love of God and confidence in God are absolutely foundational, but they are foundations for further action. An established embassy with a distinctive culture is an expression of mission, but the ambassadorial community within it prepares to engage in diplomacy. The church is sent *on* mission.

The church is intended to be a *sent* and *sending* community—a community on the move. It must maintain an "outward" orientation toward the world as well as an "upward" orientation toward God. So long as the outward orientation flows from the community's "upward" orientation, we will avoid assimilation. A fear of assimilation—that is, a lack of confidence in God and the gospel—will lead instead to an "inward" orientation of self-preservation that will damage the church's missional effectiveness.

Leadership is key to this missional effectiveness. Ephesians 4 makes it clear that Christ has given leadership gifts (embodied in apostles, prophets, evangelists, and pastor-teachers) for the purpose of equipping God's people for works of service. These works of service are meant to be "good works" in service of God's purpose in the world. They involve interpersonal relationships in the family but also economic relationships at work.[10] Believers

9. See, for example, Hauerwas and Willimon, *Resident Aliens*.

10. The "household code" lists that appear toward the second halves of New Testament letters such as Ephesians, Colossians, 1 Timothy, and 1 Peter all include discussion of the economic dimension of life, which, in that culture, was centered around the extended household.

are to do good not simply in private or in the church but also in public, where outsiders and "pagans" can see them (1 Pet. 2:12). All their work is to be done "as working for the Lord" (Col. 3:23). A believer's citizenship in heaven should make him or her stand out in the civic realm (Phil. 1:27; 1 Pet. 2:15; 1 Thess. 4:11–12; Rom. 13:6–7).[11]

Thus, church leaders must equip believers to live missional lives as workers, neighbors, and citizens in the world, not simply, or even primarily, as church members. A church whose discipleship, teaching, and training programs are oriented toward church leadership and service at church meetings, in church-led programs, and in Christian organizations (however worthy) is an "inward-oriented" community that is creating a ghetto. Mark Greene, of the London Institute of Contemporary Christianity, describes this ghetto well when he speaks of the *de facto* missionary strategy of much of the church in the West: "To recruit the people of God to use some of their leisure time to join the missionary initiatives of church-paid workers."[12]

Such a strategy is plainly inadequate, as well as unbiblical. God has so designed the church that faithful believers, scattered throughout society in all kinds of workplaces, neighborhoods, and communities, are on the frontline of missionary encounter. They do not need to "go" somewhere else to be missionally fruitful; they need to "go" into these places under the lordship of Jesus Christ. Many church leaders spend a lot of time wondering how to reach a "secular society" and a lot of energy trying to start programs and initiatives, yet they fail to see that their congregants are already perfectly placed to reach it, most of them in places that a church leader could never reach or be credible in. What these believers need is church leaders' energetic investment in biblical, theological, and missiological training to help them follow Jesus in the whole of their lives.

11. Bruce Winter has shown how New Testament teaching tended to undermine the typical patron-client relationships in Greco-Roman culture—a hierarchical system of obligation—as well as its denigration of work, which the Greeks tended to see as a base activity for slaves and those of low social status. Early Christians were encouraged to work, support themselves, and do good to others without any expectation of reciprocity. See Winter, *Seek the Welfare of the City*.

12. Greene, *People at Work*.

This is not simply to bless or baptize what people are already doing. On the contrary, we need to be as rigorously prepared and discerning to work in a retail store, investment bank, or factory as we would to do street evangelism, undertake an outreach program to prostitutes in the red-light district, or work with a Christian relief organization overseas. On the whole, however, we tend to be extraordinarily blasé and lazy about ordinary life. Very few churches provide serious help to young people or those in other life transitions in discerning their skills and gifts, learning to hear God's voice and direction, or relating Scripture to the detail of how we serve, except in circumstances involving explicitly "churchy" activities. If a young person is wondering whether they are being led to join a law firm, they can expect a few nods of interest and perhaps some prayers in their home group. If they express interest in joining a mission agency or training as a youth pastor, their experience will be wholly different. Yet surely we should be just as concerned to help someone hear God well and apply Scripture, and we should want to equip him or her for missional service, whether God is sending them into youth work or into a law practice. This reinforcement of a "sacred-secular" divide only contributes to the secularization of our culture. Equally, very few churches give sustained attention to teaching about the ideologies and stories of Western culture, the missiological challenges involved in reaching it, or what faithfulness to Christ looks like in different workplaces or in public life.

A sending church, a church on mission, will delight in equipping and sending its people not simply as apostles to faraway places but also as apostles to the marketplace, the education sector, and the elderly care facility. It will work hard to help everyone know how to read and apply the Scripture amid ordinary life so they can grow to be the best ambassador in their context. It will delight in publicly commissioning and praying over groups of construction workers, social workers, and software engineers as such people respond to God's initiative in their lives to serve him in those spheres, just as it would delight in commissioning and praying for people going overseas with a mission agency or relief organization. The key issue will not be in prejudging where the Holy Spirit is sending people but in being sure that people *are* being led by the Holy Spirit and are properly equipped to go.

God may send us into any part of his world, because his mission encompasses "all things." The scope of redemption is as wide as the scope of creation. This applies to individual Christians, but it also applies to local churches and denominations and every grouping or initiative in between. The most exciting thing about mission is that God calls us to work with him, and typically not on our own but with others. We need more of the spirit of Jonathan and his armor-bearer in the church. First Samuel 14:1–13 tells the story of the day when Jonathan basically woke up and said to himself, "Enough of the oppression of the Philistines, let's have a go and see if God will act." His armor-bearer responded, "Go ahead; I am with you heart and soul." This spirit is the spirit of hope, because it acts in the present on the basis of a confidence about God's character and actions in the future. If God has put dreams in our hearts to see his kingdom come and people delivered from the power of the enemy and reconciled to God in some area of life, let's go for it and support one another to do something about it. This text applies as much to Christians with a vision for a new business or a public campaign as it does to those with a vision for a new charity or an evangelistic community initiative.

The church *on* mission is a community of believers following the Holy Spirit. The paradigm text, in this regard, is the book of Acts. What we see there is a mixture of communal prayer, entrepreneurial responsiveness to the (sometimes odd) leading of the Holy Spirit, and surprising results.

So we see that whether as individual believers scattered throughout society, or as a local community of God's people sent to a particular place, we are to work together as ambassadorial communities confident in this missional mandate—the reconciliation of all things under the lordship of Jesus Christ. Our condition of exile turns out to be the basis for mission, not an obstacle to it.

PART THREE

AMBASSADORS OF LOVE

Exiles on Mission

9

Learn the Language

All mission is cross-cultural. The gospel is always and everywhere foreign to the culture that hears it. Ambassadors need to establish an embassy and know the mission. But they also must *learn* the language of the culture they are sent to. By this I mean that ambassadors must learn the cultural stories that form the conceptual and practical background in a given society. Our need to learn the cultural language is even more acute if this culture is one we were born into. It is precisely with such familiarity that we tend to operate with a host of unquestioned assumptions, beliefs, and feelings.

For Western Christians, the culture of Western countries is extremely familiar. The fact that we may read the Bible and the newspaper in the same written language does not mean that the thought world of the Bible and of the newspaper are the same. Being familiar with "Western," "American," or "British" cultural norms makes us prone to being co-opted into the non-Christian elements of our societies, even worshiping its false gods. Not only is this a hindrance to our faithful response to God; it also weakens our witness in society.

If we want to honor God and function effectively as Christ's ambassadors, we would do well to imitate Daniel and his friends in the posture they adopted following their exile to Babylon. They did not capitulate to the cultural stories of Babylon. But neither did they detach in order to avoid "contamination" from their pagan captors. Instead, they gave themselves to *learn* the "language and literature of the Babylonians" (Dan. 1:4). Having resolved first not to compromise their fundamental identity as God's people by eating defiled food (Dan. 1:8–16), they found that God gave them such insight and understanding into Babylonian ways that their excellence was noticed by the king himself (Dan. 1:17–20).

Like Daniel and his friends in Babylon, we need to learn the language and literature—the fundamental stories—of Western culture and do so excellently. There are two important reasons for this. First, we want our missional action in the world to be coherent and effective. We encountered this idea in chapter 3, where we first met an important statement from Alasdair MacIntyre: "I can only answer the question 'What am I to do?' if I can answer the prior question 'Of what story or stories do I find myself a part?'"[1] The stories of which a Christian ambassadorial community finds itself a part include *both* the story of God *and* the stories of the culture in which that story of God is to be told. Understanding the stories of Western culture will help us see the signs of our own times and avoid the exilic temptations arising from the disjunctions in the surrounding cultural stories with the Christian story.

But there's a more fundamental reason for learning the stories of Western culture: namely, love. It is an act of love and humility to understand well the stories of our own society. We must be careful to take seriously and not caricature the longings, fears, and hopes expressed in cultural stories, even where we conclude they are false or misleading. It is only by taking the trouble to understand our culture truly that we will be able to communicate with it in ways that will be both prophetic and redemptive. Ambassadors show respect for the host country in which they are operating, and the deepest expression of this respect is love.

1. MacIntyre, *After Virtue*, 216.

Cultural Stories and How to Read Them

As noted earlier, Jonathan Sacks has written eloquently of the central role played by storytelling in forming and passing on the core values and beliefs of any culture: "Stories tell us who we are, where we came from and what we might aspire to be. A culture is defined by its narratives."[2] Familiarity with Western culture makes it possible for Western Christians to be unaware of the cultural stories that define the culture we live in simply because they are so much part of the background texture of daily life. So *how* do we read and discern what these stories are?

In this chapter, I set out three main ways that we can do this, using an analogy between getting to know a person and getting to know a culture. If we want to know someone well, we may ask them questions about themselves, notice the kinds of things they do, and see what they're passionate about. In similar fashion, we can learn to read the narratives of our culture (or subculture) by asking good questions, observing cultural practices, and discerning motivations.

Asking Good Questions—the Worldview Approach

How do you view the world? What basic beliefs do you have about life? What is your fundamental posture toward the world? Answering these questions, whether for individuals or entire cultures, is the essence of the worldview approach. Worldview analysis has a long and fruitful, though contested, pedigree in philosophy and theology.

In his influential and valuable book *The Universe Next Door*, James Sire aims to compare all the worldviews that are in some way embodied in Western culture. Sire identifies eight basic questions whose answers fill out the essential contours of a worldview.[3] Answering them generates the basic assumptions (or "presuppositions") that constitute a given worldview. These questions are thus an excellent starting point to understand

2. Sacks, "In a World Run by MTV, Nobody Has Time to Think."
3. Sire, *The Universe Next Door*, 5th edition. Earlier editions only have seven basic questions. Sire added the eighth in this edition.

the cultural stories that surround us—and, of course, for being clear with ourselves about what we believe.

Here are the eight questions with my summary of Sire's commentary to further explain them.

1. *What is prime reality—the really real?* The most common answers to this question are either God or matter. As Sire points out, if the answer is God, we have to press further to discover what kind of God is in view.

2. *What is the nature of external reality—that is, the world around us?* This question concerns the kind of world we find ourselves in. Do we understand it as chaotic or orderly? Where did it come from?

3. *What is a human being?* Who am I? Why do I exist? Where do I come from?

4. *What happens to a person at death?* Reincarnation, transformation into another realm, and extinction are some of the options.

5. *Why is it possible to know anything at all?* This question links our answers to questions 1, 2, and 3. Given the nature of prime reality, the world, and human beings, what kind of knowledge can we have?

6. *How do we know what is right and wrong?* How do we know what to do? What (if anything) is wrong with the way things are?

7. *What is the meaning of history?* Is there any point to life? Can whatever is wrong be put right?

8. *What personal, life-orienting core commitments are consistent with this worldview?* Sire added this question in the fifth edition of the book to reflect the heart commitment that individuals may make in response to a given worldview.

Sire defines worldview as "a commitment, a fundamental orientation of the heart, that can be expressed as a story or in a set of presuppositions . . . which we hold . . . about the basic constitution of reality, and that provides the foundation on which we live and move and have our being."[4] In table 2 I summarize the nine worldviews that Sire assesses using this eight-question grid. For more in-depth analysis of each of these worldviews, I highly recommend a careful reading of Sire's *The Universe Next Door*.

The worldview approach is very helpful, but it tends to emphasize the cognitive and conscious aspects of a cultural story to the neglect of other influences on action. Human beings are not only thinkers; they are also acting and desiring creatures. These weaknesses can be balanced by other approaches.

Observing Behavior—an Aristotelian Approach

Another way to understand a cultural story (or a person) is to observe behavior and action. Aristotle is associated with an approach to understanding human flourishing in the world that emphasizes actions and behaviors, not simply beliefs and knowledge. Of course, the two approaches are not exclusive but complementary, since our observations of action will raise questions that we will want to ask and since, similarly, we will want to tease out how answers to questions of belief and knowledge follow through into action and behavior. Sometimes, of course, belief and actions are inconsistent. Learning to observe behavior and action, as well as asking good questions about fundamental beliefs, is thus very helpful in "learning the language" of our culture.

For Aristotle, our actions both develop and reveal certain character traits—virtues and vices. His ethical treatises explore what constitutes excellent (virtuous) activity and aim to persuade us to adopt patterns of life and behavior that will form these positive traits. Aristotle's approach was adapted and incorporated into Christian reflection, most notably by Thomas Aquinas.

The basis of this approach is that our ideas and assumptions about things (the "beginning" of our stories) are connected to our intentions and

4. Sire, *Naming the Elephant*, 122.

141

Table 2. Summary of Worldviews from *The Universe Next Door*

Question	Christian Theism	Deism	Naturalism	Nihilism	Existentialism	Eastern Pantheistic Monism	The New Age	Postmodernism	Islam
Prime reality?	God is infinite, tran-scendent, impersonal, transcendent, imma-nent, sovereign, and good.	God is tran-scendent but not personal or immanent. The universe runs itself.	There is no God. Matter exists eter-nally and is all there is.	There is no God. Matter exists eter-nally and is all there is.	Matter appears in two forms: objective and subjective. Only human beings make themselves who they are.	God is the one in-finite, impersonal reality. God is the cosmos. Nothing exists that is not God.	The self is the prime reality. As we grow in awareness of this, we are on the verge of a radical New Age.	There is no god. The truth about reality itself is hidden from us; all we can do is tell stories.	Allah is uniquely great, sovereign, transcendent, infi-nite, and good.
The world around us?	Created ex nihilo, with uni-form cause and effect, in an open system in which human beings have genuine agency within limits set by God.	Created as a uniformity of cause and effect in a closed system.	The cosmos exists as a uniformity of cause and effect in a closed system.	The cosmos exists as a uniformity of cause and effect in a closed system.	The objective world stands over and against human beings and appears absurd.	If something ap-pears to exist that is not God, it is an illusion. It is our oneness that gives us reality.	The cosmos, uni-fied in the self, has two manifes-tations. The vis-ible is accessible via conscious-ness; the invisible "mind at large" is accessible through altered consciousness.	Reality is con-structed through language. We can't access what is behind our language about it.	Created ex nihilo, in a closed system in that nothing happens outside Allah's will and power.
Human being?	Created in God's image, good, fallen, but capable of restoration.	Part of the determined, clockwork nature of the universe.	Human beings are complex "machines" that we are striving to understand.	Human beings are conscious machines. Free will is illusion.	Each person is totally free concerning their nature and destiny.	Atman is Brahman; the soul of every person is the soul of the cosmos.	The self is the center of the universe.	Human beings make them-selves by the languages they construct about themselves.	The pinnacle of Allah's creation. We are God's representatives on earth, with a pure and innocent nature.
What happens at death?	A gate either to fullness of life with God or separation from God.	Ambiva-lence about whether there is life after death.	Extinction of person-ality and individuality.	It is impos-sible to know. Nei-ther life nor death has meaning.	The ultimate absurdity—at death we be-come objects.	Death is the end of individual personal existence, but it changes nothing essential in an indi-vidual's nature.	Physical death is not the end of self; the fear of death goes when we achieve cosmic consciousness.	Extinction of self.	A transition be-tween this life and our eternal state, which will be paradise or hell.

Knowledge?	Though fallible, we can know God and the world because God has given us the capacity to do so and communicates with us.	There was no fall, so we can know about God and the universe simply by studying it.	We can know the universe through autonomous human reason.	We cannot distinguish between illusion and truth.	In response to the absurdity of the objective world, the authentic person must revolt and create value.	We can only realize the nature of ultimate reality by becoming it. Some things are more One than others.	Reality is what the self perceives. In a state of cosmic consciousness, reality is perceived directly.	Knowledge is a linguistic construct. Knowledge is power, and the stories we tell about the world always mask a play for power.	Allah has given us the capability of knowledge by reason and the senses. Allah also limits our knowledge.
Right and wrong?	Ethics is transcendent and based on God's character.	Ethics is limited to general revelation—the universe reveals what is right.	Ethics is generated solely by human beings and human culture.	Moral relativism is a fact. There is no rational basis for choosing values.	The good action is the consciously chosen action.	There are many roads to Oneness. To realize Oneness with the cosmos is to pass beyond good and evil and personality.	Experiencing cosmic consciousness obliterates space, time, and morality.	Ethics and meaning are linguistic constructs. Social good and purpose is whatever society takes it to be.	Found in the teachings of the Qur'an, as amplified by the Hadith and interpreted by Sharia law. We should follow all of Allah's commands.
Meaning of history?	A linear sequence leading to the fulfillment of God's purposes.	A linear sequence fully determined at creation.	A linear stream of events linked by cause and effect but with no meaning.	Determinism plus chance makes history absurd.	There is no meaning to history beyond what we make of it.	To realize Oneness is to pass beyond time. Time is unreal; history is cyclical.			History shows the sovereignty of Allah and allows people to submit to Allah.
Personal commitments?	Christians live to seek first the kingdom of God, to glorify God, and to enjoy him forever.	Life goals determined by reason or what is believed will please God.	None implied. Chosen by the individual.	There is no meaning in the universe. Any goal is arbitrary.	A core commitment to myself and my authentic self-expression.	To eliminate desire and thus achieve salvation—realization of one's union with the One.	New Agers live to realize their own individual unity with the cosmos, creating it in their own image.	The core commitments of postmodernists are in flux.	To follow divine commands in every detail with gratitude.

goals (the "end" of our stories) by our actions (the "middle"). That is, our behavior results from our attempts to achieve our goals given our assumptions and beliefs. These behaviors, in turn, shape the kind of person we become (the character traits we acquire). Figure 1 shows this connection between our actions and behaviors and the moral or cultural story that we are being shaped by.

Figure 1

How Do Stories Shape Us?

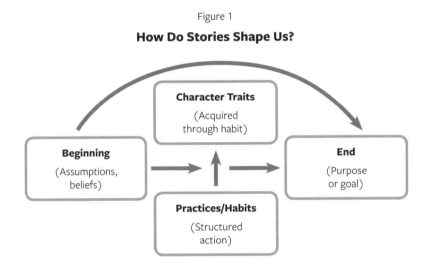

Alasdair MacIntyre stands in this tradition. MacIntyre uses the example of playing a game like chess or playing a musical instrument to illustrate how character traits are acquired and how actions make sense within a cultural story that frames them.[5] Imagine seeing and hearing a neighbor practicing musical scales and phrases on a violin day after day. What makes sense of this deliberate and purposeful action? We might guess, or confirm through inquiry, that our neighbor is part of an orchestra due to perform at the city concert hall in a few months. This makes sense to us because we are at least minimally aware of the existence of orchestras and classical music performances, even if we have never been to one and prefer hip-hop or jazz. If we thought about it, we might assume that this particular violinist was

5. MacIntyre, *After Virtue*, esp. chap. 14, pp. 181–203.

able to play a range of pieces other than the one we keep hearing, because of the evident skills that are being practiced.

From this simple account, we can draw out the four important elements of a cultural story that frame the action of playing the violin. These are illustrated in figure 2. The assumptions and beliefs we have at the beginning—before even hearing the violin being played—include various aspects of the history of music, composition, and performance; of the role of music in human life; and of the craftsmanship needed to make the delicate instrument we call a violin. The purpose or goal is the public performance of a beautiful piece of music. The practices or habits that are undertaken in order to reach the goal include repeated playing of musical scales and phrases and rehearsals with partial and full orchestra. These practices require the musician to be attentive to others, have the humility to learn from mistakes, and have the perseverance to acquire the necessary dexterity and precision to play. In turn, these character traits enhance the experience of the final performance.

We can apply this framework to a whole range of practices in our workplaces, homes, neighborhoods, and churches. The Christian practice of prayer, for instance, is based on assumptions about God's presence, interest, and availability to hear us, as well as a goal of intimate communion between human beings and God. It forces us to recognize our fallibility and need of God as we seek God's help and guidance. It cultivates character traits of humility, dependence, and resilience—traits that enhance our relationship with God and give us a source of strength in the midst of life's difficulties and challenges.

For Aristotle and MacIntyre, the whole point of moral reasoning is to provide a meaningful account of the world that, when studied and put into practice, will in fact help us lead good and virtuous lives. Aristotle argued that the fundamental purpose of human life involved excellence in the exercise of reason (which he saw as the essential human distinctive). The Christian tradition modified this goal (and some of the assumptions about human nature, God, and creation) to focus on love of God and others, since it understands our "image bearing" as the essential human characteristic

Figure 2

The Story of Playing the Violin

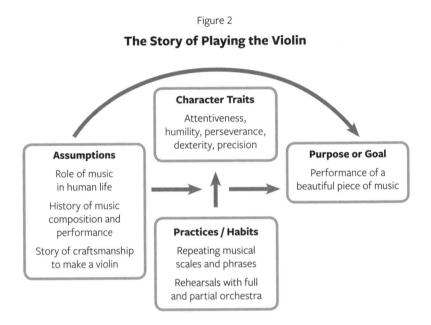

(of which reason is an important part) and union or fellowship with God as its fulfillment. MacIntyre laments that there is no longer any shared agreement about what the goal of human life is. For this reason, he argues that a "virtuous life" no longer makes sense to the vast majority of our society (hence the title of his book, *After Virtue*).

MacIntyre's book is incredibly insightful; there is no doubt that our culture has lost touch with a deeply shared moral story. Nonetheless, we have not stopped trying to think about human purpose and meaning, whether at the macro scale or with respect to how we get on in the various subcultures and communities that we live in. In a sense, we cannot avoid the connection between beliefs, goals, and behavior that Aristotle formalized. Although modern society lacks a shared moral story, we cannot avoid living by some kind of story about the world, and this inevitably shows up in our actions and behaviors. These actions and habits also inevitably shape the kind of persons we become. Consequently, I encourage my students to use this framework as a way of interrogating what the *actual* stories that people live by are.[6] Observing structured practices and habits can help us tease out what the actual cultural story of some group is, even if none of them would necessarily describe it in moral terms. Aristotle's account powerfully reveals the de facto cultural stories around us, even where they are not voiced or acknowledged.

Figure 3 is an example generated by Reuben Hoetmer, one of my students who was a Canadian varsity football player. Along with the rest of the class, he was asked to reflect on the assumptions, goals, and practices of a sphere of life that he knew well in order to better understand its internal cultural story.[7]

Figure 3

The Story of Elite Sport—North American Football

Figure 4 is an example developed as part of my teaching to explore the story of the contemporary market economy. The diagram is a collaborative

6. This interrogation is wisely directed first at ourselves, a point to which I shall return.
7. Hoetmer has continued to reflect on sport. See Hoetmer, "Michael Novak's Alternate Route."

effort. In the wake of the global financial crisis, I spoke to religiously diverse audiences of investment bankers, financiers, and business professionals in Hong Kong, Australia, the United States, and the United Kingdom. Frequently I invited the audience to help me populate this diagram and found a remarkable degree of unanimity among participants. I tended to do this by discussing first the underlying assumptions, then the goal, then the repeated practices, and finally asking the audience what character traits they thought this "story" of the market would generate in those caught up in it. The most common answers are shown in the diagram.

Figure 4

Our Story about the Market Economy

Populating this diagram collaboratively with a live audience led to very interesting conversations. Most people realized that the story contains built-in incentives to behave selfishly. This led business and financial leaders to respond in two ways. One, they started noting ways in which incentives were particularly perverse and should be changed. For instance, one real estate financier said that it was crazy that firms were given tax incentives to use debt finance.[8] Two, they started to wonder if they needed to change the story. At some events I challenged audience participants with a couple of questions: Did they believe that any of the then-proposed solutions to the financial crisis would fundamentally alter the story of the market? If the story was not changed, would the behavior change? Answers to both questions were mostly negative. At this point many participants tended to blame the government for leadership failure. I then asked them what kind of leadership they could show. Some responded by saying that business leaders needed to articulate a better reason for doing business than simply maximizing profit. In other words, they realized that the story and the associated practices needed to change if we wanted different outcomes.

I recount this example in some detail in part to illustrate how what may seem to be a very conceptual approach to reading culture can be a highly practical tool for facilitating a different kind of conversation in our workplaces and communities.

Discerning Desire—an Augustinian Approach

The Aristotelian approach we have just considered emphasizes practical rationality—a form of reasoning that connects assumptions, objectives, and actions in a logically coherent way. This is both its advantage and disadvantage. Some parts of our lives, and some aspects of culture, are dominated by practical functional matters: cooking meals, traveling to work, balancing our books each month, or attending regular medical check-ups. Some people prefer or tend to see the world in such practical terms. This is, if you like, an "engineering" approach to life that tends to think of cultural activities and institutions in terms of how they are engineered to achieve certain outcomes, just as a machine is engineered to perform certain tasks. Looking at culture to see how it works, in much the same

8. Anyone having more than a cursory acquaintance with the industry I am describing will realize how unlikely this outcome is. I barely contained my astonishment at his response myself, even though I agreed wholeheartedly. I was surprised by how the collaborative exercise, no doubt combined with the liminal moment experienced in the wake of such a huge financial catastrophe, made it possible for people to give voice to almost unthinkable ideas.

way as a good engineer might evaluate a new piece of technology, is a very helpful lens through which to look in our quest to "learn the language" of our culture. It complements the worldview approach by connecting beliefs and assumptions to structured actions and habits and by showing the results in terms of character traits and behaviors.

Nonetheless, such an approach may understate the importance of a vital dimension of human life—perhaps the most important dimension of all—the heart. Scripture tells us to "above all else, guard your heart, for everything you do flows from it" (Prov. 4:23). The "heart" is the seat of our emotions and affections, of our passion and desire. Much of what we do arises not so much from a rational calculus about how to achieve our goals as from a deep desire to realize a certain vision of life. Our imaginations become full of a certain kind of "treasure," and that is where our heart seeks to take us. Such desires can be so deep or basic that we aren't always aware of why we are behaving in certain ways or why we react as we do to events.

Augustine of Hippo was well-versed in Greek philosophy but developed his thinking in reference to the New Testament. Whereas Aristotle saw the essence of the human person as the capacity to *reason*, Augustine regarded the capacity to *love* as more fundamental. He distinguished between two main kinds of love: love of God and love of self. Whereas Aristotle believed that eventually our desires would tend to follow the results of our moral reasoning, Augustine believed that sin corrupts both our reasoning and our desire, so that both our loves and our thoughts can be disordered. In *The City of God*, Augustine develops a vision of human life and history that centers on the battle between love of God and love of self.

In his book *Desiring the Kingdom*, philosopher and theologian James K. A. Smith develops an Augustinian account of cultural stories. Like the Aristotelian account, but unlike the worldview approach, the Augustinian model centralizes our intentions and actions in the world. But what we aim at is not so much a rationally deduced objective as something desired or longed for. That "something" is what captures our imagination. At root, what we long for and desire most deeply is what we worship.

As Smith points out (in similar fashion to the Aristotelian approach of the previous section), our desires are shaped by practices that eventually internalize desire in us in the form of instinctive dispositions. The background to all this, I suggest, is not only a set of cognitive assumptions (though it is that) but also a wide range of embodied experiences that we have that frame our beliefs, and especially our imagination, about what is ultimately desirable for us. With these insights, we could rework figure 1 as shown in figure 5.

Figure 5

How Do Stories Shape Us?

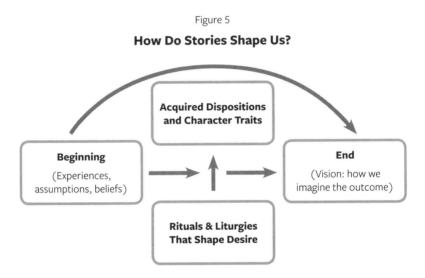

Smith accentuates the connection between worship and this Augustinian model of the person as *lover* by speaking of some practices in terms of *cultural liturgies*. In doing this he wants to focus our attention on the way that some seemingly ordinary rituals are fundamentally *religious* in nature—that is, they are "rituals of ultimate concern" that aim to form our identity and inculcate a particular vision of the good life.[9] One example of a cultural liturgy is shopping at the mall. Malls are like modern consumer cathedrals to which the faithful are drawn with the expectation of getting closer to a particular vision of the good life, a vision depicted in numerous

9. Smith, *Desiring the Kingdom*, 86.

TV commercials, advertising, and corporate images. The message embodied in images and icons wherever we look is that if we buy *this*, we'll be more sexy, more successful, more secure. Smith points out that even the architecture of the mall is designed to reinforce a sense of escape from the humdrum world into a therapeutic environment in which dreams can be realized and fears averted. We are encouraged to seek what we lack and find what we want. Despite our momentary pleasure or happiness, we soon find that there is a new emptiness that needs to be filled, that someone else has something better, that the feeling of satisfaction wears off and we are drawn back for more. Smith's key point is that the ritual of shopping at the mall is designed to *form* desire in us by accentuating what we lack and to *appeal* to that desire in order to draw us in.

Figure 6

Our Story about the Shopping Mall

It is interesting and revealing to compare figure 6—an Augustinian account of consumerism—with figure 4—an Aristotelian account of the market economy. The greatest degree of similarity is between the rational purpose and the imagined vision of the two accounts. This agreement only serves to underline the powerful religious nature of contemporary capitalism in our society[10] and the largely negative impact that it has on our dispositions and character traits. Comparison of the more rational practices of maximizing profit with the more emotion-driven impulses to meet needs that are embedded in shopping rituals shows the complementary nature of these approaches. Both can be true at once. We can quite easily rationalize our shopping behavior by thinking that we have gotten a "good deal," even though it may well be that our desire to shop at all came from something much deeper than rational calculus. Similarly, the rational calculus of economics that argues, with mathematical elegance, for the importance of profit maximization in decision-making masks the very real fear and greed that drive actual market behavior. Considering *experiences* that shape our assumptions and beliefs rounds out the more cognitive "beginning" to the cultural story central to the Aristotelian account.

The central liturgy given to the Christian community by Jesus is the Eucharist or communion. This remarkable but simple act nourishes our imagination as we gather together for a meal at which Christ feeds us in celebration of forgiveness and new life with him. It anticipates the vision of the marriage feast that awaits us in the new Jerusalem when all redeemed humanity will join in such celebration. It incorporates elements of human work (bread and wine), which are thereby honored as gifts that God will receive from us, transform, and give back to us to nourish and strengthen us. It powerfully frames our life before and after the meal in ways that cultivate forgiveness, humility, freedom, dependence, community, worship, and joy.[11]

In sum, the Augustinian approach provides an important way to read our culture. It prompts us to ask: What kind of imagination and desire does the culture seek to foster? What is its vision of the good life? What does it want us to love?

10. For more on this, see Williams, "Christianity and the Global Economic Order."
11. A profoundly powerful book that places the Eucharistic liturgy into dialogue with consumerism is William T. Cavanaugh's *Being Consumed*.

The Bible and Cultural Stories

All languages, despite their differences, share some fundamental structures. The same is true of cultural stories. These stories are commitments we hold in the form of presuppositions (whether consciously or subconsciously, consistently or inconsistently, true or false) about some aspect of reality. Those stories shape how we live, think, and act.[12]

Some of the most basic presuppositions concern our beliefs about God (or ultimate reality), the world, and human beings. We can begin to understand cultural stories more insightfully by clarifying their stance on these basic beliefs. The biblical story addresses these basic beliefs in the account of creation. Genesis 3 continues to explain what is wrong with the world by way of the account of the fall of humanity. A feeling that "something" is wrong with the world is a remarkably consistent feature of cultural stories. I know of no cultural story that thinks everything is perfectly fine just as it happens to be. Genesis goes on to reveal God's approach to dealing with the problem of the fall.

I propose that the biblical story provides a metastructure for understanding and decoding all cultural stories. That this should be so is not surprising if we believe that the biblical story is God's story that encompasses every person—indeed, everything—at all times and all places. We should expect to find that all cultural stories, no matter how "fallen," will be derivative of God's story. Each "act" of the biblical drama has a corollary in any given cultural story, and by inquiring as to what that corollary is, we can gain insight into how the cultural story works, where it can be affirmed, and where it needs to be resisted and corrected. Table 3 illustrates what I mean by showing the basic questions addressed by each act of the biblical story and how these relate to stories in contemporary culture.

Using the biblical narrative as a way of reading and discerning cultural stories can help us integrate the three approaches discussed earlier in the chapter. Most of the worldview questions are addressed in acts 1, 2, and 6.

12. This definition is an amended gloss on the definition of "worldview" given by Sire in *Naming the Elephant*, 122.

Table 3. The Biblical Story and Cultural Stories

Dramatic Act	Biblical Story		Cultural Stories	
	Shorthand Label	*Descriptor*	*Key Questions*	*Shorthand Label*
Act 1	Creation	God Establishes His Kingdom	What are the basic beliefs about God, the world, and human beings?	Basic Beliefs
Act 2	Fall	Rebellion in the Kingdom	What is wrong with the world?	Problem
Act 3	Israel	Redemption Initiated	What approach do we take to addressing the problem?	Approach
Interlude	*Intertestamental Period*	*Awaiting Messiah*	*What are the hopes and fears of this cultural story?*	Hopes and Fears
Act 4	Jesus	The Coming of the King	What is the real solution to the problem?	Solution
Act 5	Church	Spreading the News of the King	How do we implement the solution and make progress?	Progress
Act 6	New Creation	The Return of the King	What will things be like when we fully realize this?	Vision

Acts 3, 4, and 5 frame the habits, practices, and cultural liturgies of the Aristotelian and Augustinian approaches. Act 2, the interlude, and act 6 are particularly relevant to identifying desires, motives, and the imagination that fuels them.

Let's use this basic structure to comment on some of the dominant stories of our culture in simplified form.

10

Stories of the West

Of necessity, this chapter can only provide a very brief overview of the "language" or "stories" of Western culture. The danger of brevity is oversimplification. Each of the stories we will examine has a complex history and could easily be the subject of a book-length treatment. Many such treatments exist; see the bibliography and notes for further reading. On the other hand, the danger of lengthy, nuanced accounts is that it becomes easy to lose sight of the most important features. When learning a language, we begin with basic features and vocabulary and only later progress to more complex nuances of meaning. Accordingly, what follows should be treated as a cultural language *primer*, not an advanced text.

Readers are strongly encouraged to advance to a level of cultural "language" study commensurate with their own missional need and education level. The more one has been educated within the perspective of secularism, for instance, the more important it is to think about the assumptions underlying that education from a biblical perspective. The more one is engaging with others at the level of ideas and how these shape behavior, the more important it is to understand those ideas. Thus, the spiritual and intellectual laziness of highly educated Christians with a primary-school understanding of biblical theology is to be avoided. As Jacques Ellul has pointed out, if we are to love God with our minds, the first duty of a Christian is to be attentive and aware of the cultural stories around us that carry dangerous half-truths or falsehoods destructive to human flourishing.[1] This point simply underscores what we have said already about the necessity for ambassadors to learn the language and literature of the cultural context into which they have been sent.

The Stories of the (Post)Modern World

Some languages are like one another, while others differ greatly. For instance, if you know one language heavily dependent on Latin—such as Italian—then it is relatively easy to learn another "Romance" language, such as Spanish or French. Such knowledge will be of less help in learning Mandarin.

In similar fashion, there is a cluster of "languages" or cultural stories in the contemporary West that have a similar origin. These include our stories about science and technology, the economy, the person, the natural world, and the state. We will consider each of these stories in this chapter.[2] Although they are quite different, these stories do share many common themes. A particularly baffling aspect of postmodern discourse to ordinary believers is the way that many of our contemporary cultural stories have taken up what were originally ideas contextualized and directed by Christian theology and turned them in non-Christian and sometimes even anti-Christian directions. To help understand this, it is useful to begin by considering this group of contemporary stories as a whole.

Edward Pusey, a nineteenth-century Oxford scholar, provides a helpful picture of an integrated Christian understanding of knowledge: "All the sciences move like planets round the sun of God's truth, and if they left

---

1. See Ellul, *The Presence of the Kingdom*, 98–112.

2. The cultural stories I examine in this chapter are not worldviews but expressions of worldviews in particular domains of culture. I have chosen to focus at this level because we rarely encounter worldviews directly, but we frequently encounter these cultural stories in our daily lives. I strongly recommend the fifth edition of James Sire's *The Universe Next Door* for further reading and as an excellent complement to this chapter. Other summaries of the main stories of the West can be found in Ramachandra, *Gods That Fail*, and Goudzwaard, *Idols of Our Time*.

their course they would soon be hurled back into chaos."[3] By "sciences" Pusey means domains of knowledge, all of which are understood to be part of an integrated whole whose center is Christian revelation.

During Enlightenment modernity, this integrated vision of knowledge with theology at its center was modified. Enlightenment thinkers sought to replace the Christian story at the center with "secular reason." Moderns believed that reason alone could make sense of the universe, without the need for theological foundation. Some thirty years after Pusey made the statement we've just read, the idea of making sense of the universe based on reason alone came to a grinding halt in the work of Friedrich Nietzsche. Nietzsche believed that modernity had succeeded in killing God, in showing religion to be an illusion. But he then insisted that the universe did not make sense at all. There was no meaning to it. So, modernity ended up with a universe[4] without a story—a universe that is instead merely a vast, random, impersonal expanse of matter and energy, devoid of meaning and mostly inhospitable to human beings. In moving from the Christian to the secular framework, the West had exchanged one story for no story.

This shift proved to be unsustainable. Although it took a while, after Nietzsche people began to distrust those who claimed to have a story that made sense of everything. The experiences of imperialism, colonialism, and total war reinforced the philosophical argument. Since (given the "death of God") there was no real meaning or truth to be known about humanity, anyone trying to say otherwise must be a deceiver, someone out to control me, someone trying to impose their views on me. This postmodern suspicion about truth claims has increasingly fragmented our society. All the domains of knowledge that once were part of one great story of the universe have become separated and disjointed. Instead of one story, we have many lesser stories, each telling only a story fragment from a limited perspective. The

3. Edward Pusey, from a speech given ca. 1854 during a debate on university reform, as quoted in Mallett, *A History of the University of Oxford*, 331.

4. The English "universe" comes from the Latin *universum*, itself a contraction of *unus* ("one") and *versus* (from the verb *vertere*, "to turn"). The idea of "verse" as a single idea in writing comes from the single turn of a plow that creates a furrow. The "uni-verse" is thus all part of one idea—all part of the same "turn of the plow"—a coherent, integrated whole.

"no story" of modernity, which tried to build an explanatory "tower of Babel" based on reason, has been frustrated by the postmodern babble of confusion in which we now have many stories that are increasingly incoherent to each other. The uni-verse has become a poly-verse.[5]

Each of the major parts of our society has a story to tell: the story of government, of science, of our economy, of the natural world, and of the person. Each of these stories used to "orbit the sun." Each has something true and good to say. But each now thinks it is the center. Without a great story to keep things coherent, each part tends to make itself the center, to become idolatrous. Because God has been written out of each of these stories, the overall effect is what we have already referred to as *practical atheism*—the constant temptation to live as if God does not exist.[6]

In the remainder of this chapter, I'm going to use the basic shape of the biblical story we reviewed at the end of the last chapter (see table 3 in chap. 9) to analyze some of the dominant stories of our culture in simplified form. For each cultural story, I provide a short commentary to unpack it, summarize some of the main elements that the biblical story leads us to affirm or deny, and close with some reflections on the hopes and fears that arise as a result.

I have used different font treatments for assumptions about GOD, **human beings**, and *creation*. Words with technical meaning or importance are underlined.

Science and Technology: *The View of Naturalistic Scientism*

Act 1: *Basic* *Beliefs*	*Human beings* **are smart,** and that's why we are the dominant species on the planet. Our <u>reason</u> is what enables us to gain knowledge. By <u>empirical</u> observation of the world around us, we can gain knowledge about everything if only we look carefully and apply our minds to what we see. Once we understand

---

5. One could go further, as did Lesslie Newbigin, by saying that the modern university has become a "polytechnic" in which most disciplines are not only unable to talk to each other but also don't so much attempt to tell true stories about the world as simply be efficacious in controlling some aspect of reality. Pragmatism has triumphed over truth.

6. See "A Fragmented Life" in chap. 2 and "Active Listening" in chap. 5 above.

the way things work, we can use that knowledge to *control the world* through our <u>technology</u>, solve the problems we have, and make the world a better place.

Act 2:
Problem
The problem really is **ignorance**—there's still a lot we don't know. Worse still, some people choose ignorance and SUPER-STITION. They don't see that it's pointless putting weight on *THINGS THAT WE CAN'T SCIENTIFICALLY PROVE.*

Act 3:
Approach
We need to make sure that people are **better educated** to understand how <u>science</u> works and that it is the only route to real knowledge. We need to make sure that we make decisions for our society as a whole based on <u>facts</u> established by the <u>scientific method</u>, not moral value judgments that are just PRIVATE OPINIONS.

Act 4:
Solution
We had a real breakthrough in the nineteenth century. Charles Darwin established the theory of evolution as the true explanation of human origins and that has helped diminish the power of UNSCIENTIFIC MYTHS. More and more **people** have seen the value of <u>scientific reasoning</u> and **are realizing** that *the material universe is all there is* and that everything in it can be known through science.

Act 5:
Progress
So if we invest enough *resources* in science and technological development, **we can eventually figure out** solutions to all our problems. We should apply the scientific method to all fields of knowledge if we want to really understand everything.

Act 6:
Vision
If **we put our minds to it,** we can eradicate disease, alleviate suffering, and harness limitless energy without damaging our planet. We'll be able to keep making the world—and eventually other planets—better.

Commentary

This story is really a mixture of two related stories. Scientific naturalism, as propounded by people like Richard Dawkins and Sam Harris, holds that the material universe is all there is and that all that happens in it is ultimately the result of the cause-and-effect chain of the complex interactions of physical laws. There is no room for God in this view, except as a human construct. Human beings have evolved through these processes essentially by chance, and there is no underlying purpose or meaning to life or the universe except what we decide to construct.[7] The second story that follows from this is that of scient*ism*. Scientism extends the use of the scientific method from studying material phenomena (physics, chemistry, biology, etc.) to studying human behavior, especially in the so-called social sciences of economics, psychology, sociology, political science, anthropology, geography, and law. This would not be problematic were the use of such analytical methods subservient to an approach to the study of human behavior that treats the person as a subject and not simply as an object. The attempt to understand human and nonhuman worlds by the same methodology is to make a serious category mistake.[8] But scientism holds that such application of the scientific method will discover the universal laws and principles that govern human behavior and will thus enable experts and policy makers to design societies on a "rational," "scientific" basis. Overall, as Neil Postman observes in his book *Technopoly*, the combination of these beliefs gives rise to a faith in science as a comprehensive belief system able to give meaning and direction to life.[9]

Affirmations and Denials

The biblical story should lead us to affirm quite a lot of this story. First, we can affirm that human beings are uniquely able to reason and govern the world, and that our reason enables us to discover more about how the world works and how to harness this knowledge for the good of others. Second, we can affirm that this story still holds to a vision of truth—that the human mind can grasp something corresponding to the fundamental reality of the world we perceive outside the mind. This belief places a value on education of all people, and Christians should encourage a search for

7. For a more detailed exposition of naturalism, see chap. 4 of James Sire's *The Universe Next Door*.

8. For more on this, see Williams, "Christianity and the Global Economic Order," 407.

9. See Postman, *Technopoly*, chap. 9.

truth and knowledge without fearing that it might undermine Christian belief. All truth belongs to God, and seeking after it is to be encouraged. Third, we can affirm that studying the created world is worthwhile for its own sake—simply to wonder and learn about what God has created.

There are, of course, some denials as well. The most obvious concerns God's existence. Adherents of this story might consider, if the human mind has randomly evolved, why did it evolve in such a way that we have rationality capable of understanding the deepest secrets of the universe? A further major problem the absence of God (and therefore also of true moral goodness) creates for those who hold this view is the problem of real moral evil. Evil and suffering can be explained only by appeal to ignorance, belief in false stories, and bad luck. The best response to humans' intrinsic self-centeredness that can be given in this view is to say that through education and willpower we should learn to overcome it. This denial of what the Bible calls sin—and the corresponding overconfidence in the good use to which technological power might be put—is a cause for great concern. At its worst, scientism's confidence in the ability of experts to govern society for the best is a thinly veiled form of totalitarianism, ably described and prophesied by C. S. Lewis in *The Abolition of Man*. In response to a deterministic approach to the social sciences, biblical faith insists that while the "heavens" declare the glory of God whether they want to or not, human beings have freedom of choice to glorify God—or not—through their own agency.[10] Human society and human behavior cannot be reduced to physical explanations and laws without dehumanizing people and robbing them of their God-given dignity and responsibility as moral agents. We would be much closer to the truth if we reclassified the social sciences instead as disciplines under the humanities, since they explore what it means to be human.

Hopes and Fears

This story expresses some of our cultural longings. We hope science can help solve our most pressing problems: climate change, the need for

10. See, for example, Ps. 19.

nonpolluting energy, and illness and disease and the suffering they cause. We're also inspired by scientific discovery, whether it concerns the rich diversity of life on earth or the vast reaches of space. These longings are to be affirmed. Christians should aim to be excellent scientists and enthusiastic supporters of such science who pray that God would give wisdom to researchers seeking cures to diseases, pursuing improvements to health care, and discovering more about the universe God has made.

Christians also need to foster a conversation about the morality of scientific activity. Many in our society fear the power of technology and have grown increasingly distrustful of scientists, especially as stories of corruption and illegal experimentation have become more widespread.[11] The issue here is not so much an attempt to stifle research as to nurture a moral imagination. It is a commonplace but mistaken notion that technology itself is morally neutral and it is only what we do with it that is morally good or bad.[12] It certainly does matter what we do with any given technology, but the creation of a technology is also *always* a moral act. All creativity comes from the imagination, which is a moral faculty. In our imagination, our deepest desires run free. We create out of the horizons of our imagination. One dimension of those horizons is moral—a vision of human flourishing and the common good. If that vision is diminished, we will not see its possibilities. What does it say about the state of our imagination that our movie theaters are awash with dystopian films about killer viruses, evil scientists, and amoral robots? How can Christians nurture a vision for the place of science that is both excellent and moral?[13]

11. McGill University's Margaret Somerville captures this concern well. Following revelations that a South Korean scientist had illegally used employees' eggs to clone embryos and sell harvested stem cells to countries that banned such human cloning, Somerville said, "When you have things like this happen . . . it's a blow to the whole notion that you can trust scientists. Then people say, 'What else are they doing that we don't know about?'" See Abraham, "Star Scientist Hatches Cloning Controversy."

12. Examples of technology that fail to be morally neutral (accidentally or otherwise) include recruitment software biased toward male applicants or soap dispensers that recognize white skin but not black skin. These more obvious examples should alert us to a much broader problem with the notion of the moral neutrality of technology.

13. For further reading, see Lewis, "The Empty Universe"; Dawkins, "Is Science a Religion?"; Plantinga, *Where the Conflict Really Lies*; McGrath, *Inventing the Universe*; and Collins, *The Language of God*.

The Economy: *The Ideology of Free-Market Capitalism*

Act 1:
Basic
Beliefs

Human Beings are <u>individual</u>, <u>rational</u> choosers. They know what they want, and they make <u>choices</u> between alternatives based on what they think is most likely to give them the best outcome. The *planet has a lot of <u>resources</u>* available for people to use.

Act 2:
Problem

There are limits on what people can use. The first limit comes because there are costs involved in using things and not enough resources for everyone to do whatever they want. *<u>Scarcity</u>* means we must <u>compete</u> for *resources*. **People's choices are also LIM-ITED** in societies that don't prioritize individual choice.

Act 3:
Approach

We need to organize society so that scarce *resources* can be al-located to individuals in a way that <u>maximizes</u> the happiness generated by having wants satisfied.

Act 4:
Solution

The <u>perfectly competitive market</u> system will do this. We need individuals and firms to be able to own *resources* and buy and sell with each other as they want in order to <u>maximize</u> personal and corporate <u>profit</u>, and then prices will automatically <u>incen-tivize</u> people to <u>exchange</u> just the right amount of everything to maximize the system's satisfaction level.

Act 5:
Progress

Now we need to work to <u>deregulate</u> all the barriers that exist to free exchange and trade. We need to remove LIMITS ON CHOICE in every market, and we need to spread markets everywhere, including to those areas of life where people exchange things in ways that are less efficient at allocating scarce *resources*. Ex-amples of areas we could improve are where things are owned by the government, the public, or NOBODY[14] instead of by private in-dividuals and firms and where we have MORAL HANG-UPS about buying and selling something, like sex, DNA, or body parts.

Act 6:
Vision

The more we spread markets to every part of our society and get rid of limits on what kind of choices individuals can make, the happier and more satisfied we will be.

14. Examples would be air and water.

Commentary

There are many defenses of free-market capitalism. This version, based on the story of mainstream neoclassical economics, is core. Mainstream neoclassical economics, as taught in the world's major universities, is perhaps the best example of the problem of scientism just discussed. Most economists understand themselves as studying the "science of choice" in which the object is to examine how individuals rationally optimize when facing alternative choices and how society can best be ordered to facilitate the process of this optimization. This attempt to identify laws that govern economic behavior systematically excludes moral discourse about human economic relationships from its deliberations and analysis. Its academic success has given it such enormous influence that huge swaths of public policy are determined by the pronouncements of economic experts.

Although this theoretical account, and the neoliberal economic order that it underpins, has received enormous criticism, it remains highly influential. Critics have undermined the intellectual foundations of this story. Nobel Prize winner Joseph Stiglitz has shown that the conditions necessary for perfect competition are unrealizable (mainly because we never have perfect information, and the information that we do have is not equally available to all parties in a transaction). Joseph Schumpeter demonstrated as long ago as the 1940s that the wealth-creating success of capitalism has little to do with perfect competition. All of this undermines the case that a system of individual actors operating in deregulated markets constitutes the optimal arrangement for society, yet this has not prevented economists, policy makers, and businesspeople from continuing to support such arrangements. The more pragmatic supporters tend to argue that the present system is the best there is. The more intellectual argue that the theory (i.e., the story summarized above) does not need to be true; it only needs to work. The result is the rather ironic and unscientific outcome of a social science that tries to remake the world in the image of its theory rather than adjusting its theory to the reality of the world.

Affirmations and Denials

Again, there is much to affirm in this story from a biblical perspective. First, it recognizes the importance of human agency in choice. Second, it conveys and upholds a notion of human freedom in making those choices (an interesting distinction from the story of scientism). Furthermore, it values creative work undertaken in support of another person and the free exchange of that work with others at a freely agreed-upon price (i.e., private property and markets). There is also much to deny in this story from a biblical perspective. Human beings find their happiness not through individual satisfaction of ever-increasing material desires but as persons-in-relationship. We are here to steward and cultivate the earth in ways that honor God and bless others, not simply to plunder the planet for whatever we can get for ourselves. Scarcity should not be defined in terms of unrestricted human desire and should also be distinguished from finitude. As creatures we are finite, and as moral agents we ought to respect the limits present in creation to the exercise of our desires. This entails appreciating "enough." Within such a perspective, the earth may not have an infinity of resources, but it is characterized by abundance, not scarcity.

Similarly, the human person has limits and is dehumanized if defined by productive efficiency. This story fails to acknowledge God and therefore fails to acknowledge any place for ethical direction in economic activity. In the biblical story, economic activity is an expression of worship and is inherently moral and purposeful. This means it can also be immoral and idolatrous. Excluding God and a moral compass, and reducing the human person to a materialistic individualist, leads to a dehumanizing vision for economic life and an economic system that tends to favor the rich and powerful and alienate the poor and weak. Scripture is suspicious of all human centralization of power, whether in business or the state, so the biblical solution is not to give more power to the state but to limit the scope of the market and to insist on market behavior being governed by moral and relational norms. Christians can affirm the value of work, enterprise, and wealth creation without affirming individualism and materialism. This might involve starting social enterprises or seeking to influence businesses to pursue the common good and treat profit as a necessary condition for existence but not as their primary goal.

Hopes and Fears

This story impacts us all at a very personal level because of the centrality of work to human dignity. Work is often the focus of our hope for a better life—to be able to provide for ourselves and others, to be able to exercise our gifts and contribute to society. In the story of mainstream economics, work is a "bad"—a disutility that we undertake only if paid. This is why economists often see welfare payments as adequate compensation for people who don't have work. Christians should strongly affirm the importance and dignity of work and do what they can to provide such opportunities for others. Many in our culture, however, experience great frustration in work. They have a sense of meaninglessness and a longing for work that has more purpose. They also have a sense of exploitation and a longing for the rewards of work to be fairly distributed. For many people, it seems that the system is rigged against them and that no matter how hard they work, they are always struggling to afford basics such as housing or healthy food. Some feel that they are in a state of constant anxiety and at the mercy of powerful interests. A particular feature that symbolizes and amplifies these hopes and fears is debt. Individuals are encouraged to take on debt and "buy now" rather than wait. Many struggle under the tyranny of servicing unmanageable debts. The combined debts of the rich Western countries are several times their combined incomes. What does this imply about our economic story? Lesslie Newbigin suggests that "a society without [a belief in the future] spends everything now and piles up debts for future generations."[15]

15. Newbigin, *The Gospel in a Pluralist Society*, 112. For further reading, see Williams, "Capitalism"; Heilbronner, *The Worldly Philosophers*; Buckley and Casson, "Economics as an Imperialist Social Science"; Hay, *Economics Today*; and Schluter, "Relational Market Economics."

Personhood: *The Construction of a Postmodern Identity*

Act 1: *Basic* *Beliefs*	REALITY CANNOT BE KNOWN DIRECTLY but is <u>socially con-</u><u>structed</u> by human language. **Individuals have complete <u>moral</u> <u>autonomy</u>.** They have the <u>right</u> to decide who they want to be and how they want to live so long as they don't harm other people. Nobody has the right to coerce them.
Act 2: *Problem*	There are moral, religious, and traditional limits on identity and behavior that TRY TO RESTRICT the kinds of things that individuals do or the kind of <u>identity</u> that they want to create for themselves. These ideas often privilege power and oppress others.
Act 3: *Approach*	We should be <u>suspicious</u> of all <u>stories</u> about the *world* that try to tell other people what to do. These <u>metanarratives</u> are coercive. **Nobody knows what is true,** so anyone who says they do is just trying to impose their opinion on others. We've gradually been getting rid of all of these stories and have learned not to trust anyone who tries to tell them.
Act 4: *Solution*	There is no identity that is given to us, only the identity that we make for ourselves. We **make our identity by telling stories** about ourselves that work to get us what we want. Since all REALITY is socially constructed, we expose things we don't like as the social constructs of others and articulate in their place the stories that create the reality that we do want.
Act 5: *Progress*	We need to deconstruct the identities given us by family, religion, nation, *ethnicity*, and *biology*. We don't need to be restricted by these identity markers but can narrate the identity we want.[16]

16. If this seems far-fetched, consider that in the same month Caitlyn Jenner appeared on the front cover of *Vanity Fair*, an African American civil-rights worker in the United States was discovered to have falsified information about her ethnicity. Although born to white parents, Rachel Dolezal told reporters, "I identify as black." CNN reported her opinion that she was "socially conditioned (to) be limited to whatever biological identity was thrust upon me" (Greg Botelho, "Ex-NAACP Leader Rachel Dolezal: 'I Identify as Black,'" CNN, updated June 17, 2015, http://www.cnn.com/2015/06/16/us/washington-rachel-dolezal-naacp/). Again in the same month, the Canadian *National Post* ran an article about "transabled" people— those who feel they are an imposter in their healthy body and want to become an amputee or deaf or blind. See Sarah Boesveld, "Becoming Disabled by Choice, Not Chance: 'Transabled' People Feel Like Impostors in Their Fully Working Bodies," *National Post*, June 3,

Act 6:   In the future nobody else will tell us who we are, and we'll be
Vision   able to experience life how we want and create whatever kind
of personal identity we prefer, independent of our location in
space, *time*, and a particular physical *body*.

Commentary

The postmodern suspicion (or "incredulity") toward metanarratives began as a much-needed dethronement of the prideful confidence in human reason that characterized modernity. Fascism, communism, socialism, and capitalism were all rightly criticized for privileging power and making unsupportable truth claims. For a while, postmodernity was a healthy protest movement against the worst excesses of modernity, insisting that human beings not be enslaved by false ideologies. As N. T. Wright has said, postmodernity preached the "fall" to the arrogance of the enlightenment.[17] Unfortunately, postmodernity's discovery of the subjective dimension to knowing gave it the tools to deconstruct "objective" claims to truth but not the means of reconstructing a more epistemologically humble approach to reality. The result has been an ongoing process of deconstruction in which all claims to knowledge of the external world, in any arena, are "unmasked" as nothing more than stories that some people tell about the world. Postmodernists don't believe that reality is knowable. Instead, the argument is that we create language about the external world that may be more or less efficacious and stories about our lives that may give us a sense of meaning, but none of this proves anything about what is actually the case. The radical postmodern doubt that truth is knowable extends not simply to matters of religion, morality, and ethics but also to matters of science and our knowledge of the material world. On this account, *all* truth claims are simply stories we tell to try to make sense of and control our lives.

In the postmodern story, public-policy discourse becomes a battleground to achieve rhetorical effectiveness. By and large, the modernist experts and

---

2015, http://news.nationalpost.com/news/canada/becoming-disabled-by-choice-not-chance
-transabled-people-feel-like-impostors-in-their-fully-working-bodies.

17. See, e.g., Wright, "The Dangerous Vocations," 2.

technocrats of the various social sciences that have been guiding public policy in recent decades have retained their rhetorical advantage for the time being and thus retained the levers of power, but developments are sufficiently rapid as to make it likely that this will be less true by the time this book goes to print. However, one must be clear in acknowledging that postmodern epistemology implies nothing less than anarchy, because it is rooted in a complete loss of trust of the other. The only story I can really trust is my own, though even here others are more likely to give credence to my story if I am from a group considered to be marginalized rather than if I am from a group considered to be privileged.

The arena in which this radical doubt has had greatest play thus far concerns personal identity and morality. One might observe (in postmodern fashion) that this is no accident given the rhetorical power of the utilitarian individualism that has successfully colonized public discourse. Deconstruction is a negative process. It can strip away moral restraint and meaningful traditions, but it cannot reconstruct anything substantive in their place. It is a sad irony that postmodern individuals who freely deconstruct social and sexual morality and then reconstruct alternative lifestyles for themselves on a repeated basis imagine that they are freely expressing their individuality. It would be more accurate to say that they have simply become pawns in the rhetorical game played by free-market capitalists and utilitarian individualists. The ideas that I can choose to have sex with whom I want or divorce my gender or ethnic identity from my physical body are extensions of consumerism into the realm of personal identity. The body has become commoditized and traded by its occupant. In some cases this "trade" may be free, but in others people who are confused and vulnerable are effectively being co-opted into someone else's ideology. Commercial interests are quite happy to play along with this process, because it generates more transactions.[18] Political interests are happy to grant rights, because it generates more votes. But the idea that rejecting my own embodiment somehow increases my freedom is a tragedy in our generation. It is a modern form of

18. It is noteworthy here that the original "LGB" activists were profoundly anticapitalist, but gay-pride events are now routinely sponsored by multinational corporations.

Gnosticism to imagine that "I" can increase "my" happiness by treating my body as a commodity to be exchanged in order to "become my true self."

Affirmations and Denials

Certainly postmodernists are right to challenge the mistaken, arrogant result of modernity's assertion that we could attain certain objective knowledge about the world through reason. This used to be the element of postmodernity that I would emphasize in speaking with students, especially evangelicals, who tended to regard everything postmodern as godless without seeing the truth of postmodern critiques of modernity.[19]

A biblical perspective agrees that human beings cannot acquire certain objective knowledge of the world. To do so would require that we could step out of the world, escape the limitations of the particular time and place in which our presuppositions have been formed, and apprehend reality fully and nakedly in every detail. In other words, it would require that we were God. Only God has certain objective knowledge of anything. However, a biblical perspective denies that this means we are condemned to always being stuck within the prison of our own subjective experience. Rather, the Bible tells us that all knowledge begins with trust. It is "fear of the LORD" (i.e., a reverent, worshipful trust in God) that is the beginning of all wisdom and knowledge (see Prov. 1:7; 9:10). Trust in something is foundational to all our knowing as human beings. All of our progress in the natural sciences is the result of assuming things we cannot prove, such as an ordered universe in which rational laws obtain and don't randomly change over time or place. Historically, the kind of trust in the coherence of human reason with the external world such that could give rise to anything resembling modern science has only emerged in those cultures influenced

19. Evangelicalism has had a blind spot in this regard, because it developed as a movement during the modern period and largely as a response to modernist critiques of orthodox belief and the accuracy and reliability of the Bible. Evangelical epistemology has been modernist by instinct, and in this respect evangelicalism needs to change, shifting to a humbler posture learning "under" Scripture rather than over-confidently pronouncing "over" it. Much of mainstream evangelicalism has made this shift, though some evangelicals have simply adopted postmodern epistemology uncritically, with predictably negative consequences (see the discussion of "revisionist" emerging churches in chapter 1).

by the Abrahamic faiths, and especially by Christianity.[20] Trust in the Creator God as revealed in Scripture gives us a connection to objective reality and a reason to believe both that our sense perception is adequate and a means by which our mistakes can be corrected. God has communicated with us via the Scriptures, and Jesus promises that the Holy Spirit will lead us into truth. All of this requires an active humility and accountability not only to Scripture and to the leading of the Holy Spirit but also to the wider community of the church through time and space to help correct the limitations of our own finite perspective.

I also believe it is important to affirm the postmodern desire to give voice to those who have been oppressed and victimized. Christians should never endorse or use power for the oppression or coercion of others and should actively promote justice for those who have been mistreated (Matt. 20:25–28). To do otherwise is completely contrary to the spirit and example of Jesus. Unfortunately, what is now developing within postmodern identity politics is a culture of victimhood in which "offense" is taken as a rhetorical weapon in ways that are extremely destructive to human community and trust.

While I will not repeat here the denials of individualism that I make elsewhere, one further denial that deserves to be noted concerns the idea that freedom and happiness are functions of individual expression of the will. Rather than making themselves freer (and, consequently, happier) by deconstructing all moral and traditional codes that bind them to other people, postmodern individualists find themselves increasingly alienated. Insistence on autonomy leads to isolation, alienation, and loneliness.

Hopes and Fears

This story about personhood and identity responds to a real fear about the abuse of power to control and restrict my ability to "find myself." It seeks justice for those who have been oppressed or marginalized by the

---

20. Specific reasons for this are posited by the philosopher Michael B. Foster in a series of articles published in the 1930s, commencing with "The Christian Doctrine of Creation and the Rise of Modern Natural Science."

powerful. It also fears loneliness and is perpetually anxious about how to answer the question, "Who am I?" Above all, it longs for meaning and the significance found in "authenticity." It longs for trustworthiness.[21]

The Natural World: *The Philosophy of Environmentalism*

Act 1: *Basic Beliefs*	*Human beings* are animals—a species of primate. Like all other life forms, human beings are part of the planet's _ecosystem_ and dependent on it for life. Nonhuman life ought to be part of our *concern for a healthy _environment_*.
Act 2: *Problem*	Human beings have become **uniquely destructive** to the ecosystem, on which we and all other life depend. Our species has become so successful that a wide range of other species has become extinct or face extinction, and *the _biosphere_* itself has been altered. **Human greed** is causing largely *irreversible _climate change_* with potentially catastrophic results.
Act 3: *Approach*	**Human beings need to change** their attitudes and behaviors toward the environment. We need to act to *protect and conserve the environment* and the planet's _biodiversity_. We need to LIVE IN HARMONY with one another and WITH NATURE.
Act 4: *Solution*	There is no straightforward or simple solution to these problems. The idea that the market will solve these problems is nonsense. Technological changes may help, but there is no simple scientific solution. The changes we need require **large-scale collective action**.
Act 5: *Progress*	We need to **act together** to abandon fossil-fuel energy, *protect the world's forests and oceans*, shift to sustainable farming, and remove toxins and pollutants from the supply chain. We need **to free people** from the domination and exploitation of powerful oppressors, such as those driving economic globalization.

21. For further reading, see Lasch, *The Culture of Narcissism*; Berger, "Western Individuality: Liberation and Loneliness"; Fish, "Postmodern Warfare"; and Smith, *Who's Afraid of Postmodernism?*

Act 6:
Vision

If we are successful, we can **build a society** in which the earth is given a voice alongside those of **all people groups** so that all can live interdependently in HARMONY with one another in a sustainable manner.

Commentary

Of the five major stories of contemporary Western culture that I consider in this chapter, environmentalism is unusual in a number of ways. First, it is the only story that explicitly recognizes a moral failing in human nature: it sees human greed, selfishness, and aggression behind the destructive and wasteful behaviors that threaten the planet. Unlike the view of scientism, environmentalists don't think that education alone is sufficient to change behavior. They want much more regulatory intervention and peer pressure to change incentives and behavior. Perhaps because of this, environmentalists tend not to put their hope in quick fixes such as "technology will save us" or "the market will save us." Unlike the stories of capitalism and postmodern identity, environmentalists don't celebrate unrestrained choice. They believe there are limits to our choices that we must learn to respect.

If all of the other stories are, in one way or another, legacies of modernity, environmentalism is more of a protest story, especially a protest against unbridled consumerism. Environmentalism tends to be less materialist as a philosophy, giving more space for a spiritual connection with the earth. Often this is little more than the kind of "biophilia" popularized by scientist E. O. Wilson.[22] But sometimes it moves toward a form of pantheism in which nature is divinized and worshiped, particularly in the deep ecology movement. This sensitivity to a spiritual dimension when connected to concern for others presents a tension for environmentalists. If humans are just one life form among many, why is it that of all the species on the planet, only human beings exhibit concern for other species? A final observation is that environmentalism's concern for biodiversity and nature often develops into social concern, especially for the poor (since

22. Wilson defines "biophilia" as "the urge to affiliate with other forms of life." See his *Biophilia*, 85.

the poor typically suffer disproportionately from environmental disasters),
and advocacy of a form of democratic localism, because local democratic
governance tends to protect local ecosystems more effectively than arrangements where citizens feel disempowered.

Affirmations and Denials

There is a great deal to affirm in this story from a biblical perspective.
Human nature tends to be viewed less individualistically and more relation-
ally than in the other stories. The desire to protect and conserve nature is an
instance of human obedience to God's command in Genesis 1–2 to protect
and cultivate the earth. There is also greater recognition of a moral and spiritual dimension to human life, even though sometimes this strays into the error
of pantheism. The vision for democratic localism and socioeconomic justice
aligns with biblical concerns to avoid concentrations of economic and state
power and for an increase in decentralized empowerment and responsibility.

In terms of denials, the first would be that human beings are not *merely*
another species and that to treat them as such is neither consistent nor safe.
The environmental movement itself is already wrestling with the consis-
tency point, recognizing that only the human species cares for or is willing
to act to help other species. Somehow, humanity seems to bear a unique
responsibility. Second, the danger of not acknowledging human uniqueness
is that it then becomes possible to denigrate humanity as a parasitical species
that needs resisting to bring balance back to nature. In reality this would
mean some human beings resisting others, bringing us back to a form of
totalitarianism. Such an attitude is not prevalent in the mainstream environmental movement, but it is present on the margins. It sometimes shows
up in the mainstream as a blanket suspicion of all business and wealth-
creating activities. Finally, the deeper problem is that this philosophy has
no understanding of a personal God and no concept of redemption capable
of transforming human behavior. It then becomes very easy to give way
to despair. The effect of sin in the form of human greed and selfishness is
obvious, and these effects seem everywhere to be beyond control. If there is
no God capable of intervening and no remedy for sin except more vigorous

campaigning, it is easy to become demoralized and despairing and perhaps turn to less democratic methods to achieve change.

Hopes and Fears

The hopes of the environmental movement for conservation, sustainable living, and democratic participation are hopes that Christians can affirm enthusiastically. Much of the environmental movement shares a genuine love for the natural world and experiences enormous grief at the loss of habitats, biodiversity, and individual species. Supporters are often involved in specific conservation projects, and their sense of loss or fear of loss may be linked to these projects rather than to more general worries about climate change. The latter is clearly of concern, however, and especially so in the Global South, where the effects of climate change, including rising sea levels and severe weather events, will more likely impact contexts with fewer resources to cope. For people in such countries, there is real concern that the rich world can afford to ignore their plight because the impact of continued emissions will affect them much less. In the rich Western world, we may fear the cost or inconvenience of the lifestyle changes required. But the poor in Western countries are particularly vulnerable to increases in energy or transportation costs arising from government attempts to change consumer behavior.[23]

The State: *The Ideology of Secular Pluralism*

Act 1: Basic Beliefs	**Everyone has the right to their own <u>autonomy</u>.** People have a wide variety of religious and moral beliefs. It is not possible to establish the truth of these beliefs. The role of the state is to protect people's rights and promote a harmonious society.
Act 2: Problem	The problem is that differences of <u>belief</u> lead to conflict, and this conflict can turn violent. **Human society needs to be ordered to avoid violent conflict.**

23. For further reading, see Bouma-Prediger, *For the Beauty of the Earth*; Harris, *Kingfisher's Fire*; Wilkinson, *Earthkeeping in the Nineties*; Suzuki, *The Sacred Balance*; and E. Wilson, *The Creation.*

Act 3: *Approach*	We need to separate government authority from religious au-thority. The state needs to be <u>NEUTRAL</u> WITH RESPECT TO RE-LIGIOUS BELIEF while allowing freedom of religion.
Act 4: *Solution*	The solution is to KEEP opinions about religion and morality that cannot be proven IN THE PRIVATE REALM and base public policy only on arguments that can be articulated in the neutral <u>language of reason</u> and on *facts that can be established through the empirical and rational methods of science.*
Act 5: *Progress*	The public sphere needs to be purged of all traces of religious belief, language, and practice. Morality and RELIGIOUS BE-LIEF MUST BE CONFINED to the <u>private sphere</u> and NOT BE ALLOWED TO INTRUDE into <u>public life</u>.
Act 6: *Vision*	Such an approach will create a <u>tolerant</u> society in which people with a wide variety of beliefs are able to work and live together harmoniously.

Commentary

Modern secularism has deep roots in Christian theology. The idea that everyone, including the king, is subject to the same non-arbitrary law finds its source in the Old Testament. Similarly, although Israel was a divinely instituted theocracy, the prophets had the authority to challenge state power in God's name, and kingship required the assent of the tribal elders. The Christian tradition advocates church-state separation for two main reasons. The first is the denial that the state is god or should be divinized. Thus, Jesus' comment that one should "give back to Caesar what is Caesar's, and to God what is God's" (Matt. 22:21) directly challenged the idea that Caesar *was* God (despite the pretensions of the imperial cult). The second arises from the biblical tradition of decentralized power and the avoidance of corruption. Thus, not only is the state corrupted by becoming too closely aligned with religion, but the church is also corrupted by becoming too closely aligned with political power. The modern version of secularism was a response to the religious wars that took place in the early part of the seventeenth century following the Reformation. It was the initiative of

Christians, aghast at the resulting devastation, to insist that the state act neutrally with respect to different expressions of faith. The state was to allow faith to be expressed in public so long as no particular denomination or sect received a particular political advantage from the state. Thus secularism was intended not to keep religious expression out of the public arena but to protect the whole community from the influence of a state dominated by one particular sectarian interest.

A further idea was added to this core in the late-eighteenth and nineteenth centuries. Enlightenment philosophers, such as Voltaire and Rousseau, advocated use of a neutral public language as the preferred medium to express public-policy arguments. This development sought to exclude expressions of belief and morality from the public square and only allow "facts" based on the empirical and rational methods of science to be admissible in public discourse.

Affirmations and Denials

On the affirmation side, a biblical perspective endorses a form of the separation of church and state and the protection of a safe environment in which a diverse range of views, including non-Christian religious and irreligious views, can be expressed. Biblical faith strongly upholds freedom of conscience and freedom of religion, because God does not coerce but rather invites us into relationship. A biblical perspective also agrees with the idea that a primary function of the state in a fallen world is to prevent violent conflict and safeguard people's security and rights.

These affirmations, however, need to be qualified by a number of denials. Most significant, biblical faith resolutely denies the idea of a neutral language of reason or of a morally neutral public square. There is no such thing. It is one thing to say that the state ought not to privilege a particular religious group qua religious group and quite another to say that the state ought to be neutral toward all of the *ideas* of all religious groups. This is nonsense.

A few examples should suffice to demonstrate this. Consider first the role of women in society. Quite obviously, the state in Western countries does not act neutrally toward the Islamic community's beliefs on this matter; our laws are much closer to a Judeo-Christian perspective than to an Islamic one. Defenders of the idea of a language of neutrality claim that it is important that whatever arguments are made in public discourse be made in the form of a language that is "neutralized" of any sectarian content. Again, this is simply not possible. All language concerning human behavior is value-laden.

As a second example, consider the assumption made within the story of secular pluralism that human beings have "individual moral autonomy." Closer inspection of this phrase will reveal that it is a secular humanist distortion of the Christian idea of personal freedom. Humanism is a comprehensive worldview, not a neutral perspective. The language of "autonomy" betrays the truth that secular pluralism is a carrier of secular humanism and thus privileges irreligious worldviews over religious ones.

This observation brings us to a further denial. The way that secular pluralism in Western societies currently operates has allied the humanist notion of individual autonomy with a degenerate form of utilitarianism, creating, in effect, a de facto state religion. Autonomous individuals are deemed to know best what will make them happy and are encouraged and permitted to pursue their own interests as they see fit. The good of society is equated with the largest number of individuals being able to satisfy their individual visions of happiness. This pursuit of individual happiness is supported by the state through the allocation of individual rights (and support for the capitalist and postmodern drive for ever-widening individual choice). New rights are claimed by individuals on a regular basis. Any group of individuals that shouts loud enough is able to claim new rights, and the state then arbitrates between competing rights via legislation and the courts. The reality is that almost every time this occurs, new rights for individuals are granted at the expense of the more community-oriented moral vision of most religions.

The consequence of this is that the state progressively dominates all institutions in civil society between itself and the individual and abrogates power to itself. The human person increasingly finds that every aspect of life is defined only in terms of individual choice and individual rights. Such a life is no longer related properly to others. The maintenance of this colonizing tendency of the state relies on the exclusion of substantive moral discourse from public life. The myth of moral neutrality enables the technocratic expertise of elites to control the levers of power. Here, again, is a creeping form of totalitarianism.

Hopes and Fears

The story of secular pluralism responds to a fear of state-sanctioned imposition of religious or nonreligious ideologies on the general population. It contains within it a hope for a reasonable and reasoned debate. But this secular framework is increasingly under strain. Postmodernity is rapidly undermining confidence in any of the stories that typically hold national communities together, including the story of secular humanism. There is not only a growing fear of being deceived and a longing for leaders we can trust but also a growing fragmentation and divisiveness in public discourse that reveals the underlying fragility of Western societies.

This gives rise to further fears. If we lose our ability to disagree in an ordered and reasonable way, the democratic nation-state itself becomes increasingly untenable. Around the world, democratic forms of government seem to be giving way to more autocratic forms, whether Marxist, nationalist, or Islamic. Western leaders fear a loss of control, and Western voters are dismayed by a lack of leadership or fear an increasingly aggressive and elitist form of secularism determined to stay in control.[24]

Conclusion

In this chapter we've been reviewing some of the main stories of Western culture and, while doing so, seeing how the structure of the biblical story can help us understand them and identify what we can affirm as well as

24. For further reading, see Arendt, *The Origins of Totalitarianism*; Baggini, "The Rise, Fall and Rise Again of Secularism"; Chaplin, *Talking God*; O'Donovan, *The Desire of the Nations*; and Taylor, *A Secular Age*.

what we need to deny. Table 4, at the end of the chapter, compares the five major stories we have examined side by side with Christianity.

A few observations can be made by way of comparison between these stories. First, some of these stories reinforce one another. As may be apparent from the foregoing account, there is a great deal of overlap between the stories of capitalism, postmodern identity, and secular pluralism. These three together are the prime carriers of a corrosive utilitarian individualism. Sadly, while postmodernists imagine they are freely constructing their own identities, in reality their lives (and everyone else's) are increasingly dominated by the power of big business and big government. The more we refuse the disciplines (and freedoms) of the moral law, the more we will find ourselves vulnerable to the manipulation of commercial interests and political power. Second, scientism is a story that enables the technocratic influence of economists, social scientists, and policy makers and thus indirectly supports the story of contemporary capitalism. Third, environmentalists typically have the most antipathy toward free-market capitalism and ideology of choice. Environmentalism is also probably the cultural story that is closest in affinity to Christianity because of its understanding of the fallibility of human beings and the importance of stewarding the created world. Finally, the story of postmodern identity is probably most at odds with Christianity because of its Gnostic rejection of the created world and its collapse of all truth-claims into a will to power.

These stories are only some of the main cultural stories of the contemporary West, and this chapter has provided only an initial outline of them. For further reading on each story, see the works listed in a footnote at the end of each section.

Some mixture of these five main cultural stories will dominate the cultural narratives of whatever sphere of life we encounter—whether a neighborhood, a workplace, or a particular age or interest group. But all of the various spheres of life will also have their own subcultures. It's important to give our attention and time to learn the stories of the subcultures we are in. The pattern I've used in this chapter is one that could be used for any cultural story.

Table 4. Stories of the West and the Drama of Scripture

	Naturalistic Scientism	Free-Market Capitalism	Postmodern Identity	Environmentalism	Secular Pluralism	Christianity
Act 1: Basic Beliefs	Humans can use reason to understand and control the world.	People know what they want and make rational choices about how to get it. The world contains resources we can use.	All reality is socially constructed. Every individual decides who they want to be. Nobody else has the right to coerce them.	Human beings are part of the ecosystem like everything else. Human life is totally dependent on the ecosystem of the planet.	There are diverse peoples in the world with many opinions of what life is about. We all need to get along.	God made everything and gave human beings the ability to rule the earth in relationship with him and with one another.
Act 2: Problem	There's a lot we don't know, and some people believe things that can't be proven.	Unfortunately, there aren't enough resources. Scarcity means that we have to compete.	There are moral and traditional limits on identity and behavior.	Humans have become so dominant and are living so wastefully that the entire ecosystem is threatened.	People try to persuade others of their opinions. People who disagree can fight and kill.	People choose to live away from God; as a result, they become confused, selfish, and weak.
Act 3: Approach	We need better education so that our society is based on knowledge, not ignorance.	We need to allocate scarce resources in the way that creates the most satisfaction of wants.	One by one we've been getting rid of stories about the world that limit individual identity choice.	We must radically change our behavior, especially in the economic realm. This is the only planet we have.	We need to separate church and state, and the state needs to be strictly neutral about religious belief.	God worked with a particular group to show everyone how things could be different. They realized they needed God's help.

Act 4: Solution	Now we know the universe is all there is, and we can know it through science.	The perfectly competitive market system will do this for us automatically.	We make our identities by exposing the stories that other people tell about us as social constructs and by narrating our own stories that work for us.	Some people think science or the market will save us, but they can't and they won't.	We need to keep religious belief in the private realm, out of public debate.	God came in the person of Jesus, not just for one group but for everyone, to sort out the mess. He proved this by rising from the dead.
Act 5: Progress	We should apply scientific methods to all areas of life. If we invest enough resources, we can solve all problems.	We just need to get rid of all barriers to trade and exchange in every market and spread markets everywhere.	We can reject the identities given to us by family, nation, religion, race, and biology. We can construct the identity we want in their place.	We should work together now to abandon fossil fuels, shift to a sustainable economy, and be rid of oppressive economic power.	We must make sure that public discussion is allowed only in a neutral, nonreligious language.	Jesus invites us now to work with him to accomplish this. He promises to help us, forgive us, and heal us. He is restoring our relationships with him, with one another, and with creation.
Act 6: Vision	Eventually we can get rid of disease and suffering and can have limitless energy.	When everything is exchanged in such markets, we will have the best society it's possible to have.	In the future, our essential self should be freed to define its identity without any constraint from our biology or culture.	If we are successful, we can live interdependently in harmony with one another and with nature.	By basing public life on arguments that can be proved only by scientific reason, we'll have a more tolerant society.	In the end, Jesus will return to put things right and live with us in a renewed creation. But he doesn't want to coerce people. He wants them to choose while they can.

11

Cultural Translation

"Know the Gospel; Know Culture; and Translate" is a slogan of the Venn Foundation in New Zealand.[1] It captures something vital about the nature of ambassadorial mission. We have seen the process by which ambassadors are commissioned and sent to establish an embassy in a host culture. They must know the mission and dedicate themselves to learning the language and culture of their context—as explored in the last three chapters. But as important as all this is, it is only the precursor to ambassadorial work. Ambassadors engage in diplomacy. Their mission is complete only when they have effectively translated and communicated the message they have been given by the sending country into the language of the host country so that it can be received. This "diplomacy" is the fullest manifestation of their purpose. Similarly, the fullest experience of ambassadorship is a Christian community translating the gospel into the host languages of all the many receiving cultures and subcultures into which it is sent.

In this chapter, I want to use the notion of "cultural translation" to mean more than, say, the translation of this sentence into modern Italian.

1. "About," Venn Foundation, accessed September 5, 2019, https://www.venn.org.nz /about/.

I want to find ways of communicating the gospel in the context of societies where the cultural stories from the previous chapter have gained a degree of explanatory power. That is, I'm interested in how we communicate the meaning of the gospel in a culture that has lost sight of that meaning and may routinely misunderstand the gospel because of a latent but fading cultural memory.

Translation involves the transfer of meaning from a *source* language system into a *target* language. But rarely do different language systems map onto one another easily. The difficulty of rendering the Greek text of the New Testament into English, for instance, will be evident even to native English speakers who have no trace of koine Greek if they compare the differences of word choice among modern English translations. These differences illustrate the varied ways that translators try to render meaning between the two languages accurately. Our languages are not simply different codes for talking about the same set of meanings shared between cultural groups. Rather, languages carry and embed the different cultures and meanings of the communities who use them. The cultural assumptions and understandings of the Greco-Roman world and of the New Testament authors are significantly different from those of the twenty-first-century West. Translation, then, is primarily a complex communication between two cultures in which language is the vehicle or medium.[2]

In this chapter, I aim to explore what it means to communicate the message of the gospel in actions and words, in the varied contexts of life and work, and through the varied media of contemporary Western society. Our goal is to communicate this message in such a way that it makes sense to the culture of which we are a part and is faithful to the culture in which it was birthed. Western societies have become a place where the cultural narratives explored in the previous chapter have gained a degree of explanatory power. These societies are places in which the gospel needs

---

2. The discipline of translation studies documents this "cultural turn" as taking place during the last few decades of the twentieth century. See Trivedi, "Translating Culture vs. Cultural Translation." The basic concept of cultural translation has been understood, though not always put into practice, by missiologists for somewhat longer.

to be retranslated. I want to talk about this communication as translation because doing so highlights the *foreignness* of contemporary culture to the gospel. This sense of foreignness is something that Western Christians have largely lost. Western cultures have been greatly impacted by Christianity in the past, are still full of its symbolism, and have a few vestiges of Christianity as a civil religion. As a result, it is easy for contemporary Western Christians to imagine that citizens of these societies understand the basic tenets of Christianity. This problem is magnified by the historic mind-set of Christendom in the church. To speak of the "translation" of the gospel in the West reminds us that Western society is the frontline of mission for Western Christians.

The primary communication barrier we face is not a linguistic one but a cultural one—the gap between the culture of the kingdom of God and the culture of the individualistic Western society in which the gospel is to be communicated. Indeed, there are gaps (plural) between the culture of the kingdom of God, the culture of individualistic Western society, and the culture of the contemporary church. A genuine exercise of cultural translation will not leave the church unchanged.

To translate is an innovative process that will harness all of our gifts in every sphere to which God has sent us. "Translation" provides us with a rich and highly practical model for understanding what it means to be sent into the world as God's ambassadors, telling God's story of reconciliation. I will argue that, rightly understood, to translate *is* to be on mission.

A Model of Cultural Translation

What then is this model of cultural translation? Translation occurs as an interaction between three main elements: a source language, a receiving language, and a context for communication. By "languages" here we mean cultural stories. In particular, we are focusing on an interaction between God's story (our source language) and the story of Western culture (or a subset of it—the receiving language) in a particular context. We have already rejected the idea that there is a simple encoding and decoding of meaning going on, because each story contains quite different sets of meanings and assumptions. Translation is a complex reorientation of language in which these stories are juxtaposed and placed into dialogue in a particular context.

Scholars of literary theory, anthropology, linguistics, critical theory, and cognitive science are drawing increasing attention to the way in which language shapes how we think, how we see the world, and the broader culture that we inhabit and develop. We should not be surprised by this power of language to construct social reality and even shape how we understand and interact with the natural world. Human beings image a God who spoke creation into existence, whose speech sustains the being of heaven and earth, and whose simple command stopped the sun, stilled the storm, and calmed the waves.

God's word is performative. It accomplishes what it says. When Scripture tells us that God watches over his word to see it fulfilled, we are being told that God's authority, power, and attention are released and focused in and through his speech so that his words endure—remain true and effective—forever (Jer. 1:11–12; Isa. 40:8; Mark 14:49). His words cannot be controlled (2 Tim. 2:9) or amended (Matt. 5:17–18). Humans, as God's image bearers, also have incredible power because of our language ability, which distinguishes us from all other species. Scripture repeatedly warns us, therefore, to be careful with our words. Language has great power for good and for evil.

Knowing the power of language to generate cultural reality is both revelatory and imprisoning. On the one hand, postmodern literary and cultural theorists and cognitive scientists have gained enormous insight into how cultures are formed and shaped, especially concerning the power of language and culture to alter our experience of reality. But this knowledge has led to a dead end because of the hypersubjectivism that usually accompanies it. To say that all culture is a linguistically and socially generated reality—constructed from the mythmaking that human beings engage in—has led to the conclusion that all cultural norms and values are *nothing more than* the ideas created by particular groups of people. All cultural stories, in this view, are simply stories we invent to help us survive in the world or achieve power over others. They have no objective referent or meaning beyond those that we invest in them. If, as Jonathan Sacks says, "a culture is defined by its narratives,"[3] and if those narratives are simply stories we tell to create social reality around us, then this radically relativist conclusion seems inescapable.

But if God has spoken and told us the true story of the world, if that speech has come among us in the writings of Scripture and as a human person, and if God continues to speak now to uphold, persuade, and reveal that story to us, then it is possible for us to break out of the prison of our own storytelling. This is the potential of cultural translation. The goal is to release the power of God's speech into a given community, including, of course, our own. Amazingly, God has entrusted his people with the ability to be his witnesses—that is, to speak and testify about him. We have been given both the Scripture and the Holy Spirit, who will help us understand Scripture and lead us into truth. Effective cultural translation takes place when, under the guidance of the Holy Spirit, we are empowered to tell God's story in such a way that the reality of Jesus is experienced.

Translation as Mission

In a journal article discussing cultural translation, Boris Buden and Stefan Nowotny explain the root meaning of "translate" as a "carrying across" from one place to another, an act that can be applied to people as well as to words: "One can culturally translate people—for a political purpose and with existential consequences."[4] This definition can help us understand why translation is uniquely characteristic of Christian faith. Missiologist Andrew Walls puts it like this: "God chose translation as his mode of action for the salvation of humanity. Christian faith rests on a divine act of translation: 'the Word became flesh, and dwelt among us.'"[5] The sending

3. Sacks, "In a World Run by MTV, Nobody Has Time to Think."
4. Buden et al., "Cultural Translation," 196.
5. Walls, "The Translation Principle in Christian History," 24.

of the Son involved the translation of God into humanity. As Walls goes on to explain, this translation of divinity into humanity made clear the message, "This is what God is like." All our translations of the biblical story are rooted in this fundamental translation and share its purpose to reveal God in Christ.

Following Walls, we can go further and highlight that translation is akin to conversion. When a foreign concept is translated into a new culture or language, it must be expressed using the words and meanings that already exist in that cultural-language system, but the words and meanings are *redirected* to express the new concept. In similar fashion, Christ redirected and transformed human nature, both to express the character of God and to show what a truly human life is like. The extent to which a person or a culture absorbs and responds positively to this newly revealed meaning of God in Christ is the extent to which it has *converted* to Christ.

The discipline of translation studies has a rather ambivalent attitude toward the idea of "cultural translation." This is not because there is any quibble with the idea that translation is all about the culture conveyed in language but rather because of the political dimension of the translating act.[6] Instead of seeing translation as a simple transfer of meaning, it is understood as a social relation between two cultures, and like any social relation, this relation can be subject to power dynamics. Consider the case of a refugee seeking to enter the West. They may be subject to a whole host of policies and citizenship tests to ensure that they "integrate properly" into Western culture. The cultural exchange in this relation is very one-sided. In effect, migrants are "translated" into the culture and values of Western pluralism in a way that renders their voice nearly mute. A similar point could be made about the history of the church. Acts 15 records how some of the Jewish Christians, who made up the vast majority of early believers, wanted to impose circumcision and the Mosaic law on the newly converted Gentiles. Fortunately, the Jerusalem church heeded

6. See the discussion forum on cultural translation in Buden et al., "Cultural Translation."

the words of the apostle Peter: "God, who knows the heart, showed that he accepted [Gentiles] by giving the Holy Spirit to them, just as he did to us. He did not discriminate between us and them, for he purified their hearts by faith. Now then, why do you try to test God by putting on the necks of Gentiles a yoke that neither we nor our ancestors have been able to bear?" (Acts 15:8–10).

The translator has the power to shape both the way that a given "foreign" community is understood and how that "foreign" community receives a cultural message. Under the guidance of the Holy Spirit, what we see in this account from Acts 15 is not the "Judaizing" of the Gentiles but rather the Christianizing of the Gentiles *and* of the Jews in ways that purified and preserved the cultural distinctiveness of each community. In the context of Christian mission, our power to translate carries with it two responsibilities. First, we need to be careful not to communicate what are merely localized cultural practices as if they are part of the gospel message and carry the same authority. Many of our practices may be perfectly benign or even positive in our context—how we dress, take communion, or sing songs, for instance—but become stifling if imposed as part of what it means to be a follower of Jesus. The early church had to learn that circumcision was a localized cultural practice that need not be extended to other converts to Christ. Second, we must be careful to allow the Holy Spirit to bring forth an expression of faith in terms that are authentic to the community and subculture that is receiving the gospel message. That requires being open to quite different ways of acknowledging Christ's lordship than the ones we may be used to.

Our goal in translating the gospel into the culture and subcultures of the West is not to homogenize, much less eradicate, the cultures that we encounter but rather to help *redirect* them toward God and his purposes for human life. Whether in our neighborhoods, workplaces, or communities, we look for ways in which the culture can be redirected. Often these opportunities will arise at those points of cultural discontinuity that we highlighted in the previous two chapters—points of incoherence between beliefs, values, and actions and places where hopes and fears are expressed, especially by the weak and marginalized. These are places where we should be looking to see what God is doing.

Our tendency can be the opposite: when intellectuals show interest in faith, we want them to become more practical; we want businesspeople to become less entrepreneurial; and we want young people to behave like older people. Similarly, we tend to focus on what is wrong with a culture rather than on what can be affirmed and to what good it points. We need to make space for all to be themselves in Christ so that intellectuals redirect their thinking toward understanding and explaining the world in the light of faith, businesspeople redirect their entrepreneurialism toward the common good, and young people redirect their energy and radicalism toward Christ. This redirection, if received by the community in focus, is a reorientation of that community toward Christ. This reorientation may, in turn, alter our own understanding of the gospel, just as the Gentile conversion altered the understanding of the early church.

Translation is not a one-way action. It is a social relation that transforms both linguistic and cultural communities. There is both sending *and* receiving. We see this most profoundly in the incarnation. By humbling himself and allowing himself to be translated into humanity, Jesus transformed humanity and gave it a completely new beginning. All that is good about humanity is redeemed and perfected in Christ, and all that destroys and diminishes human nature is defeated by him on the cross. Yet divinity, too, was changed. At the center of the trinitarian life of God, seated on the throne at the right hand of the Father, ruling the universe, there is now a human being.

Our translating activity is always a retranslation of that original translation of the Word of God into human flesh and human language. Whenever we are translating, our work can be compared and checked against the master copy of Jesus and Scripture, as well as against other faithful translations undertaken elsewhere in Christian history and geography. It is essential that we remain humbly dependent on the Holy Spirit to lead both us and those receiving the gospel message. The majesty of God and the diversity of human culture mean that every act of translation, for each culture and subculture that turns to Christ, in each generation, has the potential to add something fresh to our understanding of God. This adds a further dimension of wonder and worship to mission as translation: who knows what we will see of God and his character if we allow an authentic expression of faith to grow up in the subcultures of the contemporary West, including those, for instance, of postmodern youth, social media, biosciences, derivative traders, or the newly arriving refugee communities?

The kind of cultural translation that I am advocating is not a *precursor* to mission; rather, it *is* mission. It involves being sent to a community, listening humbly, communicating responsibly, trusting the Holy Spirit with the response, and being open to receive and learn more of God through those whose receipt of the gospel message leads to acceptance and thus conversion.

Cultural Translation and Scripture

In principle, translation of this kind occurs whenever we read the Bible. Scripture is the source language; our own beliefs, practices, and assumptions constitute the receiver culture; and the exchange between the two takes place in some kind of context, such as a sermon or a Bible study. The result may be an effective translation, in which case some part of God's story will be made more manifest in (i.e., be translated into) our lives. As a result, we will participate more fully in the mission of God.

However, this is not always our experience. The legacy of modernity and the alienated mind-set we can so easily fall into shape how we view the Bible, who we think it is addressed to, and what context we think it is to be read in. In sum, these have robbed Scripture of its life and power for many of us.

The Bible is an increasingly unpopular book in modern secular culture. Quoting it or promoting it in public discourse is liable to lead to a negative reaction. Like Jesus, the Bible can feel embarrassing, so there is an assimilation pressure to leave the Bible behind, whether literally or metaphorically, in the way we inhabit our vocation. The Bible's role is further denuded in the mentality of the ghetto. On the one hand, even evangelicals who pride themselves on being biblicist[7] reduce the text to a pietistic tool—a way of accessing an inward experience, often asking only, "What does this mean to me?" We may read a text such as the exodus account, for instance, and see only a type of our deliverance from sin. But before it can function effectively to teach us about slavery to sin, the text tells us about an actual enslavement of Israel by the Egyptians. We often miss the force of this. When God says to Pharaoh (through Moses), "Let my people go, so that they may worship me" (Exod. 8:1), do we imagine that God wants his people freed so they can sing songs in the desert? For the Bible, work *is* an expression of worship. Enslavement to other human beings *is* enslavement to a false god. The fulfillment of God's desire, expressed in this command to Pharaoh, was not some kind of "Worship-Fest Sinai" but the Israelites' entry into the promised land and the division of that land among the tribes and families so that they could work it and live in a way that honored God as he dwelt among them.

On the other hand, we tend to not only spiritualize the text but also privatize it. If you ask how the Bible is relevant in their workplace, many Christians will answer in terms of personal relationships and evangelism. They cannot see how it might relate to the actual work they do or the industry or occupation they work in. Once we see the text primarily in terms of our inward piety, we easily assume that it has nothing to say about our public life. The story of Jesus and Zacchaeus in Luke 19, for example, is often told in terms of Jesus' compassion for the outcast, alongside Zacchaeus' determination to see Jesus and his subsequent repentance, forgiveness, and conversion. It certainly is all these things. What is usually missed, in this case, is the public dimension of his repentance. As a tax collector, Zacchaeus was in a position to exploit his fellow Jews under the protection of Roman power. His restitution of wrongs was not simply generosity but justice, and those paying taxes would experience this and his

7. David Bebbington is well-known for his identification of four markers of evangelicalism: crucicentrism, conversionism, biblicism, and activism. See *Evangelicalism in Modern Britain*.

subsequent work as a significant structural change in society. When John the Baptist called on people to produce fruit in keeping with repentance (Luke 3), they asked him what he meant. His answer related to work and money: tax collectors should stop extorting, soldiers should stop making false accusations and be content with their pay, and people should share their possessions. Do we expect our conversion to Christ and our reading of Scripture to address these very public parts of our lives?

In addition to thinking of the text as primarily a pietistic tool, addressed only to our personal lives, the mind-set of alienation has tended to distort the work of biblical scholarship such that the Bible's meaning is assumed to be only accessible to those with specialist training. The clerical mind-set of Christendom that assumes cultural Christianity and thus concentrates on the personal edification of the flock is also prone toward a scholasticism that further removes the text itself from the ordinary believer and his or her life in the world. Rarely is scholarly knowledge of Scripture used to help form an integrating center for understanding the world, in which theology plays its proper role as "queen of the sciences." Instead, it is easier to maintain religious truth as a domain of knowledge unto itself. Such an approach only encourages further secularization. It reinforces the common notion that the only way to embody Scripture in our lives is to obey a command or to practice a principle. If we read the Old Testament primarily as a set of types of personal salvation in Christ, and read the New Testament as a privatized personal faith manual, then we will find very few commands or principles of relevance to our ordinary lives. Our questions about the text can become increasingly esoteric. Pastors may be expected to function as "Bible answer man," but rarely does this mean that ordinary believers gain a deep appreciation of how Scripture addresses all the spheres of their work activities or the public issues discussed in the media. Instead, people grow more confused about how to read and interpret the Bible and less confident in its relevance to ordinary life.

The upshot of all this is that, far too often, Scripture (the source language) is seen as a pietistic tool and/or a specialist religious text to be interpreted by experts. The implied audience (receiver language) is assumed to be Christians in their private lives and specialist scholars. The context for reading and translating its message is assumed to be a quiet time, one's personal life, a Bible-study group, a sermon, or a seminary class. None of these are wrong in themselves. But taken as a whole, they reinforce both a ghetto mentality and a vulnerability to assimilation. We see the church as a private reading community with a specialist interest in Scripture, not as a public witnessing community who embodies the text for ongoing dialogue with the culture. A privatized and fragmented Bible is easily absorbed by the competing narratives of Western culture. There is practically nothing in the pietistic or scholastic mode of reading that could help us creatively engage the Western stories of individualism, materialism, and the will to power. The Gnostic tendency of postmodern culture that we saw in the previous chapter is sadly mirrored by the Gnostic way in which we read Scripture.

By way of contrast to all this, Lesslie Newbigin tells the story of an encounter he had with a Hindu scholar in India who said to him: "I can't understand why you missionaries present the Bible to us in India as a book of religion. It is not a book of religion—and anyway we have plenty of books of religion in India. We don't need any more! I find in your Bible a unique interpretation of universal history, the history of the whole of creation and the history of the human race. And therefore a unique interpretation of the human person as a responsible actor in history. That is unique. There is nothing else in the whole religious literature of the world to put alongside it."[8]

This perspective is remarkable, but it is not unique. Two features of the Bible have consistently struck those who have studied it as a piece of literature: its narrative unity and its unique authority.[9] Scripture contains a lot of stories (narrative is recognized as the Bible's main genre), but it also forms one single, rich, overarching story. We have already discussed this in previous chapters. Moreover, just as Jesus' contemporaries were amazed

---

8. Newbigin, *A Walk through the Bible*, 4.

9. A selection of the diverse range of scholarly work on this includes Frei, *The Eclipse of Biblical Narrative*; Frye, *The Great Code* and *Words with Power*; Newbigin, "The Bible as Universal History," in *The Gospel in a Pluralist Society*; Alter, *The Art of Biblical Narrative*; Auerbach, *Mimesis*; and Mangalwadi, *The Book That Made Your World*.

at the authority with which he taught, so scholars and readers have been struck and amazed by the authority that the Bible carries. In its own terms, this is because "all Scripture is God-breathed" (2 Tim. 3:16). We can talk about this authority in terms of doctrines of inspiration and inerrancy, though such formulations can hide as much as they reveal.[10] To say that Scripture is God-breathed is to say that when we read the Bible, we are only a breath away from the God who made us and who gave himself in love to rescue us from ourselves. The authority of the Bible is the authority of an artist for his creation, of a parent for his child, and of a lover for his beloved. It is a passionate, intimate, committed authority, not one that is aloof, distant, and unmoved by our response. Scripture is God's love letter to humanity. To read it only as a set of rules to be obeyed or principles to be believed is to do violence to what Scripture is.

Translating with Scripture

Cultural translation of the gospel requires a rediscovery of scriptural authority by the contemporary church. The authority of the Bible as God's speech has been undermined by liberals and evangelicals alike. Whereas liberals have tended to maintain the broad scope of scriptural application to all of life but undermine its authority by subjecting it to the prior assumptions of secularism, evangelicals have maintained the primary authority of Scripture's voice but increasingly narrowed the domain over which it is effectively permitted to speak. The opportunity now is to release the power of Scripture as God's speech, in the power of the Holy Spirit, in all domains of life. This involves learning to communicate Scripture—whether in words, actions, or cultural symbols—so that the reality of Jesus can be experienced.

When we read and study Scripture for ourselves, the authority of the text is operating on and in us. Reading is *transformative*. Translation, on the other hand, is *performative*. In cultural translation, we aim to *perform*

10. For a helpful discussion on this point, see Goldingay, "Inspiration and Inerrancy," in *Models For Scripture*, 261–83.

196

the text so that its authority operates not only on us but *through* us. It is vital that we do not attempt such performance without having previously experienced something of the text's transformation in our own lives and experience. Performance, though, is not completely distinct from transformation, nor translation from reading. Rather, translation and performance are proper parts of our response to the text—outcomes of our own transformation.

Just as careful reading requires attention to the different genres of Scripture, so effective translation is also sensitive to genre. Scripture includes narrative, law, proverb, hymn, history, parable, poetry, apocalypse, and epistle. Each type of writing communicates in a different way. Putting this differently, the authority of the Bible works differently through its various genres. Some texts command us, others reveal the character of God and human nature through story, others inspire and shape our imagination about the world or our future. We are exhorted, warned, encouraged, taught, excited, and comforted. In all of this, the authority of God is operating, but in quite different ways. Sensitivity to the ways in which different scriptural genres operate authoritatively will help us *perform* those texts with appropriate authority.

Biblical scholar John Goldingay identifies four main models for understanding and interpreting Scripture.[11] His approach is to allow Scripture itself to identify and determine the way we understand and read it. His four models correspond to four types of genre in Scripture: narrative, instruction, prophecy, and experienced revelation (such as the wisdom and apocalyptic books).

- *Narrative* is described by Goldingay as a witnessing tradition, because it aims to pass on testimony to the story of God's dealings with Israel and humanity. Its function is to portray a pattern of events in order to express a vision to which we respond with more storytelling and worship.

11. See Goldingay's *Models for Scripture* and its companion volume, *Models for Interpretation of Scripture*.

- *Instruction* material includes Israel's law and similar authoritative commands in the New Testament. Its aim is to proscribe an obligation on us and, by virtue of its divine source, to elicit both delight and obedience.

- *Prophecy* is an inspired word in which typically God is speaking to and through human beings. It functions to confront us with God's perspective on reality in order to secure our repentance or to comfort and inspire hope.

- *Experienced revelation* often involves the reverse of prophecy, in the sense that it is the scriptural record of human beings speaking to God and reflecting before God on their experiences. It draws us to "overhear" an exchange between someone else and God, and it functions not to teach us about that but to invite us to imitate. Thus, for instance, the psalms are intended not to teach us about prayer but to lead us to pray.

Goldingay summarizes the differences and relationships between these four major types of Scripture as follows: "What a narrative tells a story about, an instruction text expresses an ethic, a prophecy turns into warning and promise, and experiential-revelatory material makes a matter for reflection and prayer."[12]

We are now able to appreciate what it might look like to unlock the power of Scripture in and through the act of cultural translation. In what follows I will unpack and illustrate what the performance of Scripture might entail for each genre, though I shall follow a different ordering of the four types than does Goldingay.

Wisdom: The Knowledge of Experience

The wisdom literature (what Goldingay calls "experienced revelation") models attentiveness to reality as it is and in the presence of God. The psalms are full of every kind of raw human emotion—from joy and gratitude (e.g.,

---

12. Goldingay, *Models for Interpretation*, 7.

Pss. 21; 30) to doubt, depression, envy (e.g., Pss. 13; 22; 73), and vengeful anger (e.g., Ps. 137). These human emotions are expressed with brutal honesty before God. Ecclesiastes is an extended meditation on life without God. Song of Songs celebrates romantic and sexual love. Job and Lamentations plumb the depths of personal and communal suffering. Proverbs attends to the created and human world—and the typical patterns of life that occur—in ways that give insight into the nature of human affairs and our relationship with God. Apocalyptic literature—like the book of Daniel and the Revelation of John—similarly aims to help God's people see the reality of a crisis experience (in these cases, the Babylonian exile and the Roman persecution) in the light of God's sovereignty and involvement in the world.

What is common to this genre is a refusal to dilute either the reality of our experience of the world or the reality of God. Often we can feel that our anger, for instance, has to be modified and controlled before we can talk to God about it, or that sexual pleasure is not an experience that is appropriate to even consider in God's presence. Our tendency is to try to collapse the apparent gap between the human and divine realities. One way we do this is through some form of pretense about our human situation—for instance, by pretending we are not really angry or by spiritualizing our anger as righteous indignation in order to justify it. Another is to make God like us and assume that he feels the same way we do. Finally, we may simply give up on God because we think the gap is unbridgeable and that God is too removed from us either to care or to help.

The wisdom genre deals with the gap in a different way: through juxtaposition. Neither human nor divine reality is denied. Each is honestly portrayed. The gap is bridged as we attend to our experience, as it is, *in the presence of God*. To perform these texts is to imitate them, to juxtapose human experience and gospel promise, to bring the community that we have been sent to before God in conscious prayer. Part of the role of an ambassador is to accurately represent a foreign culture to the home government. To use another biblical term, this is a priestly function. We are attentive to those in the spheres of life to which we have been sent. We look and listen. We are careful to listen to what people say, observe what they do, and empathize with what they long for and fear. This work—the work of reading our culture that we discussed in chapter 9—brings a new kind of knowledge when we undertake it in God's presence. If we hope to reach the tech industry, young mothers, or our work colleagues, we will have to begin by listening and observing well enough that we can represent the views, actions, hopes, and fears of participants as they would themselves. The first place to represent them is before God in prayer.

As we do this, as we bring human realities into God's presence, we begin to see and experience how divine reality engages with the human condition. The more we are steeped in the wisdom texts, the more we will find the Holy Spirit highlighting the relevance of a particular proverb or psalm, for instance, to this particular context. Moreover, if we do this not as detached observers but as participants in people's lives, we will begin to see where God is already working. Our perspective and understanding of what is happening will change. We will begin to see that, far from there being an unbridgeable gap, God is present and active in our lives. This very personal knowledge is profoundly different from simply gathering data and information, though that too has value. There's a neighborhood in Vancouver, Canada, where I used to live, known for its abject poverty, homelessness, and drug addiction. Charities and policy experts frequently bandy about social statistics and indicators, and many worthy initiatives and programs are started on the basis of them. But a different starting point for action was modeled by a friend of mine who committed simply to being present and prayerfully listening to the stories of residents, week after week, for months. This immersion brought insight and knowledge that could not be captured in statistics. And the very act of being heard impacted those who shared their stories.

In sum, what happens when we immerse ourselves in reality in this personal way, before God, is that our experience of a situation changes. We begin to see it and feel it as God does. Just as the Gospel writers frequently attest to the times when Jesus was motivated to act by compassion for people, attentiveness can help us re-experience reality in the light of God's heart and truth. This re-experiencing is the foundation for gospel change.

Narrative: The Story We Live By

Wisdom literature helps us pay attention to the world's needs. This is certainly a crucial first step, but it is not sufficient in itself. In addition to sharing God's heart for people in their need, we also need God's vision for people made whole. As Goldingay highlights, narrative functions in Scripture to give us a vision of God's purposes for human life and of how God works in the details of our messy history to realize those purposes. If we have already done the work of reading the culture to which we've been sent, we have a sense of the internal story it tells itself. To perform the narrative genre of Scripture is to renarrate that internal story of our workplace, neighborhood, or group *within* the overarching story of God's purposes for the world. This renarration often will include a range of affirmations and denials of the culture's internal story that combine to form the redirection of the cultural story that cultural translation involves.

The biblical drama provides the starting point and outline for this work. Whether we are focused on an engineering business or young people at risk, we begin by asking about the role our topic of focus plays in creation, how it has been affected by the fall, and so on through the drama of the biblical story. On the way, we look for specific biblical stories that relate to all or some of the aspects of the sphere of life in question. This process is not mechanical, based on a Bible word search (though that may be useful), but is prayerfully discerned. This is, by way of example, how Jesus responds to a question on divorce. Table 5 reproduces Matthew 19:3–12 rearranged to highlight the various elements of the biblical drama to which different verses refer. You can read the story in textual order by starting at the top and moving down at the same level of indentation, then back to the top and reading down the second and then third levels of indents.

My focus here is to see Jesus' teaching as an exemplar of biblical theological reasoning. Jesus answers the Pharisee's question by renarrating "divorce" within the biblical narrative, starting at creation and continuing in dialogue with his disciples all the way to the perspective of the

Table 5. Jesus on Divorce: Matthew 19:3–12

[3] *Some Pharisees came to him to test him. They asked, "Is it lawful for a man to divorce his wife for any and every reason?"*	
[4] *"Haven't you read," he replied, "that at the beginning the Creator 'made them male and female,'* [5] *and said, 'For this reason a man will leave his father and mother and be united to his wife, and the two will become one flesh'?* [6] *So they are no longer two, but one flesh. Therefore what God has joined together, let no one separate."*	Act 1: Creation
[8] *Jesus replied, "Moses permitted you to divorce your wives because your hearts were hard. But it was not this way from the beginning."*	Act 2: Fall
[7] *"Why then," they asked, "did Moses command that a man give his wife a certificate of divorce and send her away?"*	Act 3: Israel
[10] *The disciples said to him, "If this is the situation between a husband and wife, it is better not to marry."*	Interlude: Hopes and Fears
[9] *"I tell you that anyone who divorces his wife, except for sexual immorality, and marries another woman commits adultery."*	Act 4: Jesus
[11] *Jesus replied, "Not everyone can accept this word, but only those to whom it has been given.* [12a] *For there are eunuchs who were born that way, and there are eunuchs who have been made eunuchs by others. . . .* [12c] *The one who can accept this should accept it."*	Act 5: Church
[12b] *"And there are those who choose to live like eunuchs for the sake of the kingdom of heaven."* (Matt. 22:30: "At the resurrection people will neither marry nor be given in marriage; they will be like the angels in heaven.")	Act 6: New Creation

new creation. To perform the narrative genre of Scripture is to similarly renarrate a given sphere, context, or topic within the drama of Scripture.

The impact of the sacred-secular divide means that we will typically find it relatively easy to do this for topics related to personal relationships but much harder for broader areas of life such as education, work, or government. This difficulty is a feature not of the text but of our narrow theological conditioning. After all, the drama of Scripture itself encompasses all things in heaven and on earth with no exception. My experience in working with students is that it may take some hard work to get going, but it is incredibly rewarding in the end to be able to see one's sphere of ambassadorial service more clearly within the biblical story. The best people to do this kind of biblical theology are the people who know the sphere best. So the best people to think through a biblical theology of engineering, gardening, or community leadership are the engineers, gardeners, and leaders who are deeply involved in those spheres of life and committed to thinking and acting biblically within them.

Table 6 illustrates the kind of output that is possible from such an exercise. The questions in the table illustrate the kind of prompts that I've found help students get into the exercise. One column provides, for reference purposes, a relatively generic biblical theology of work, generated as a short summary of a course I've been teaching on that topic for the last decade at Regent College. Another is a very specific reflection on a particular workplace context by one of my students, whose job involved responsibility for the maintenance of a fleet of commercial helicopters. I've picked this example because it seems, at face value, to be an extremely difficult sphere of life to develop a theology about. Of course, such an exercise represents only one person's perspective and will be enhanced by discussion with others. The point is not to generate the definitive biblical position on helicopter maintenance (or anything else). Rather, the point is to actively use Scripture to help us envision or repurpose a particular sphere of work so that it is redirected toward Christ. This may seem like a strange idea, but consider the alternatives: Is our sphere of influence fine as it is, or is it that God doesn't care about such things? The weighty witness of Scripture is that things are not fine and God does care because he cares both for his creation and for every single one of his image bearers. This exercise builds on the previous one of attentive listening by helping us avoid developing a lopsided vision for a sphere that fails to take account of the whole pattern of the biblical story.

Prophecy: Naming Reality

Prophecy is often associated with predicting the future. But scholars highlight the role of the prophet as an intermediary, one called by God to speak on his behalf to particular communities at particular times.[13] The

13. Hermann Gunkel's form-critical work on the typical prophetic speech pattern laid the foundations for this conclusion, which can be explored more fully in the excellent collection by David Petersen, *Prophecy in Israel*.

Table 6. Repurposing: An Example

Biblical Story	Questions/Prompts	Work	Helicopter Maintenance[a]
Act 1: God Establishes His Kingdom	What can be affirmed as part of God's creation purposes in your sphere? How does it fit the cultural mandate of Genesis 1–2?	*Work is designed as worship in God's temple-creation.*	• Helicopters are examples of human creativity that unlock the potential of creation and extend our ability to steward the planet. They cultivate a sense of wonder and risk. • Planning maintenance to sustain function imitates God's sustaining of his creation, and human cooperation and teamwork reflect the creation mandate.
Act 2: Rebellion in the Kingdom	How is your sphere affected by the fall? Consider relationships with God, self, others, and creation.	*Fallen work defaces God's image.*	• The fall is evident in the way that human error arising from distraction, poor communication, and stress can result in machine malfunction, fatigue, and accidents. • Human errors are amplified by dishonesty, deception, laziness, pride, self-interest, and greed.
Act 3: Redemption Initiated	How does the story of Israel, and the law given to Israel to help them function as a model nation, speak to your sphere?	*Redeeming work helps restore God's image and lead people to Christ.*	• God's wisdom for Israel is reflected in the laws and industry regulations that protect from employer abuse of staff, dishonest parts suppliers, deficient training, and so on (cf. Israel's health and safety laws); and professional institutions that promote best practice (cf. certain roles of Levites). • Wisdom on planning, teamwork, communication, and especially Sabbath is relevant.
Interlude: Awaiting Messiah	What are the hopes and dreams in your sphere? What are the frustrations and longings?	*People often pursue their longings, hopes, and dreams through work.*	• Helicopters can be used to explore the wonder of creation—but this can become an arrogant desire to control. • People long for healthy work schedules, environments, and safe outcomes. • Unrealistic expectations, dishonesty, and accidents are fears.

Act 4: The Coming of the King	How is the gospel good news in your sphere? Consider the foolishness, wisdom, and power of the cross; suffering and humility overcoming evil.	*Sacrificial work is how God overcomes evil.*	• The gospel is good news in this context because it brings freedom from the burden of pride and reputation—"settling with power"[b] (Mark 4:35–41). • The gospel brings freedom from debilitating responsibility—e.g., the "Jesus nut."[c] • The gospel gives proper value and worth to people: "I am not a machine."
Act 5: Spreading the News of the King	What does it look like to witness to the gospel in your sphere? How does the gathered life of the church relate to it, and how does the church equip/relate to individual Christians scattered into that sphere?	*Empowered work participates in God's ongoing mission in the world.*	Witnessing to God's story in this context includes • modeling a revolutionary nonutilitarian work ethic, • showing how to grieve without blame, and • teaching and equipping people in terms of accountability, Sabbath, honesty, integrity, and communication.
Act 6: The Return of the King	In what sense might this sphere be fulfilled when Christ returns? Could it become part of the "glory and honor of the nations" offered in worship before the throne?	*Sanctified work will be offered up before God's throne in the new creation.*	• In the new creation, there will be fullness of joy in harnessing creation's potential for the glory of God, but without stress in work or potential loss of life.

a This column is based on answers generated from graduate assignments by Kevin Peters, director of maintenance for a commercial helicopter company in British Columbia, Canada. From a young age, Peters was inspired by the stories of missionary aviators. In his early career he worked for charities and mission agencies as a helicopter mechanic in South America and Africa. When circumstances led to a return to Canada, he felt that his ambitions and calling were blocked and became disheartened. He almost left the industry altogether, but gradually and gently God began to show him that he could be just as missional with helicopters in Canada as in Colombia. His team, colleagues, customers, and suppliers are now those he seeks to serve as an ambassador for Christ.

b "Settling with power" refers to a situation requiring counterintuitive behavior on the part of pilots to avert disaster in the case of a helicopter getting caught up in its own downwash of air when descending.

c The "Jesus nut" is the nut on Bell helicopters so named because it is the most critical component connecting the rotor assembly to the helicopter body, and its failure will lead to catastrophe. Both "settling with power" and the "Jesus nut" are cultural stories of his industry that Peters uses as touchpoints for the gospel.

content of prophetic messages revolved not so much around predicting future events as around God's messages of hope, challenge, and promise designed to draw his people away from sin, false gods, or despair and back into relationship, faithfulness, and hope. Sometimes God's promises contained or implied specifics about the future, but these were rarely understood to be far in the future. This understanding is apparent from the fact that one test of a false prophet is that what they said would not happen. This test would have little force if prophetic messages regularly involved long-range futurology. The predictive elements of prophetic messages are well described as announcements about the future—of what God has decided to do—rather than as long-term predictions.[14] The key point here is not the predictive nature of some prophetic messages but that the focus is on speaking God's messages to a given community. Thus, the prophets have rightly been seen primarily as *forth*tellers rather than *fore*tellers.

Goldingay's summary of the prophetic genre is that it functions to confront us with God's perspective on reality in order to bring about change. The emphasis on change is important. God's intent in speaking to us is to bring about repentance, or to instill hope, in ways that profoundly alter our behavior and redirect us back to faithful relationship with him. The prophets were those who spent long periods of time in prayer and solitude to hear God speaking, but they were also those known for their rhetoric and poetry. The prophetic literature contains striking use of metaphor, imagery, and rhetoric designed to convey a message that would impact a person's will and emotions along with their intellect. It is replete with metaphorical language in which God's people are likened to animals (cows, donkeys), plants (vines, grain), a mother, a son, a (faithless) wife, and so forth. A similar range of metaphors is used to speak of Israel's behavior and of God's actions. The prophets use extreme figures of speech to overcome our inbuilt tendency toward conservatism. For instance, Jeremiah likens those who gather riches unjustly to a partridge hatching eggs that it doesn't lay

14. As argued by Gene Tucker, who concludes that prophetic messages are essentially concerned "with a future within history and society as presently known." See "The Role of the Prophets and the Role of the Church," in Petersen, *Prophecy in Israel*, 168.

(Jer. 17:11). Amos and Isaiah liken the Israelites' oppression of the poor to trampling them underfoot and crushing the people like grapes from a vineyard that has been devoured (Amos 8:4–7; Isa. 3:14–15). Micah likens Israel's leaders to cannibals (Mic. 3:1–3)!

Recent studies of the role of metaphor in shaping how we think and behave affirm the power of the prophetic use of metaphor. In the classic study *Metaphors We Live By*, George Lakoff and Mark Johnson develop the argument that, far from simply being poetic figures of speech, metaphors actually function as lenses through which we see the world. For instance, Lakoff and Johnson highlight the way in which the concept of arguing in our culture is structured and enacted through the metaphor of warfare. We "defend," "attack," and "win" arguments. This metaphor actually shapes the way we argue, creating a confrontational or adversarial context. Lakoff and Johnson ask us to imagine what shape our arguing might take if we adopted instead the metaphor of dance. Then we might focus more on cooperating, taking turns, and elegance. Equally, we could ask what the dominant metaphors in our own spheres of mission are and how we might work to change them. In my sphere as an economist, the dominant metaphor is "business as competition"—we do business to beat other companies at making money. What would it be like if we began to think about business and economic activity using the more biblical metaphors of stewardship or cultivation, doing business to help people and creation flourish? Metaphor, then, is actually a very powerful vehicle for meaning and authority. We could almost say that metaphors are (or can be) prophetic. My point here returns us to one made earlier in this chapter: language is powerful and acts to shape the way we perceive reality and function within it. Prophetic language deliberately uses metaphor to expose reality as God sees it and to motivate us to change our behavior as a result. Our performance of this genre has the same objective.

A historical example is provided by the seventeenth-century Moravian Christian and educationalist John Amos Comenius. Comenius was motivated to improve educational opportunities for all children, especially the poor. As he reflected on the creation account of Genesis 1–2, he noticed how education began as Adam and Eve encountered, experienced, and named the different animals in the garden. From this observation, Comenius developed the idea of educating children in a "garden of delight" in which knowledge developed as a part of play and worship and in which moral formation was understood through the extended metaphor of pruning and nurture. For Comenius, this biblical reflection led to promotion of an instructional scheme, commencing with *kindergarten*, which remains highly influential to this day.[15]

Notice how performance of the prophetic genre relies and builds on our earlier focus on wisdom and narrative. Prophets could not possibly function without a deep understanding of God's purposes and character. They knew the story of God well. But they also had to be those who were attentive to the circumstances around them, as well as to what God was saying. A frequent pattern for the prophets is to look and pay attention to something, hear God speaking about it, and be given a specific message to deliver on God's behalf. In sum, where the wisdom genre prompts us to listen and look at the way things are and narrative enables us to see and envision how things could be, prophecy is what brings the dynamic movement from where we are toward where God wants us, along the path that he chooses.

Having paid attention and immersed ourselves in listening to and looking at a context in God's presence, we make ourselves available to hear what God may speak to us and through us. We may find our attention drawn to some particular aspect, story, or metaphor that has arisen from our attentive immersion. One student of mine had a heart to work with young people at risk—those from broken homes or those struggling with serious addictions or mental illnesses. Her attentiveness to their situations and the way they described them in their own language led to her identification of the "battlefield" or "war zone" as a primary metaphor for their experience of life, with an endless series of obstacles to be overcome, with

15. I am indebted to David Smith, who coauthored a paper exploring the role of metaphor in education, for this example. See Shortt, Smith, and Cooling, "Metaphor, Scripture and Education."

occasional attacks from "enemies," and with little-to-no experience of personal care for them as individuals. Another student working with the same demographic group in another place also identified "war" and "battle" as a relevant metaphor to understand their experience of the oversexualized culture of the West. These reflections, discerned and tested in prayer, began to develop into confidence to speak on behalf of these young people— both to give voice to the reality of the situation and to hold accountable those enabling it—such as social media networks that fail to police advertising and behavior that preys on addictions, pornography, and loneliness. These reflections also brought focus to God's invitation and promise to be our strong tower and refuge who cares for each one of us.

Instruction: Design for Living

Cultural translation is about communicating God's story—whether in words, actions, or symbols—in such a way that people experience the reality of Jesus. We've talked about this kind of communication as being a *performance* of Scripture that, when undertaken with the guidance and creativity inspired by the Holy Spirit, can release the world-creating power of God's speech into any and every situation. We've already considered wisdom, narrative, and prophecy as genres whose performances help give voice to the reality being experienced, provide vision for how our sphere could develop, and release prophetic insight to motivate and inspire change.

At face value, instruction, or law, seems to be the least promising genre for us to consider. Typically, we regard the law in Scripture as something that no longer applies to us and that we are glad not to be under. It seems to be the very antithesis of the kind of creative performance of the gospel that we are discussing. Scripture itself does not share this negative view of the law, however. Certainly, the law should not be understood as a means to become righteous before God, an approach that would negate the grace offered to us in Christ. And yet both Jesus and Paul uphold the law as God's righteous wisdom, able to lead us to Christ (Gal. 2:21–25; 4:1–7) and from which not one "jot or tittle" shall be removed (Matt. 5:17–20 KJV). Moses presents the law not as a means of forgiveness, punishment, or merit but rather as God's gift of wisdom to his people to enable them to flourish and prosper. It is also meant to serve as a testimony of God's wisdom to the surrounding cultures (see Deut. 4:5–8). Two questions arise from this summary: Has God's wisdom changed? Does our culture still need to be led to Christ?

It seems to me that the answer to the first question is no, and to the second, yes. Biblical scholar Richard Bauckham puts it like this: "God and his purposes for human life remain the same in both testaments. . . . We cannot apply [Old Testament] teaching directly to ourselves, but from the way in which God expressed his character and purposes in the political life of Israel we may learn something of how they should be expressed in political life today. . . . None of it applies directly to us, as *instructions*, but all of it is relevant to us, as *instructive* (c.f. 2 Tim. 3:16)."[16]

The Old Testament law, then, is understood as God's wisdom for life given in the cultural context of Israel. It embodies God's design, not as a blueprint to be slavishly copied in all other cultural contexts, but rather as an example to be creatively but faithfully imitated. Psalm 119 is a massive hymn of praise to the wisdom of God's law, describing it in terms of "great riches" (v. 14), something to be longed for (v. 20), that which is trustworthy (v. 86) and righteous (v. 106), "sweeter than honey" (v. 103), and a "lamp for [our] feet" (v. 105). The rich and detailed material of the law is embedded in the story and history of God's dealings with Israel and deserves to be interpreted in that context. If we're prepared to receive it with the same care and diligence as the psalmist, we will find it richly instructive in discerning how to embody the kind of prophetic message that arises from careful performance of the previous three genres. Jesus gave us an important hermeneutical key in his answer to the expert in the law recorded in Matthew 22:35–40. Asked which is the greatest commandment, Jesus answered by quoting Deuteronomy 6:5 and Leviticus 19:18:

16. Bauckham, *The Bible in Politics*, 6.

"Love the Lord your God with all your heart and with all your soul and with all your mind" and "Love your neighbor as yourself." He concluded, "All the Law and the Prophets hang on these two commandments."

The starting point for performing these texts in our cultural context is to join the psalmist in praying for wisdom and discernment to understand and apply them to our lives (see Ps. 119, esp. vv. 12, 18, 27, 33, 46, 66, 91, and 125). If our previous work in translating and performing the wisdom, narrative, and prophetic texts in ways appropriate to our spheres have not already identified stories and passages concerning which particular aspects of the law are relevant, then we can generate a list of such passages and ask of each one: How does it orient us toward God, and how does it help us love our neighbor? For instance, Deuteronomy 22:8 indicates that one way we love our neighbor is that when we are building our house, we put a parapet on the flat roof so that it can be used without the risk of people falling off. This health and safety principle can be extended into other areas of life beyond roof design. Similarly, Leviticus 19:9–10 tells us something about love for God and neighbor in the context of an agricultural harvest. We love the poor and the foreigner by leaving them something to gather to provide for themselves. We don't have an agrarian economy today, but might this text suggest ways in which business owners could offer "gleanings" of work, around the "edge" of their "harvesting," for those in need to provide for themselves with dignity?

US businessman Don Flow reflected on the rather obscure passages in the law about just weights and measures (e.g., Deut. 25:13–16) and then reengineered his automotive dealerships in response. He was aware that the typical industry model of sales and pricing tended to favor white, middle-class, well-educated men. This demographic tended to benefit from the emphasis on bargaining, whereas the less educated, the poor, minority groups, and women ended up paying more for the same vehicle. Flow realized that this was contrary to the biblical norm of treating each person fairly and equally in exchange.[17] So he redesigned his pricing so that everyone paid the same for the same vehicle, while maintaining business margins. Over

17. See, for example, Lev. 19:35–36; Deut. 25:13–16; Prov. 11:1; Amos 8:4–6; Hosea 12:7–8.

time, the result was an increase in trust, a lowering of transaction costs, and a growing business.[18]

Words of Power, Words of Life

In a society that has become imprisoned inside the socially constructed reality of its own cultural stories, God's speech is liberating and empowering. When God speaks, we hear "words of eternal life" that break through the fog of our confusion and the chains of our distrust. As ambassadors of Christ, our goal, under the inspiration and empowering of the Holy Spirit, is to so communicate the Scripture in the host languages of all the receiving cultures to which we have been sent—whether in words, actions, or symbols—that the reality of Jesus is experienced and people are set free. We do this as we perform the various genres of Scripture, each according to its own authoritative voice, and redirect people and cultures back toward God and his purposes. To be able to do this, Scripture itself must be freed from the traditions we have imposed on it that reduce it to a therapeutic tool or an academic specialism for use by religious people in their private or scholarly lives. The words of Scripture are the words of God, capable of creating and re-creating the world around us as he has designed it, freeing us from false narratives and confusion, and drawing us back into relationship with him in Jesus. They are words of power and love that are public, for all humanity, in all contexts, and at all times. It is time for the church now to take up these words once again with confidence, to wield them with grace and truth, to draw the mighty sword of the Spirit, and to learn again how to use it.

18. Flow is a Regent College alumnus who was interviewed for the ReFrame film series produced by my team at the Marketplace Institute in 2014. His ongoing desire and progress in integrating his faith with his work has been documented elsewhere. See "Strangers and Exiles," video, 39:48, ReFrame Course, episode 8, accessed August 28, 2019, https://www.reframecourse.com/episodes/episode-8; and "Don Flow: How Do You Live Faithfully," Faith & Leadership, February 15, 2010, https://www.faithandleadership.com/don-flow-how-do-you-live-faithfully.

12

Pilgrimage

A Way of Being

Foxes have dens and birds have nests, but the Son of Man has no place to lay his head.

Matthew 8:20

As the Father has sent me, I am sending you.

John 20:21

Ambassadors need to know their mission, learn the language of the culture they are sent to, and translate their message of love through words, deeds, and lifestyle. This "kingdom diplomacy" that we have been examining in the last several chapters cannot be reduced merely to a series of communication acts. Taken together, our words, actions, and the whole posture of our lives as an ambassadorial community constitute a kind of relationship with our society. But what kind of relationship? We've spoken about our situation in terms of exile and of our posture as that of purposeful ambassadors who know they are in a foreign land intentionally, but we need to add a third metaphor to round out the biblical witness—that of pilgrimage.

When we are in the world as it is, we are in exile from our true home. Our experience of exile, though, need not take us further away from home but rather can be a context in which we are journeying closer toward home. As individual Christians and as a community of believers, we are *followers* of Jesus. We are anchored fundamentally in him, not in a geographic place, political identity, or social status. Jesus leads us first to know the Father. It is this that roots us in our identity as God's people and detaches us from a worldly identity. As we continue to follow Jesus, he leads us into the world to be his ambassadors, carrying on his ministry of reconciliation. But Jesus also leads us toward our true home. We are headed toward the promised land of God's full and final coming as King, the promised new creation in which heaven will come to earth and everything will be made new. Jesus tells us to put our treasure there, that he has gone ahead to prepare a place for us there, and that we should eagerly await his return from there, because it will mean that our journeying is finally over, we can see him face-to-face, and we will dwell with him in a renewed creation that has been purified completely from sin and its effects.

Biblical scholars understand the Jewish exile as a kind of return to the wilderness. The church, too, is in a kind of wilderness on its way to the promised land. This situation is not one that we typically delight in. But it is where God has sent us. Our journey in the wilderness is not a wandering or a waiting time, unproductive except as a way to pass the time. The wilderness is a place of dependence, learning, struggle, blessing, and purification. Pilgrimage, though transitional, changes us and the society of which we are a part.

Becoming God's People

I enjoy hiking. I've had the chance to walk a few stunning trails, like the Inca Trail in Peru, the Milford Track in New Zealand, and the Juan de Fuca Trail on Vancouver Island's west coast, but mainly I've appreciated an afternoon's ramble along the footpaths of England or the trails of the Pacific Spirit Regional Park in Vancouver. Walking is a great way to spend time with others. My memories of those major hikes are full of conversations with my wife, children, friends, and other walkers we've met on the journey. There's something about the rhythm of walking together, side by side, that makes conversation very easy. We're not looking at each other; instead, we're enjoying the view and looking out for the path. This common focus, away from the normal structures of life, seems to liberate a more intimate and easy discussion. The more lengthy and demanding the hike, the more intense this effect can be. A challenging hike, in which we need to rely on each other and work together, can forge deep relationships.

This kind of experience of deep, spontaneous community during a journey is considered in depth by the anthropologist Victor Turner in his study of pilgrimage. He develops and employs two concepts that are helpful to us. The first is *liminality*—the quality of ambiguity that exists in the middle of the transition between one fixed social structure and another. Often, liminal experiences are moments that take place during rituals, such as marriage or coming-of-age ceremonies, or initiations, such as baptisms. The gap between asking and answering a marriage proposal or between a baptismal vow and its response is a brief experience of liminality, since our answer and decision at each of these points can lead into a whole new set of life structures and possibilities.

Teenage years in modern society can be difficult precisely because they are often experienced as a kind of extended limbo between childhood and adulthood with little guidance for how to move out of that limbo and into adulthood proper. Other examples include graduation or times between old and new job roles. A journey can often create a kind of liminal experience when we are temporarily free of the responsibilities and structures of life as we travel from one destination to another. Religious pilgrimage is a form of journeying in which this liminal experience of "breaking free" is pursued quite intentionally for devotional purposes. At a larger scale, liminality may describe the experience of immigrant communities caught between the home that they have left and the home they have not yet found in the country they seek refuge in. In this sense, the condition of exile is itself characterized by a kind of liminality. Our experience of liminality may be a freeing one that reminds us of our deeply held values and releases creativity, or it may be a negative one that unsettles us and brings a sense of insecurity. Much will depend on how the transition is led and structured for us by appropriate leaders.

To this notion of liminality, Turner adds the idea of *communitas*, by which he means a particular kind of social structure. Communitas is characterized by fellowship, an emphasis on our common humanity and equality, rather than being dominated by recognized social hierarchies. Turner uses the example of religious pilgrimages to explain how the liminal experience of the journey can give rise to a social experience of communitas in which members of different social classes, races, and groups can mix and converse as equals in a way that would be difficult or impossible in normal life because of the expectations created by the hierarchical structures of society.

The notion of the Christian life as pilgrimage works closely with that of Christian identity as strangers and exiles in the world. Both reinforce a more permanent sense of liminality. Usually, liminal moments are brief, and the experience of communitas that Turner describes is equally short-lived. But it is possible for social structures to develop around the liminal experience that enable that experience to be extended over time and to gain more permanence—a condition of "normative communitas," in Turner's language. There is evidence that Turner realized that the entire Christian life can be thought of in these terms following his conversion to Christian faith in 1958.[1] Entry into the Christian faith through repentance and baptism puts all Christians into a common community of believers following Jesus back toward our true home in God's unmediated presence. There is an extraordinary social experience of oneness and fellowship on this journey among those who recognize Jesus Christ as Lord and Savior. The very first believers were known as followers of *the* Way (see, e.g., Acts 9:2; 24:14). The church *is* a pilgrim people following the Way of Jesus in the world.

Pilgrimage establishes and nurtures our new identity as Christ followers, changing us in the process. We experience the life of Jesus and the presence

---

1. Turner described Eden, as well as the community of the kingdom established at Pentecost, in terms of communitas. See Larsen, *The Slain God*, 183.

of the Holy Spirit in a huge variety of people: men and women from diverse cultures, races, and socioeconomic groups. We find that we belong in this family of God, and like any family we share the ups and downs of life on the journey. We learn to celebrate together and lament together, often through the intimate shared disciplines of prayer, confession, and forgiveness. Fundamentally, the rhythms of the journey—following Jesus by attending to his word, obediently putting it into practice in our lives, confessing our sins, receiving forgiveness and guidance, offering our worship and service—all combine to shape us, to make us fit for the journey, and to prepare us for entry into the promised land of the new creation. In the language of Augustinian desire that we encountered in chapter 9, pilgrimage structures a cultural liturgy for the church throughout time.

It is important to emphasize that this pilgrimage is not a journey from earth to heaven. The Bible does not envision the Christian life as a kind of Gnostic escape from material reality. Nor is it a metaphor for building heaven on earth, for establishing some kind of ideal communitarian experiment in which the kingdom of God is fully realized through human effort. Instead, we are journeying through time on earth and in heaven simultaneously. The journey's goal is the marriage of heaven and earth that will take place only when Christ returns and the Lord's Prayer is fully answered as heaven comes to earth and God's will is done "on earth as it is in heaven" (Matt. 6:10). In other words, the pilgrim people of the church are not a large crowd traveling through the world, touching or impacting it as little as possible, nor are they a group trying to take it over and settle down. Rather, Christians are called to journey through the world in ways that bless it and help prepare it for the coming of God, joining God in his work of renewing all things.

Blessing God's World

Unlike modern embassies, the Christian embassy is mobile. The Christian community is a community of emissaries, roving ambassadors for Christ in the world. How do we understand this juxtaposition of metaphors for

Christian mission, of the combination of the ambassador and the pilgrim? Normally we think of an embassy as a fixed residence in the midst of foreign territory. We understand that an ambassador might shuttle back and forth between the home country and the foreign one for the sake of accurately conveying messages. A roving ambassador suggests that the relationship is only preliminary, but a permanent embassy makes diplomacy seem more serious. Are these metaphors simply misaligned and confusing when pushed together, or is there something to learn here?

One practice observed in some modern diplomatic services may help shed light on this. There is a recognition that living in a foreign country and being surrounded by its culture for an extended time can lead to an ambassador or diplomat "going native" and subtly realigning his or her loyalties away from the home country and toward the foreign one. For this reason, diplomatic staff are usually reassigned on a regular basis. Theologically, this speaks to the danger of assimilation, of the temptation to settle down and fit in, and of the need to keep being renewed in our Christian identity. Perhaps as individuals we may find that God moves us on from situations or activities that are perfectly good in themselves in order to keep drawing us closer to himself, preventing us from settling for lesser things. But how does this relate to the people of God as a whole? We can make sense of individuals being reassigned, but what do we mean when we say the whole Christian community is on a journey?

The answer lies, I suggest, in understanding that the journey itself is part of the ambassadorial message of the church. The state of being on a journey, on the Way toward God's promised future, is prophetic. It proclaims our conviction that the world as it is in its fallen state is not a place to settle, to get comfortable in, but rather a place to leave in pursuit of the world that Jesus wants to give us. When we seriously engage with the world around us but do so with our eyes clearly fixed on a different place, we naturally encourage those around us to look in the same direction, to be reoriented toward God's intended future for them. Our way of being on pilgrimage invites others to join us on the journey and to follow Jesus themselves.

Again, to speak of leaving the fallen world in pursuit of the world that Jesus wants to give us does not at all mean giving up our work as plumbers, financiers, or medical doctors in order to become paid pastors, youth leaders, or church planters. Rather, it means that whatever work we do, we do it "as for the Lord and not for men" (Col. 3:23 ESV). We fit pipes, design pension schemes, and care for the sick all with our gaze on Jesus, in a manner that is worthy of the Way of Christ that we are traveling on. The Way of Jesus is characterized not by the pursuit of political power, material gain, or personal pleasure but by service for the good of others, generosity to those in need, and contentment and joy in our restored relationship with God.

The Old Testament contains several prophetic pictures of this pilgrimage of God's people back toward him and of the impact they have as they journey. Psalm 84 begins with a vision, "How lovely is your dwelling place, LORD Almighty," toward which the psalmist yearns to travel. A few verses later it celebrates both pilgrimage and its effects:

> Blessed are those whose strength is in you,
>> whose hearts are set on pilgrimage.
>
> As they pass through the Valley of Baka,
>> they make it a place of springs. (Ps. 84:5–6)

The Valley of Baka is an inhospitable desert whose name also conveys the meaning of tears and suffering.[2] Isaiah 35 portrays a similar picture in which the desert comes to life as the redeemed people of God travel through it on the Way of Holiness. The desert of suffering symbolizes the world in its fallen state. As God's pilgrim people travel through the world, they bless it so that it comes to life and can sustain future pilgrims. The fallen world is not discarded as useless, nor cultivated for settlement, but becomes part of the journey. It is reoriented so that it serves God's purposes to draw everything in creation back to himself.

---

2. In Hebrew, "Baka" sounds like the verb for weeping and probably refers to a tree or shrub that grows in arid places.

This ministry of bringing life to the desert is another picture of mission. It enriches the idea of "seeking the welfare of the city" that the Jewish exiles were encouraged to adopt, and it grounds the notion of mission as translation that we explored in chapters 8 and 11. Reorienting our neighborhoods, workplaces, and communities through gospel translation is fundamentally about choosing and bringing life to a desert.

What is striking about this picture is that it is not those who are settled in the world but the people of God—those who are traveling along the Way as they follow Jesus—who become the ones who offer hospitality and bring life.[3] Often in such situations it is those who are hungry and thirsty who are most open to accept hospitality. It is the poor in spirit, who know their need of God, who are most eager. This means that mission will often be most immediately effective on the margins of society rather than at its center. We see this pattern in Jesus' ministry. Much of his focus was on ordinary people, as well as the sick and marginalized, rather than with the elites (who, for the most part, tended to resist his message).

But why is mission often more effective on the margins of any given society? It is not because God doesn't care about the rich and powerful but because those at the center, who have the power and wealth, have the most to lose from the gospel's invitation and thus most strongly resist it. One way of understanding conversion is as acceptance of the invitation to leave a settled life in the fallen world and begin the pilgrimage toward God that following Jesus involves. As a pilgrim people, the church in its existence, as well as in its activities and words, is inviting others to come along on the journey.

In terms of the anthropological concepts in this chapter, the church provokes the world into an experience of liminality, of transition from

---

3. Another way of putting this irony is that it may be precisely because we are on a journey, following Jesus to know God, that we may be willing to remain physically stable and present to people. Much of the hypermobility of the modern world is a symptom of malaise and dissatisfaction—a restless searching for meaning and life. To remain in one community over time is to become a spring of life to that community and thus to help them find the start of the only journey that really matters.

being settled in one's fallen life to being unsettled in it and ready to follow Jesus, through the death and resurrection of baptism, into a new life. A society that is structurally designed to settle down in acceptance of the assumptions of a fallen world and to keep God out is provoked by a pilgrim people who are structurally designed to maintain a state of liminality and communitas in God's presence. Such provocations are most likely to succeed in contexts that evoke what Turner calls "the subjunctive mood" of the social process, in which "suppositions, desires, hypotheses, possibilities, and so forth, all become legitimate."[4] These are essentially contexts in which artists, poets, priests, and prophets can speak into society in ways that challenge its basic assumptions. Examples might include not only carnivals, festivals, theater, and film but also public debates and the rituals of the political process. At a smaller organizational or neighborhood scale, these contexts can form whenever the need for change is recognized in a dissatisfied group. Again, these liminal contexts can be identified by considering what the hopes and fears of a given cultural story are (see chaps. 9 and 10) and how best these desires and concerns might be shared and explored.

One of the most important things that Christian pilgrims can bring to such contexts is time and presence. We are probably familiar with the way that houseguests from afar have a knack for asking penetrating questions and opening up deep conversations that don't seem to come up when we socialize with friends and neighbors whom we see more frequently. Equally, we may recognize the sense of presence that we can offer to others when traveling abroad that we might not inhabit in our day-to-day lives. There is something about the traveling mind-set that can free the mind and spirit and enable a deeper and more prescient engagement. When this presence carries with it and conveys the stillness of the Holy Spirit, then our presence will communicate his presence. If we remain attentive to what Jesus is doing and saying, then we will be able to identify and engage with contexts in which people can be drawn into a liminal experience of encounter with God.

4. Turner, *The Ritual Process*, vii, cited in Ashley, *Victor Turner and the Construction of Cultural Criticism*, 30.

Us and Them

Blessing from the margins is not always welcome. Feeding the hungry, caring for the sick, insisting on fair dealing with the relatively weak and powerless, speaking up for those who cannot speak for themselves, and spending time with the lonely can all be seen as a threat. The gospel is not always received as good news: to some it is the smell of death and doom (2 Cor. 2:16).

Turner speaks of communitas as a kind of anti-structure that symbolizes an ideological rejection of—or at least a substantial corrective to—the dominant social order.[5] The church as a prophetic community—an embodied communitas that calls society to be reoriented toward Christ—challenges the spiritual order of society, the idolatries and ideologies that keep people captive and prevent them from hearing the gospel. We challenge these powers, in the name of Christ, to "let my people go." This challenge arises simply from the church's existence, so long as we maintain our identity as a pilgrim people. To settle down is to have become, at least partially, defeated by the spiritual powers of our age. But when we inhabit our identity and begin to live out of it and bless the world, the church becomes literally terrifying to the spiritual powers of death and darkness. To a spiritual order that maintains control through the fear of poverty, pain, insecurity, humiliation, and death, the church is an existential threat.

Given these spiritual dynamics, how then does the church as God's pilgrim people relate to temporal power? In the contemporary debate, there are some who argue that the church should remain on the margins of society, concentrate on being itself, and avoid the danger of contamination that comes with any engagement with worldly power. Others argue that the worldly centers of power should not be abandoned, because they too must be made subject to Christ. To caricature, one view has it that Christians should eschew worldly influence, concentrate on our gathered life together, and reach out to those on the margins with works of service and mercy; the other view believes that we should be politically active, speak

5. See Turner, "Liminality and Communitas," chap. 3 of *The Ritual Process*.

truth to power, and seek to change the institutions and legal structures of society to better serve the will of God on earth.

This question and these debates about how we relate to power are taking place, of course, in the significantly changed context of the end of modernity in the West. There are important nuances to be found in these alternative viewpoints, reflecting different assessments and motivations. Thus, for some, keeping out of worldly affairs and focusing on the purity of Christian life may be appealing because of an unexamined dualism between the secular and the sacred, in which Christianity is about the personal and private and not the social and public. For others, the motivation may be quite different. Some Christians may fully understand that the gospel has public and social claims but consider that the church has become so compromised by its entanglement with power during the modern era that a season of "fasting" from political influence will help realign our hearts with the true spiritual power that must be at the center of all Christian mission. Equally, it is clear that some of the calls for more political involvement, and indeed the actual activities of some Christian lobby groups, are motivated essentially by a desire to stop the loss of Christian influence and regain legal and political control of national life. This is a battle to control the worldly settlement, not to call it onto a journey of pilgrimage. On the other hand, others may be concerned to maintain a Christian voice and not capitulate to the ideology of secular pluralism and its pressure on the church to retreat from the public square and from public witness.

From this brief sketch there are two points I want to highlight. The first is that our battle is "not against flesh and blood" (Eph. 6:12). The church's warfare is directed toward the spiritual powers that bind people and societies, not toward the people and societies who are bound by them. To think that we can exist on the margins of society in some pure, generous, and "nice" community is to ignore the reality of the spiritual battle that is taking place all around us. Equally, to engage in aggressive pronouncements and political maneuvers against secular proponents of abortion, gay marriage, and secular humanism is to be fighting precisely the wrong kind of battle.

223

The second point is that a pilgrim church will necessarily make different kinds of relationships in the course of its journey. With some, the relationship may be close, welcoming, and open, whereas with others it may be more frosty or even hostile. How the church relates to power will be in large measure a function of the kind of relationship it has with the society it is journeying through. Such was the situation with Israel's prophets. Nathan's relationship with David and Isaiah's relationship with Hezekiah are examples of prophetic relationships with power when power itself is relatively God-fearing and God-oriented. These prophets were welcome advisors in the royal court. But when a society becomes apostate, the situation changes. Elijah's relationship with Ahab and Jezebel, Amos's relationship with the Northern Kingdom of Israel, and Jeremiah's relationship with the Southern Kingdom of Judah are examples of prophetic relationships with power in situations of relative apostasy. In these examples, the prophet was pushed out from the center of influence and had to operate increasingly from the margins, often facing hostility, persecution, and imprisonment.[6] These examples of relative faithfulness and apostasy all took place within an Israelite society that essentially accepted the biblical witness. But we also have examples of faithful witness in more clear-cut pagan societies, such as Joseph in Egypt, Daniel in Babylon, and Esther in Susa. In all cases, the call of the prophet was not to become the king or to take over the government but to be a faithful witness and representative of God and God's message. The appeal of the prophets, even to the most unbelieving culture, is a redemptive one—an appeal to heed God's word and receive God's blessing.

What does this mean for us today? In most Western countries, the church as an institution and Christianity as a message are being pushed toward the margins. So far, the kind of persecution experienced by Western Christians has been relatively minor: some social mockery and hostility and occasional economic disadvantage. Depending on the country in question, some vestiges of Christianity's cultural privilege remain. What kind of

---

6. See R. Wilson, *Prophecy and Society in Ancient Israel*. Wilson's careful study distinguishes central and peripheral intermediary prophets. See esp. pp. 30, 56, and 83.

attitude ought we to have concerning the influence we have lost and that which we retain?

The examples of Israel's prophets suggest that it is faithful witness that ought to be our primary objective, not regaining lost power or retaining influence. It is precisely at times such as these, when we are pressured to conform to a dominant secular society, that we may be tempted to compromise faithfulness in order to retain "influence." I hear frequently that we must be careful what we say or do lest we lose the remaining influence we have at the center of power. Such an attitude betrays a vulnerability to the temptation to assimilate. It is the breeding ground not of faithful witness but of false prophecy. It falsely assumes that "influence" derives from being on good terms with the influential rather than from being obedient to the Most Influential. It also assumes that the loss of the church's power is necessarily a bad thing and wholly outside of God's will. There is little doubt that the institutional church has been guilty of abuse of the power and influence it has had during the Christendom and modern eras. Should we perhaps consider the possibility that God is removing temporal power from the church for its own good? However we answer this last question, the point remains that the faithful witness of the Christian community will ultimately give us the kind of enduring influence that is truly missional rather than merely worldly.[7]

This does not mean, however, that Western churches should withdraw from public discourse or engagement. Being situated more on the margins of society may be good for the church's humility, purity, and identification with the weak and marginalized. It also should help us function more independently of worldly power and the need to appease it. This is true only if we are provoked to more deeply identify with Christ and our prophetic call to follow him rather than spend all our time on the margins simply wishing we were back in the center. The witness of Israel's prophets is that being on the margins does not in any way preclude speaking to

7. On this point I agree wholeheartedly with James Davison Hunter's call for faithful presence. See the conclusion of *To Change the World*, 238–86. Hunter links his argument explicitly to the "new paradigm" of exile (278).

the center. It's also important to remember that whereas the institutional church may have been relatively marginalized, this does not mean that all individual Christians are thereby also absent from influential roles in society. Scripture is replete with examples of occasions when God led specific individuals into positions of significant influence during seasons when the formal institutions of power were lukewarm toward God, apostate, or straightforwardly pagan.

The primary work of the pilgrim church as it travels along the Way of Christ is to demonstrate the transforming love of God in the desert places of our fallen world and to invite individuals, communities, and societies to join it on this journey of following Jesus back to a restored relationship with God. The church's relationship with power (or money or reputation) is to be understood spiritually. Can the institutions that support temporal power, money, and reputation become subservient to the Way of Christ? Can they help rather than hinder people and communities to follow Jesus? To the extent that they are willing and able to help, the church must encourage and affirm them, but to the extent that they become barriers and blockages, they must be opposed. This opposition must be understood in terms of spiritual warfare, not temporal power politics. Crucial to an appropriate posture is that the church has confidence in God and the power of the gospel to overcome any ideology or idolatry that tries to hold people and communities captive.

Now and Then

In this final chapter, I have rounded out the biblical witness on exile and mission by developing the notion of pilgrimage to supplement that of the purposeful ambassador. The fundamental relationship of the church in the world can be understood within this paradigm of a pilgrim people of God traveling as a roving ambassadorial community through the fallenness of the world along the Way of Christ. This community journeys along, inviting individuals, communities, and societies to leave their settled life in this fallen world and join the pilgrimage toward God and the fullness of

Christ's kingdom. We've seen that as we journey along this way, we become a community fit for the journey and ready to enter into the promised land of God's fullness. As we travel through the desert of the fallen world, we can bring the love and life of God to neighborhoods, workplaces, and communities as we reorient them toward Christ and his kingdom. We can expect to face resistance and opposition, because there are spiritual powers that seek to bind and captivate humanity to remain settled in its fallen state. But we can also expect victory against these spiritual powers, because we are confident in Christ's victory and the power of his gospel, against which the gates of hell cannot stand.

Like any journey, this Christian pilgrimage sometimes seems arduous, as if it will never end. We may grow weary of opposition or disillusioned if we don't seem to see transformation around us. We may find the company of fellow pilgrims much easier than the challenge of relating to those "settled" communities we're traveling through. Again, like any journey, our experience of it is impacted by the kind of expectations we have of it. In this respect there are two kinds of mistake we can make concerning our expectations of the journey.

The first is to expect too much too soon—to think that everyone will join the journey immediately and that the whole desert will become a garden as we travel through it. The danger of this mind-set is that we become fixated on the desert instead of on our journey's destination, focused on sin and brokenness but gradually losing sight of our hope in the return of Christ, who alone has overcome death and can fully renew all the deserts of this fallen world. We act as though the fullness of the kingdom is in our hands, but eventually we will become overwhelmed, lose heart, and become disillusioned. In our effort to help, we may also do a lot of damage trying to impose by sheer force of will, charisma, or worldly power our own idea of the garden of Eden on some particular corner of the world.

The second mistake, of course, is to expect too little—to see the desert and be fearful of it lest it suck the life out of us. In this mind-set the destination becomes everything and the journey something to be endured. Rather than leave the desert a place of springs, we leave it untouched. Our faith is focused on the cross and the need for forgiveness of sins, but we've lost sight of, or confidence in, the resurrection and the outpouring of the Holy Spirit to transform our lives and those of others around us now. Our life in the world becomes at best a form of endurance training and at worst a minefield full of temptations and distractions to be avoided. It is hard to love and bring life to those whose lifestyles and communities we fear. Evangelism is conducted by means of daring raiding parties into hostile territory, but most of life is lived among the safe community of fellow travelers. A focus on hurrying toward the destination means we have little time or inclination to care about the quality of the road we travel on or invest in the communities we travel through. Why bother about environmental damage, business practices, or international justice if all that matters is making peace with God before you die?

Both of these mistakes—of over- and underrealized eschatologies—lose sight of the true nature of the journey, because they lose sight of Jesus, the journey's destination. In the first case, the journey becomes all about transformation of the world, and in the second, all about escape from it. In both cases the focus is on the sin and brokenness of the world rather than on Jesus himself. We think either that the world must be completely fixed or that it can't be fixed at all and we must keep away from it as much as possible.

But Jesus himself modeled something quite different. He was not afraid to be among the worst of sinners (prostitutes, terrorists, and corrupt financiers were all among his associates). But though he healed and transformed many lives, there was much sin and brokenness in Israel that Jesus did not heal during his earthly life. Many remained sick, lonely, or outcast; the exploitation of religious and political power continued; extremes of wealth and poverty persisted; unbelief was widespread. Jesus focused not on the immediacy of sin and brokenness around him but on the Father by whom he had been sent and to whom he would return. He did what he saw the Father doing and spoke what he heard the Father speaking. He sought to please the Father in all he did, becoming obedient even to death on a cross.

This is our model. We have been called to take up our cross and follow Jesus into the world, to speak his words and do his works as his body on earth in the power of the Holy Spirit. Our focus as we follow him is on his actions and his words so that our experience of journeying through the world is one in which Jesus is present with us, acting and speaking by his Spirit. The focus is not on sin and brokenness but instead on what Jesus is doing and saying. In this way, we remain in him and bring his life in his way at his time. Yet at the same time as we experience Jesus powerfully *with us* by his Spirit as we journey through the world, we also anticipate and long for his bodily return in the future, which will mark the end of our pilgrimage.

The New Testament speaks of Christ's return "on the clouds of heaven, with power and great glory" (Matt. 24:30). Unlike the incarnation, which was private and humble, his second coming will be public and awe-inspiring. In the Old Testament, the coming of God in glory and power is also spoken of from the perspective of God's people in exile using the image of a highway being prepared in the desert for God to enter and reclaim his royal city and his people. "In the wilderness prepare the way for the LORD, make straight in the desert a highway for our God" (Isa. 40:3). Malachi speaks of this preparation in terms of a messenger who will tell of God's coming (Mal. 3:1), and later, in Isaiah, the preparation of the road is spoken of in terms of removing obstacles from the path of God's people. John the Baptist had this ministry of preparing a way for Jesus by announcing the need for repentance and getting ready for God's coming (e.g., Matt. 3:1–3). The gospel itself, as announced by Jesus, also plays this role: "'The time has come,' he said, 'The kingdom of God has come near. Repent and believe the good news!'" (Mark 1:15). This is also the ministry of the church—to prepare the way for Christ's return by announcing the gospel in and through all that we do.

Our journeying, our pilgrimage, is precisely about making a highway in the desert that prepares for and invites the coming of the Lord Jesus. These activities are essentially the same thing, because God wants everyone to be ready when he comes. As the pilgrim people of God travel through this fallen world, bringing life, making springs in the desert, we create a roadway that points toward our destination. Our lives become signposts

229

for others to follow. Just as Jesus endured the shame of the cross for the joy set before him (Heb. 12:2), so we are sustained on the journey, even as we "[participate] in his sufferings, becoming like him in his death," because of the hope of a resurrected body in which we shall know Christ and see him face-to-face (Phil. 3:10–11). For us, this anticipation is also that of a bride awaiting her groom on her wedding day.[8]

Time to Move Out

What I have described in this book amounts to a fundamental reorientation of the church in contemporary Western culture. We need to reevaluate not only our cultural context but also our sense of identity and mission. I have sought to give biblical metaphors we can inhabit to help us in this reorientation: metaphors of exile, ambassadorship, diplomacy, translation, and pilgrimage.

For some time the church in the West has given its main energy and focus to propping up institutions and models that are clearly no longer fit for purpose, to accommodating to or judgmentally critiquing Western culture, and to anesthetizing ourselves to the missional challenges we face through our Christian consumerism and pietistic withdrawal.

It is time to face up to the missional challenges of our generation; to sharpen our focus, perception, and prayer lives; to resolutely seek awareness of what God is doing so as to follow him; and to harness our resources as if we mean business.

It is time to move out and once again become a people of the Way.

8. In the Jewish marriage customs that Scripture uses to teach us, there would be a significant gap between the marriage contract and betrothal, on the one hand, and the wedding celebration and consummation of the marriage, on the other. During the gap, the groom would go away to prepare a home for the bride and, at a time set by the groom's father, would return, with an element of surprise, to claim his bride. While waiting for the groom to return, the bride would consecrate herself and prepare her bridal gown.

Bibliography

Abraham, Carolyn. "Star Scientist Hatches Cloning Controversy: South Korean Admits Violating Ethics Code." *Globe and Mail* (Toronto), November 25, 2005, Canada in Context, A1.

Alter, Robert. *The Art of Biblical Narrative.* New York: Basic Books, 1981.

Arendt, Hannah. *The Origins of Totalitarianism.* New York: Schoken, 1951.

Ashley, Kathleen M. *Victor Turner and the Construction of Cultural Criticism: Between Literature and Anthropology.* Bloomington: Indiana University Press, 1990.

Auerbach, Eric. *Mimesis: The Representation of Reality in Western Literature.* Translated by Willard R. Trask. Princeton: Princeton University Press, 1953.

Augustine, Saint. *The City of God.* Translated by Marcus Dods. New York: Modern Library, 1993.

———. *Confessions: A New Translation.* Translated by Peter Constantine. New York: Liveright Publishing, 2018.

Baggini, Julian. "The Rise, Fall and Rise Again of Secularism." *Public Policy Research* 12, no. 4 (2006): 204–12.

Bartholomew, Craig G., and Michael W. Goheen. *The Drama of Scripture: Finding Our Place in the Biblical Story.* 2nd ed. Grand Rapids: Baker Academic, 2014.

Bauckham, Richard. *The Bible in Politics: How to Read the Bible Politically.* Louisville: Westminster John Knox, 1989.

Bebbington, David W. *Evangelicalism in Modern Britain: A History from the 1730s to the 1980s.* London: Unwin Hyman, 1989.

Berger, Peter. "Western Individuality: Liberation and Loneliness." *Partisan Review* 52 (1985): 323–36.

Bockmuehl, Klaus. *Listening to the God Who Speaks: Reflections on God's Guidance from Scripture and the Lives of God's People.* Colorado Springs: Helmers and Howard, 1990.

———. "Recovering Vocation Today." *Crux* 24, no. 3 (Sept. 1988): 25–35.

Bonhoeffer, Dietrich. *The Cost of Discipleship.* Translated by R. H. Fuller. London: SCM, 1948.

———. *Life Together.* Translated by John W. Doberstein. New York: Harper & Brothers, 1954.

Bosch, David J. *Transforming Mission: Paradigm Shifts in Theology of Mission.* Maryknoll, NY: Orbis Books, 1991.

Bouma-Prediger, Steven. *For the Beauty of the Earth: A Christian Vision for Creation Care.* 2nd ed. Grand Rapids: Baker Academic, 2010.

Brueggemann, Walter. *Cadences of Home: Preaching among Exiles.* Louisville: Westminster John Knox, 1997.

Buckley, P., and M. Casson. "Economics as an Imperialist Social Science." *Human Relations* 46, no. 9 (1993): 1035–52.

Buden, Boris, Stefan Nowotny, Sherry Simon, Ashok Bery, and Michael Cronin. "Cultural Translation: An Introduction to the Problem, and Responses." *Translation Studies* 2, no. 2 (2009): 196–219. https://www.tandfonline.com /doi/full/10.1080/14781700902937730.

Cavanaugh, William T. *Being Consumed: Economics and Christian Desire.* Grand Rapids: Eerdmans, 2007.

Chaplin, Jonathan. *Talking God: The Legitimacy of Religious Public Reasoning.* London: Theos, 2008.

Church of England. *Breaking New Ground: Church Planting in the Church of England.* London: Church House Publishing, 1994.

———. *Mission-Shaped Church: Church Planting and Fresh Expressions of Church in a Changing Context.* London: Church House Publishing, 2004.

Collins, Francis S. *The Language of God: A Scientist Presents Evidence for Belief.* London: Pocket, 2007.

Congar, Yves. *Jalons pour un théologie du laïcat.* Paris: Cerf, 1953.

Dawkins, Richard. "Is Science a Religion?" *Humanist* 57, no. 1 (January/February 1997): 26–29.

Diehl, William. *Ministry in Daily Life: A Practical Guide for Congregations.* Herndon, VA: Alban Institute, 1996.

Driscoll, Mark. "A Pastoral Perspective on the Emergent Church." *Criswell Theological Review* (Spring 2006): 87–93.

Ellul, Jacques. *The Presence of the Kingdom*. 2nd ed. Colorado Springs: Helmers and Howard, 1989.

Farley, O. William, Larry Lorenzo Smith, and Scott W. Boyle. *Introduction to Social Work*. 12th ed. Boston: Pearson Education, 2011.

Fish, Stanley. "Postmodern Warfare: The Ignorance of our Warrior Intellectuals." *Harper's Magazine*, July 2002, 33–40.

Foster, Michael B. "The Christian Doctrine of Creation and the Rise of Modern Natural Science." *Mind* 43 (1934): 446–68.

Foster, Richard. *Celebration of Discipline: The Path to Spiritual Growth*. New York: Harper & Row, 1978.

Frei, Hans. *The Eclipse of Biblical Narrative: A Study of Eighteenth and Nineteenth Century Hermeneutics*. New Haven: Yale University Press, 1974.

Frye, Northrop. *The Great Code: The Bible and Literature*. London: Routledge & Kegan Paul, 1982.

———. *Words with Power: Being a Second Study of the Bible and Literature*. San Diego: Harcourt Brace Jovanovich, 1992.

Gay, Craig M. *The Way of the (Modern) World: Or, Why It's Tempting to Live As If God Doesn't Exist*. Grand Rapids: Eerdmans, 1989.

Goldingay, John. *Models for Interpretation of Scripture*. Grand Rapids: Eerdmans, 1995.

———. *Models for Scripture*. Grand Rapids: Eerdmans, 1994.

Goudzwaard, Bob. *Idols of Our Time*. Leicester, UK: Inter-Varsity, 1984.

Greene, Mark. *People at Work*. Presentation at Lausanne Congress, Cape Town, 2010. http://conversation.lausanne.org/en/resources/detail/11359/.

Guder, Darrell, ed. *Missional Church: A Vision for the Sending of the Church in North America*. Grand Rapids: Eerdmans, 1998.

Guinness, Os. *The Call: Finding and Fulfilling God's Purpose for Your Life*. Nashville: Thomas Nelson, 1998.

Hardy, Lee. *The Fabric of This World: Inquiries into Calling, Career Choice, and the Design of Human Work*. Grand Rapids: Eerdmans, 1990.

Harris, Peter. *Kingfisher's Fire: A Story of Hope for God's Earth*. Oxford: Monarch, 2008.

Hauerwas, Stanley, and William H. Willimon. *Resident Aliens: Life in the Christian Colony*. Nashville: Abingdon, 1989.

Hay, Donald A. *Economics Today: A Christian Critique*. Leicester, UK: Apollos, 1989.

Heilbronner, Robert L. *The Worldly Philosophers: The Lives, Times, and Ideas of the Great Economic Thinkers*. Rev. 7th ed. New York: Simon & Schuster, 1999.

Hirsch, Alan. *The Forgotten Ways: Reactivating Apostolic Movements*. Grand Rapids: Brazos, 2009.

Hirsch, Alan, and Michael Frost. *The Shaping of Things to Come: Innovation and Mission for the 21st-Century Church*. Rev. ed. Grand Rapids: Baker Books, 2013.

Hoetmer, Reuben. "Michael Novak's Alternate Route: Political Realism in *The Joy of Sports*." *Journal of the Philosophy of Sport* 45, no. 1 (2018): 22–36.

Hunter, James Davison. *To Change the World: The Irony, Possibility, and Tragedy of Christianity in the Late Modern World*. New York: Oxford University Press, 2010.

Kraemer, Hendrik. *A Theology of the Laity*. Philadelphia: Westminster, 1958.

Kuyper, Abraham. "Sphere Sovereignty." In *Abraham Kuyper: A Centennial Reader*, edited by James D. Bratt, 461–90. Grand Rapids: Eerdmans, 1998.

Lakoff, George, and Mark Johnson. *Metaphors We Live By*. Chicago: University of Chicago Press, 1980.

Larsen, Timothy. *The Slain God: Anthropologists and the Christian Faith*. Oxford: Oxford University Press, 2014.

Lasch, Christopher. *The Culture of Narcissism*. New York: Warner Books, 1979.

Lausanne Committee for World Evangelization. "Business as Missio." Lausanne Occasional Paper no. 59. Pattaya, Thailand, 2004.

———. "Marketplace Ministry." Lausanne Occasional Paper no. 40. Pattaya, Thailand, 2004.

Lewis, C. S. *The Abolition of Man: Reflections on Education with Special Reference to the Teaching of English in the Upper Forms of Schools*. Oxford: Oxford University Press, 1944.

———. "The Empty Universe." In *Present Concerns: Ethical Essays*, edited by Walter Hooper, 81–86. London: Fount Paperbacks, 1986.

The Life of St. Samson of Dol. Translated by Thomas Taylor. Translations of Christian Literature, series 5, Lives of the Celtic Saints. London: SPCK, 1925.

Lindsay, D. Michael. *Faith in the Halls of Power: How Evangelicals Joined the American Elite*. Oxford: Oxford University Press, 2008.

MacIntyre, Alasdair. *After Virtue: A Study in Moral Theory*. Notre Dame, IN: University of Notre Dame Press, 1984.

Mallett, Charles Edward. *A History of the University of Oxford.* London: Methuen, 1927.

Mangalwadi, Vishal. *The Book That Made Your World: How the Bible Created the Soul of Western Civilization.* Nashville: Thomas Nelson, 2011.

Marsden, George M. *Fundamentalism and American Culture.* New York: Oxford University Press, 1980.

McGrath, Alister E. *Inventing the Universe: Why We Can't Stop Talking About Science, Faith and God.* London: Hodder & Stoughton, 2015.

McLaren, Brian. *A New Kind of Christian: A Tale of Two Friends on a Spiritual Journey.* Hoboken, NJ: Wiley & Sons, 2001.

———. *The Story We Find Ourselves In: Further Adventures of a New Kind of Christian.* Hoboken, NJ: John Wiley & Sons, 2003.

Miller, David W. *God at Work: The History and Promise of the Faith at Work Movement.* Oxford: Oxford University Press, 2007.

Morrison, Chanan. *Gold from the Land of Israel: A New Light on the Weekly Torah Portion from the Writings of Rabbi Abraham Isaac HaKohen Kook.* Jerusalem: Urim Publications, 2007.

Mouw, Richard. *Called to Holy Worldliness.* Philadelphia: Fortress, 1980.

Newbigin, Lesslie. *Foolishness to the Greeks: The Gospel and Western Culture.* Grand Rapids: Eerdmans, 1986.

———. *The Gospel in a Pluralist Society.* Grand Rapids: Eerdmans, 1989.

———. *The Open Secret: An Introduction to the Theology of Mission.* Grand Rapids: Eerdmans, 1978.

———. *The Other Side of 1984: Questions for the Churches.* Geneva: World Council of Churches, 1983.

———. *Proper Confidence: Faith, Doubt, and Certainty in Christian Discipleship.* Grand Rapids: Eerdmans, 1995.

———. *A Walk through the Bible,* London: SPCK, 1999.

Niebuhr, H. Richard. *Christ and Culture.* New York: Harper & Brothers, 1951.

O'Donovan, Oliver. *The Desire of the Nations: Rediscovering the Roots of Political Theology.* Cambridge: Cambridge University Press, 1996.

Ogereau, Julien M. "The Jerusalem Collection as κοινωνία: Paul's Global Politics of Socio-Economic Equality and Solidarity." *New Testament Studies* 58, no. 3 (2012): 360–78.

———. "Paul's κοινωνία with the Philippians: *Societas* as a Missionary Funding Strategy." *New Testament Studies* 60, no. 3 (2014): 360–78.

Oldham, J. H. *Work in Modern Society.* London: SCM, 1950.

O'Neill, Jim. "Building Better Global Economic BRICs." Goldman Sachs Global Economics Paper no. 66 (2001).

Petersen, David, ed. *Prophecy in Israel: Search for an Identity*. Philadelphia: Fortress, 1987.

Peterson, Eugene H. *Under the Unpredictable Plant: An Exploration in Vocational Holiness*. Grand Rapids: Eerdmans, 1992.

Plantinga, Alvin. *Where the Conflict Really Lies: Science, Religion, and Naturalism*. New York: Oxford University Press, 2011.

Postman, Neil. *Technopoly: The Surrender of Culture to Technology*. New York: Vintage, 1992.

Ramachandra, Vinoth. *Gods That Fail: Modern Idolatry and Christian Mission*. Carlisle, UK: Paternoster, 1996.

Richardson, Alan. *The Biblical Doctrine of Work*. London: SCM, 1952.

Robinson, Martin. *Rediscovering the Celts: The True Witness from the Western Shores*. London: Fount, 2000.

Ryken, Leland. *Work and Leisure in Christian Perspective*. Portland, OR: Multnomah, 1987.

Sacks, Jonathan. "In a World Run by MTV, Nobody Has Time to Think." *Daily Telegraph* (London), September 6, 2001. https://www.telegraph.co.uk/comment/4265412/In-a-world-run-by-MTV-nobody-has-time-to-think.html.

———. *The Politics of Hope*. London: Jonathan Cape, 1997.

Schluter, Michael. "Relational Market Economics." *Journal of the Association of Christian Economists* 13 (1992): 48–61.

Shortt, John, David Smith, and Trevor Cooling. "Metaphor, Scripture and Education." *Journal of Christian Education* 43, no. 1 (May 2000): 21–28.

Sire, James. *Naming the Elephant: Worldview as a Concept*. Downers Grove, IL: InterVarsity, 2004.

———. *The Universe Next Door: A Basic Worldview Catalog*. 5th ed. Downers Grove, IL: InterVarsity, 2009.

Smith, James K. A. *Desiring the Kingdom: Worship, Worldview, and Cultural Formation*. Grand Rapids: Baker Academic, 2009.

———. *Who's Afraid of Postmodernism? Taking Derrida, Lyotard, and Foucault to Church*. Grand Rapids: Baker Academic, 2006.

Southern, Richard. *Western Society and the Church in the Middle Ages*. London: Penguin, 1990.

Stetzer, Ed, and David Putnam. *Breaking the Missional Code: Your Church Can Become a Missionary in Your Community*. Nashville: B&H, 2006.

Stevens, R. Paul. *Abolition of the Laity: Vocation, Work and Ministry in Biblical Perspective*. London: Paternoster, 2000. Published in the United States as *The Other Six Days*. Grand Rapids: Eerdmans, 2000.

———. *Liberating the Laity: Equipping All the Saints for Ministry*. Downers Grove, IL: InterVarsity, 1984. Reprint, Vancouver: Regent College Publishing, 2002.

Stott, John. *New Issues Facing Christians Today*. Fully revised ed. London: Marshall Pickering, 1999.

Stringfellow, William. *An Ethic for Christians and Other Aliens in a Strange Land*. Eugene, OR: Wipf & Stock, 1973.

Suárez-Orozco, Carola, and Marcelo M. Suárez-Orozco. *Children of Immigration*. Cambridge, MA: Harvard University Press, 2001.

———. *Migration, Family Life, and Achievement Motivation among Latino Adolescents*. Stanford, CA: Stanford University Press, 1995.

Suzuki, David. *The Sacred Balance: Rediscovering Our Place in Nature*. Vancouver: Greystone Books, 1997.

Tawney, Richard. *Religion and the Rise of Capitalism: A Historical Study*. New York: Harcourt, Brace, 1926.

Taylor, Charles. *A Secular Age*. Cambridge, MA: Belknap, 2007.

Thomas, Keith. *Religion and the Decline of Magic: Studies in Popular Beliefs in Sixteenth- and Seventeenth-Century England*. Oxford: Oxford University Press, 1971.

Trivedi, Harish. "Translating Culture vs. Cultural Translation." In *In Translation: Reflections, Refractions, Transformations*, edited by Paul St-Pierre and Prafulla C. Kar, 277–87. Amsterdam: John Benjamins, 2007.

Turner, Victor. *The Ritual Process: Structure and Anti-Structure*. Harmondsworth, UK: Penguin, 1961.

Vancouver Foundation. *Connect & Engage: A Survey of Metro Vancouver*. 2017. https://www.vancouverfoundation.ca/our-work/initiatives/connections-and-engagement.

Volf, Miroslav. *Work in the Spirit: Toward a Theology of Work*. New York: Oxford University Press, 1991.

Walls, Andrew. "The Translation Principle in Christian History." In *Translation and the Spread of the Church*, edited by P. C. Stine. Leiden: Brill, 1990. Reprinted in Andrew Walls, *The Missionary Movement in Christian History: Studies in the Transmission of Faith*, 26–42. Maryknoll, NY: Orbis Books, 1996.

Weber, Max. *The Protestant Ethic and the Spirit of Capitalism*. Translated by Talcutt Parsons. London: Allen & Unwin, 1930.

Wenham, Gordon J. *Genesis 1–15*. Word Biblical Commentary. Waco: Word, 1987.

White, Lynn. "The Historical Roots of Our Ecologic Crisis." *Science* 155, no. 3767 (March 1967): 1203–7.

Wilkinson, Loren, ed. *Earthkeeping in the Nineties: Stewardship of Creation*. Rev. ed. Eugene, OR: Wipf & Stock, 2003.

Willard, Dallas. *The Divine Conspiracy: Rediscovering Our Hidden Life in God*. San Francisco: HarperSanFrancisco, 1998.

Williams, Paul S. "Capitalism." In *Dictionary of Scripture and Ethics*, edited by Joel B. Green, 115–18. Grand Rapids: Baker Academic, 2011.

———. "Christianity and the Global Economic Order." In *The Oxford Handbook of Christianity and Economics*, edited by P. Oslington, 402–17. Oxford: Oxford University Press, 2014.

Wilson, Edward O. *Biophilia: The Human Bond with Other Species*. Cambridge, MA: Harvard University Press, 1984.

———. *The Creation: An Appeal to Save Life on Earth*. New York: Norton, 2006.

Wilson, Robert. *Prophecy and Society in Ancient Israel*. Philadelphia: Fortress, 1980.

Winter, Bruce. *Seek the Welfare of the City: Christians as Benefactors and Citizens*. Grand Rapids: Eerdmans, 1994.

Wolters, Albert M. *Creation Regained: Biblical Basics for a Reformational Worldview*. Grand Rapids: Eerdmans, 1985.

Wright, N. T. "The Dangerous Vocations: Church, Media and Public Life in a Post-Rational World." Paper presented at the Church's Media Network Conference, RSA, London, October 20, 2016. http://ntwrightpage.com/2016/10/21/the-dangerous-vocations-church-media-and-public-life-in-a-post-rational-world/.

———. *Jesus and the Victory of God*. Christian Origins and the Question of God 2. London: SPCK, 1996.

———. *The New Testament and the People of God*. Christian Origins and the Question of God 1. London: SPCK, 1992.